FORGING A CHRISTIAN ORDER

FORGING A CHRISTIAN ORDER

South Carolina Baptists, Race, and Slavery, 1696–1860

Kimberly R. Kellison

THE UNIVERSITY OF TENNESSEE PRESS | KNOXVILLE

The America's Baptists series will bring broader understanding of the places Baptists have occupied in American life. Many of these works will be historical monographs, but the series will embrace different types of primary and secondary works, including but not limited to annotated collections of diaries, letters, and personal reflections as well as biographies and essay collections.

First Edition.

FRONTIS:
Interior of Black Mingo Church, Nesmith, South Carolina.
Library of Congress.

Library of Congress Cataloging-in-Publication Data
Names: Kellison, Kimberly R., 1967– author.
Title: Forging a Christian order : South Carolina Baptists, race, and slavery, 1696–1860 / Kimberly R. Kellison.
Description: First edition. | Knoxville : The University of Tennessee Press, 2023. | Series: America's Baptists | Includes bibliographical references and index. | Summary: "This is a comprehensive examination of the Baptist movement in South Carolina from its founding to the eve of the Civil War. The author argues that from the beginning the Baptist impulse and organization were driven by elites, who closely valued hierarchy and from the earliest times mounted a Christian defense of slavery. While the ideology of Baptists tended to emanate from the lowcountry, and there was some resistance to its details in the upcountry, Baptists ministers throughout the state fashioned a Christianized version of slavery that legitimized the institution" —Provided by publisher.
Identifiers: LCCN 2022050093 (print) | LCCN 2022050094 (ebook) | ISBN 9781621907596 (paperback) | ISBN 9781621907602 (pdf)
Subjects: LCSH: Slavery and the church—Baptists. |Slavery and the church—South Carolina. | Slavery—United States—Justification. | Baptists—South Carolina—History.
Classification: LCC HT917.B37 K45 2023 (print)
LC record available at https://lccn.loc.gov/2022050093

CONTENTS

Foreword by Keith Harper xi

Acknowledgments xiii

INTRODUCTION
1

ONE
Framing a Christian Order
13

TWO
Growth, 1760–1790: A Threat to Order
37

THREE
National Denominationalism, 1790–1830
59

FOUR
Defining Sectionalism, 1790–1830
77

FIVE
Baptist Clashes, 1830–1845
105

SIX
Sectionalism Ordained
129

CONCLUSION
The Reframing of Christian Order
153

APPENDICES
South Carolina Baptist Church and Membership Statistics 161

Notes 169

Index 215

ILLUSTRATIONS

Figures

Interior of First Baptist Church, Charleston 2

High Hills Baptist Church, Stateburg, South Carolina 44

Silver Bluff Church, near Augusta, Georgia, in 1773 52

Map

Geographical Divisions and Baptist Associations across South Carolina 104

TABLES

TABLE 1. Adherents of Charleston Church, 1708 161

TABLE 2. Population of White Baptists according to Gov. Nathaniel Johnson, 1708 161

TABLE 3. Adherents in South Carolina, 1760 162

TABLE 4. Adherents in South Carolina, 1790 162

TABLE 5. Adherents in South Carolina, 1800 163

TABLE 6. Adherents in South Carolina, 1830 163

TABLE 7. Adherents in South Carolina, 1836 164

TABLE 8. Adherents in South Carolina, 1850 164

TABLE 9. Adherents in South Carolina, 1860 164

TABLE 10. Adherents in South Carolina, 1890 165

TABLE 11. Upcountry and Lowcountry Church Growth in South Carolina, 1830 165

TABLE 12. Upcountry and Lowcountry Church Growth in South Carolina, 1834 165

TABLE 13. Upcountry and Lowcountry Church Growth in South Carolina, 1850 165

TABLE 14. Upcountry and Lowcountry Church Growth in South Carolina, 1860 166

TABLE 15. Number of Baptist Churches in South Carolina, 1750–1860 166

TABLE 16. Baptist and Methodist Membership 166

TABLE 17. White and African American Membership, Lowcountry Associations, 1860 167

TABLE 18. White and African American Membership, Upcountry Associations, 1860 167

TABLE 19. Membership, First Baptist Church, Charleston, 1795–1840 168

FOREWORD

Ask any student of Baptist history to list distinguishing characteristics for what it means to be a Baptist, and you are likely to get a range of answers. Some say Baptist identity is bound in a set of doctrinal tenets, not the least of which baptism by immersion. Others say it is more closely linked to the sort of freedom and individualism that challenges authority structures. Regardless of how one positions Baptists over time, Kimberly R. Kellison's *Forging a Christian Order: South Carolina Baptists, Race, and Slavery, 1696–1860* is certain to challenge many long-cherished notions of Baptist identity.

Kellison focuses on South Carolina Baptists over a 150-year period, and her title alone speaks volumes. These Baptists were interested in establishing an orderly society. That is, in addition to religious liberty, they wanted a "seat at the table" when it came to political power and cultural influence. Unfortunately, westward migration sometimes pitted the "upcountry" and "low country" Baptists against each other especially with regard to education, wealth, and social order. They even squabbled over fine points of church decorum.

Achieving consensus even among likeminded believers was not always easy, hence Kellison's Christian Order had to be "forged." But how? Kellison argues that South Carolina Baptists were not necessarily bound by theology or even the missionary impulse. Rather, they found common ground in their acceptance of slavery that was rooted deeply in paternalism. Tying slavery with paternalism is not new, but Kellison maintains that South Carolina Baptist leaders were among the first to articulate the tenets of a "Christian paternalism." As such, enslavers claimed that those enslaved were actually "family members," that they deserved to hear the gospel, and they deserved fair, "Christian" treatment. As such, they believed they recognized African American humanity without recognizing African American equality and without surrendering the place that they carved for themselves atop the nation's social, economic, and political structures.

There is more to say, but I will leave the rest of the story to Kim Kellison—and what a story it is! The University of Tennessee Press is proud to offer *Forging a Christian Order*, and we hope it challenges, inspires, and encourages readers to reconsider what they think they know about Baptists. One thing is certain: Reading this book may well change your view of antebellum Baptists, especially in South Carolina. We sure hope so.

Keith Harper
Southeastern Baptist Theological Seminary

ACKNOWLEDGMENTS

This study was a long time in the making, interrupted by various aspects of life, career, and family. Portions of the original research for the book were conducted decades ago, while other materials were mined more recently. Over the years, I have benefited greatly from the archival assistance of J. Glenwood Clayton and others at the Baptist Historical Collection at Furman University and from the guidance and friendship of many archivists at the University of South Carolina's South Caroliniana Library, including but not limited to Allen Stokes, Herb Hartsook, Henry Fulmer, Brian Cuthrell, and Beth Bilderback. At Baylor University, Janet Jasek and her staff have been particularly helpful in securing countless rolls of Baptist church minutes through interlibrary loan.

I am also grateful to my two readers, Edward R. Crowther and Thomas J. Little, whose incisive questions and comments sharpened and improved this book. A huge thanks also goes to series editor Keith Harper and to Scot Danforth and Jonathan Boggs at the University of Tennessee Press for their suggestions, encouragement, and patience.

My colleagues at Baylor University in the History Department and in the College of Arts and Sciences have provided academic support as well as fellowship, laughter, and friendship. I am blessed to work at an institution where colleagues exhibit genuine care and support for one another.

My parents, Bob and Larita Kellison, have given me unwavering love and support throughout my life. Their role in my personal and professional formation has been inestimable. Likewise, my brother, Todd Kellison, has been a rock, a sounding board, and an inspiration. My close friends Mona Choucair and Robyn Driskell have kept me sane with queso, white sauce, and laughter and tears.

This book is dedicated to my husband, George Stonikinis, whose true partnership in our marriage has allowed me to pursue my professional goals while also raising a family. His willingness to co-parent (and sometimes solo-parent) is profoundly appreciated. The book is also dedicated to my daughters, Emery and Rory, whose wit, courage, determination, and love are sources of joy in more ways than they will ever know.

INTRODUCTION

This book explores the growth and development of white Baptists in South Carolina from initial settlement to the Civil War. It argues that South Carolina Baptists, comprised of elite members from their founding, were in the vanguard of denominational growth and leadership in the pre–Civil War years, and that they were among some of the earliest voices advocating for a proslavery stance for church and society. The first Baptist ministers in South Carolina settled in Charles Town (hereafter Charleston) and nearby coastal areas, where concentrations of wealth were quickly established and where concerns for order and stability were paramount.[1] Although the emphasis upon personal salvation inherent in the Baptist message attracted individuals from all walks of life, early ministers built churches that spoke to and reflected the values of the elite. While opposing worldly pursuits such as dancing, drinking, and gambling, white Baptists emphasized order and hierarchy in the church and in the world. They engaged in and accommodated the slave system by turning to the Bible to defend their practices. The vision of Baptists in the Lowcountry—the rich alluvial areas along the Carolina coast—was not embraced by all. Churches in the interior portions of South Carolina, initially called the backcountry and by the nineteenth century labeled the Upcountry, fought against the ordered hierarchy and denominational vision of Charleston-based ministers, resulting in an internal culture war that lasted well into the nineteenth century. Although they divided over how elite and educated their congregations should be, Baptist ministers throughout the state reinforced racial distinctions in their churches and fashioned a Christian version of slavery that legitimized the institution. In the early 1800s, decades before most evangelicals were doing so, white Lowcountry Baptists publicly affirmed slavery as biblical and moral, claiming it as their denominational stance. In a state where slavery defined all aspects of life more deeply than in any other state, where white control and social order were more prioritized than in any other

Interior of First Baptist Church, Charleston, oldest Baptist congregation in the American South, 61 Church Street, HABS Survey, photographed by C. O. Greene, March 21, 1940. Library of Congress.

state, where political radicalism was greater than in any other state, white Baptist leaders aligned themselves with a religious system that accommodated slavery and that promised a system of social control.[2]

This study speaks to the historiography of religion and race in the American South in two significant ways. First, it challenges and complicates the standard view advanced by historians John B. Boles, Donald Mathews, Anne C. Loveland, and Christine Heyrman that eighteenth-century evangelicals exerted both a religious and a social challenge to the traditional mainstream order, maturing into middle-class denominations only in the nineteenth century. As Walter B. Shurden has shown, South Carolina Baptists presented a more bifurcated narrative. Although the nonconformist Separate Baptists settled in South Carolina in the 1760s, by the 1770s claiming a significant presence in the interior portions of the state, an earlier, and much different, Baptist tradition emerged in Charleston and other areas of the Lowcountry. Despite their status as religious dissenters, white Lowcountry Baptists set up churches that reinforced rather than contested elite social structures. They communicated with their urban brethren in

Philadelphia, Boston, and England in the early 1700s, developing by the latter 1700s a denominational presence that stressed education, wealth, and social order. Charleston Baptists worked specifically and intentionally to spread their brand of denominationalism to backcountry Separates. They were embarrassed at the ill-training of backcountry Baptists and made a conscious effort to educate and transform their behavior; they also reinforced to civic leaders that they were friends of the elite, rather than opponents of the social order. Although over time Baptists in the backcountry began to attract larger congregations, with elite and non-elite alike joining their churches, some backcountry churches resisted the denominational vision of Lowcountry churches well into the nineteenth century. Rather than developing holistically from a sect-to-denomination model, South Carolina Baptists throughout the antebellum period operated from two distinct centers of organization. Seldom united, they engaged in bitter clashes over differing versions of church order, missionary outreach, and the professionalization of the ministry.[3]

Second, this work contributes to the historiography of white proslavery thought in the American South by arguing that among white South Carolina Baptists, proslavery Christianity developed in two distinct phases: a private, religious embrace of Christian paternalism in the eighteenth century, followed in the early nineteenth century by a definitive and public construction of proslavery Christianity, one that engaged with the state over the right to provide religious instruction to enslaved men and women. By showing a clear distinction between these phases, this work complements the work of historians such as Charles F. Irons and Alan Gallay, who locate Christian paternalism—a system that provided care and benevolence to the enslaved in return for loyalty and obedience to the enslaver—as part of religious movements of the eighteenth century. Simultaneously, by showing the significant ways that Lowcountry leaders, particularly Richard Furman, forcefully shifted arguments about slavery into the public arena in the early 1800s, this work nuances broader studies by scholars such as Lacy Ford and Willie Lee Rose, who contend that Christian paternalism did not become widely accepted in southern society until the nineteenth century.

From their early settlement in South Carolina, white Baptists demonstrated a nascent form of racial paternalism that recognized the humanity of the slave while starkly emphasizing black inferiority. Turning to the Bible to justify their accommodation of slavery, white eighteenth-century Baptists gradually pieced together a set of beliefs about the spiritual care of enslaved people, formulating the beginnings of a Christian model of slavery. Similar to Charles Irons's study of evangelicals in eighteenth- and nineteenth-century Virginia, white Baptists in the South Carolina Lowcountry emphasized a strong belief in racial difference and white supremacy but also recognized that enslaved men and women should hear the gospel message and receive humane care and management. Although tentative and not endorsed by all white Baptists, this early thread of paternalism developed in South Carolina at an earlier stage than identified by Alan Gallay, who attributes its beginnings to mid- and late-eighteenth-century evangelical revivals, or by Joyce Chaplin, who argues that Late Enlightenment thought contributed to an emerging, modern humanitarian model of slavery in the second half of the eighteenth century. While revivalism as well as Enlightenment and Revolutionary beliefs strengthened paternalistic thinking among white Lowcountry Baptists in South Carolina, causing them to put greater efforts into slave evangelization in the latter years of the 1700s, the roots of paternalism in South Carolina, however tenuous, existed at an earlier date.[4]

Although religious and intellectual histories have shown that some white southerners manifested humanitarian, paternalistic attitudes toward enslaved men and women in the eighteenth century, thus challenging harsher eighteenth-century attitudes about the management of enslaved people, most scholars agree that paternalistic justifications of slaveholding did not become endemic to larger white southern culture until the nineteenth century. As historians such as Lacy Ford, Willie Lee Rose, and Jeffrey Robert Young have shown, in the early decades of the nineteenth century, white southerners advanced a broad social vision of slavery as a benevolent, domestic institution that emphasized the paternalistic ideal of reciprocal duties between the master and the enslaved. In this ideological vision of domestic slavery, enslaved men and women comprised part of the enslaver's household. Christian duty compelled the enslaver to care for enslaved men and women as he would his white household dependents, with benevolence and care. In return, enslaved men and women were to fulfill their Christian duties as loyal and hardworking servants. Although Ford and others acknowledge that aspects of paternalistic thought existed in the second half of the eighteenth century, they contend that issues specific to the early nineteenth century—the rapid expansion of the cotton economy, the extensive growth of evangelical Christianity, and the closing of the international slave trade—led to a much broader and wide-ranging social articulation of paternalism throughout the slaveholding South.[5]

This book contends that white Baptists in Lowcountry South Carolina—a region dominated by hierarchical relations—played a pivotal and early role in advancing a public defense of Christian slavery in the nineteenth-century slaveholding South. In Lowcountry South Carolina in the 1790s, where a white minority population lived in constant anxiety over control of enslaved men and women, news of revolt in Saint-Domingue led to heightened fears of black violence. Additionally, at the turn of the century, reports of antislavery sentiment among evangelical denominations ran rampant. Fearful of being associated with antislavery evangelicals and, in turn, of being labeled as an enemy of the planter and urban elite, Richard Furman and other white Lowcountry ministers orchestrated a major transformation in the Baptist construction of paternalism. Engaging publicly with the state over the right to evangelize to enslaved men and women, white Lowcountry Baptists developed a more cohesive and absolute justification of slavery, one that allowed no room for question about the social benefits of owning enslaved people and treating them in a Christian manner. The Bible sanctioned slavery, Furman and others argued, so long as it was practiced in a Christian manner, with the master bestowing protection and care to all members of his household, white and black alike, and with enslaved dependents serving the benevolent master with loyalty and obedience. Applying this biblical understanding to the relations between enslavers and enslaved people and treating enslaved people as part of the domestic household promoted rather than threatened the social order, Baptist ministers contended, providing the best solution to the fear of slave rebellion. Rather than appearing as an insurgent movement that took hold only in the nineteenth century, Christian paternalism in the South Carolina Lowcountry developed as an alternative social model within Baptist circles throughout the 1700s, was shifted forcefully and strategically into the public sphere in the early 1800s by Richard Furman and like-minded ministers, and contributed powerfully to the emergence of a public legitimization of proslavery Christianity—in other words, to the larger "domestication" of slavery described by Rose, Ford, and others. Staking their claim as preservers rather than opponents of the social order and basing their proslavery vision on a Christian paternalism developed in the eighteenth century, white Lowcountry Baptists of the nineteenth century emerged as some of the earliest architects of a public vision of racial salvation, white superiority, and a Christian vindication of African enslavement.[6]

The scope of this work focuses primarily on white Baptists, and often upon religious rhetoric articulated and advanced by white ministers. But people of color and white women also played a crucial role in the growth of Baptist churches.[7] Sharing a conversion experience and joining a church brought believers of all backgrounds together in an exclusive spiritual setting. Church members, both black and white, referred to themselves as "brother" and "sister" and disciplined one another to encourage moral and biblical behavior.[8] Enslaved people as well as white women sought opportunities for leadership in Baptist churches, forcing white men to acknowledge their significance as Christians and to recognize their shared sense of human and spiritual belonging. Yet spiritual roles did not translate to equal social opportunities for white women or for enslaved people, either within or outside the walls of the church. White women enjoyed a more flexible status than enslaved people: although official leadership remained in the hands of white men, in numerous Upcountry congregations white women exercised more formal governing roles, frequently voting on ministers and sometimes voting alongside white men in disciplinary cases. Lowcountry churches, by contrast, excluded white women from any type of formal governance, instead relegating them to more gender-specific activities.[9] While white gender relations varied from Lowcountry to Upcountry churches, formal roles for African Americans were much more restricted. Black Baptists sought a spiritual home where their humanity could be fully recognized, both spiritually and ecclesiastically. Black male preachers sought, sometimes successfully, to preach to racially mixed congregations, and black men frequently exercised semi-official leadership roles among other free and enslaved black members. However, black Baptists operated in churches that, just like the world, separated them from the social privileges of whiteness. In Lowcountry and Upcountry alike, white Baptists crafted a Christian model of slavery that provided order and security and that consistently reinforced racial difference and white supremacy. No matter how much they recognized that black members had spiritual gifts that could rival those of whites, white Baptists found common ground in a shared belief that viewed black men and women, both enslaved and free, as racially inferior.[10]

Baptists became a prominent presence in South Carolina both numerically, socially, and culturally in the pre–Civil War years. Church adherence, while small in proportion to the overall population for much of the eighteenth century, increased from a conservative estimate of 3–4 percent of the state population in 1760 to 10.1 percent in 1830 to 25.8 percent in 1860.[11] Black populations did not increase substantially in biracial churches until the late 1700s, but prior to this time white (and sometimes black) ministers preached to enslaved men and women on Lowcountry plantations who may not have officially joined Baptist churches. Starting in the late 1700s, both Upcountry and Lowcountry churches attracted white and black members within a biracial setting. In Upcountry congregations, whites usually outnumbered enslaved members, while in the Lowcountry, enslaved men and women often outnumbered white members, at times exponentially. By the late antebellum period, African Americans were close to 50 percent of South Carolina Baptists, with the strongest presence in the coastal and middle sections of the state.[12] Overall membership projections are likely low, as churches rarely reported accurate membership numbers every year, and nonmembers frequently attended Baptist services. Baptist churches increased numerically because of the widespread denominational efforts of Lowcountry Baptists to train successive generations of educated clergy and to promote organized missionary efforts, but growth also occurred because of the remarkably wide appeal of the Baptist message. Because conversion implied a transformational and deeply personal relationship with Jesus Christ, whites and blacks could be attracted to a church that offered them significantly different understandings of Christian order. For black South Carolinians, Baptist churches provided an alternative belief system that allowed them to affirm dignity and self-worth, to resist the dehumanization of slavery and racism by walking with a God who offered salvation to the dispossessed as well as the powerful. White Baptists, both elite and non-elite, found in Baptist teachings and practices not only individual spiritual sustenance and meaning but a moral and religious justification of a social order that legitimized racial slavery, white dominance, and black inferiority. Through their insistence that Christian slavery was both biblically based and the solution to threats of civil disorder, white ministers bestowed sacred meaning to a larger cultural attitude condoning slavery and white dominance. These competing belief systems carried forth into the postbellum years, when white Baptists looked to the Bible to legitimize racial segregation, and when black Baptists, who had by this time left white-controlled churches, continued to find in scripture an affirmation of their human dignity and religious equality.[13]

This book is arranged chronologically. Chapter 1 documents the formation and growth of early Baptist churches in South Carolina, arguing that Baptists, from the start of settlement, established congregations that accommodated rather than challenged the prevailing social order of the economically stratified Lowcountry. The first Baptist church in the British southern colonies began in Charleston in the late 1600s. Between the 1730s and 1750s, settlers formed additional congregations along the coastal areas. Following a period of stability under the leadership of their first pastor, William Screven, Charleston Baptists experienced several decades of volatility that included ministerial changes, division over theological views of Calvinism, and a literal court battle over the use of their meeting house. By the 1750s Pennsylvania native Oliver Hart assumed leadership of the Charleston church. In addition to bringing more unity and stability to the Charleston congregation, Hart ushered in a new phase of Baptist growth in South Carolina. He took the first steps toward building a Baptist denomination in the South by organizing Lowcountry churches into an associational model and by establishing a Baptist-supported society to train aspiring ministers. Throughout the 1700s, white Baptists also participated in and accommodated the institution of slavery. White ministers preached to enslaved people and encouraged their membership in Baptist churches, and leading ministers and members owned enslaved people. Some Baptists struggled to reconcile the more brutal customs associated with eighteenth-century slavery with Christian modes of thinking. Turning to the Bible, they began to fashion a rudimentary Christian model of slavery—a Christian paternalism—that recognized the humanity of the slave while speaking deeply into the racial differences between Africans and Europeans. During the 1700s this model of slavery remained in a developmental stage. Churches did not enforce a uniform perspective on slaveholding, and Christian paternalism remained an individualized, private matter discussed at times in congregations but not in the larger context of the state. Only later, with a new generation of ministers and a conflagration of social concerns at the turn of the nineteenth century, did the model of Christian slavery emerge in a stronger, more public, and more decidedly proslavery form.

Chapter 2 covers the years 1760–1790 and discusses the appearance and fast-paced rise of a second group of Baptists known as the Separates. Separate Baptists migrated from New England to Virginia and later to Sandy Creek, North Carolina, where they established a number of congregations in the region. In the early 1760s, some Separates moved into South Carolina and Georgia. Separates eschewed pastoral education and were more likely to give white women leadership and preaching roles. As such, they alarmed established Lowcountry ministers, both Baptist and Anglican. White Baptists in the Lowcountry attempted to forge a union with Separate Baptists, but neither side could find a path toward unity. The American Revolution, rather than uniting Baptists, showed their fault lines. Most Lowcountry Baptists supported the cause of the patriots, viewing religious liberty an important part of their fight against British rule. Separate Baptists were more mixed—some remained strongly loyalist—and many of their congregations were displaced after the fighting. White and black Baptists also debated the fate of slavery in the wake of the revolution. Some black Baptists fled with the British in search of freedom. Those who remained enslaved continued to protest slavery in various ways, including through religion. In parts of western South Carolina and across the border in Georgia, where Separate Baptist influence was strong, some enslaved men and women established independent black congregations. In the more strictly ordered area around Charleston, whites exercised greater oversight over black congregations, disallowing the formation of independent black churches. Rather than advocating for religious independence for the enslaved, whites in the Lowcountry increased their missionary efforts toward them, articulating more collectively the need to evangelize and care for enslaved men and women within the church. At least one white Baptist minister voiced antislavery views in the 1770s, but most white Baptists in the post-Revolutionary years, rather than promoting emancipation, endorsed greater benevolence toward enslaved peoples, seeing it as their Christian duty to preach to and to provide moral uplift for a race they believed to be inferior. For white Baptists in late-eighteenth-century South Carolina, the Christian model of slavery increasingly became the only possible answer to revolutionary calls for liberty and freedom.

Chapter 3 focuses on strategic efforts to expand Baptist operations between 1790 and 1830. During these years, Baptists lobbied successfully for a state constitution that recognized their religious freedom. They raised funds to educate and train ministers, promoted domestic and foreign missions, and created various denominational models to carry out their elite evangelical vision. Richard Furman, who was converted as a Separate Baptist but who, by the 1790s, had become fully immersed in the world of Lowcountry Baptists, served as the driving force behind these aggressive efforts to professionalize and denominationalize Baptist churches. With Furman's forceful leadership, Lowcountry Baptists led the way in forming a national, state, and regional denominational organization. They were integral in the creation of the first national Baptist denomination in the United States, the Baptist Triennial Convention (1814), put into place the first state convention in the southern states (1821), and established the first Baptist seminary in the southern states (1826).[14] The vigorous organizational work of Lowcountry leaders was challenged by Baptists in the backcountry (commonly referred to as the Upcountry by the early nineteenth century), who refused to join denominational efforts, arguing that the Bible nowhere sanctioned extra-congregational missionary or educational efforts. Upcountry Baptists saw a tremendous explosion of churches and converts in the early 1800s, during the season of the Great Revival that swept through many southern states, but many of their churches remained fundamentally disengaged from Lowcountry congregations in terms of organizational and professional vision and ideology. Although Lowcountry Baptists succeeded in convincing some Upcountry churches to support wider denominational efforts, an internal culture clash continued to separate Baptists from achieving state-wide unity and harmony.

Chapter 4 addresses the public emergence of a white Baptist proslavery argument in the late 1700s and early decades of the 1800s (1790–1830). During these pivotal years, white Baptists argued with the state about the right to evangelize enslaved men and women, in the process advancing a more direct and public legitimization of slavery than had been their practice in prior decades. Concerned that events of the late 1700s and early 1800s would lead to their branding as antislavery advocates and that they would lose their denominational influence among Lowcountry elites, Lowcountry ministers, under the aggressive leadership of Richard Furman, enlarged and transformed the Christian model of slavery—one that called for a Christian *practice* of slavery but did not collectively expound on slavery as *morally right*—to a proslavery argument vindicating slavery as moral and biblical by envisioning it as both a Christian duty and a Christian *right*. Furman, who believed that ministers should play an active role in shaping the social and political order, became one of the South's earliest proslavery advocates, speaking decisively for his denomination and silencing those in Baptist circles who took a differing stance. The Bible explicitly condoned slavery so long as it was practiced according to Christian means, Furman proclaimed.

Moreover, Christian paternalism not only benefited the enslaved by providing moral and material care and protection, it also assured that enslaved men and women would remain loyal and obedient to their Christian masters, thus preserving the social order by preventing slave insurrection. So important was Christian paternalism to the safety of the white community, Furman believed, that church and state should cooperate to ensure that the religious instruction of slaves continued unimpeded. Although Upcountry whites did not take as public a stance about slavery as did those in the Lowcountry, white Baptists in both sections of the state increased their evangelization efforts to enslaved men and women in the early 1800s. Ironically, as white Baptists in South Carolina forged a Christian denominational order that was national and international in scope in terms of education and missions, they also created a sectional existence built squarely on the protection and biblical justification of slavery. During the early 1800s, these two divergent stances—denominational nationalism and a sectionalism built upon slavery—coexisted with one another in a way that would be impossible to reconcile in years to come.

Chapter 5 traces continued divisions within Baptist congregations over denomination building, as well as the growing sectional divide within the national Baptist denomination. Between 1830 and 1845, white denominational Baptists increased their attempts to fold all churches into the state organization and to create a united front for missions and pastoral and religious education. Their concerted and aggressive efforts reached a peak of resistance in some Upcountry congregations, causing a small number of churches to identify as Primitive Baptists and eliciting much division and conflict within other church bodies. As divided as they were over missions and education, over church and worship style, white Baptists throughout the state were more unified in their religious defense of slavery. They forged a united front against abolitionist critiques of their morality and increased their efforts to evangelize to enslaved people, becoming more proscriptive about how churches should do so. Simultaneously, they called for more segregation in worship, sending clear indications of a two-tiered worship system within physical religious spaces. When northern Baptists demanded the exclusion of slaveholders from national denominational efforts, white Baptists in South Carolina worked closely with other white southern Baptists to form a new, sectional denomination dedicated to missionary work that included the concerted evangelization of enslaved people. Fully breaking with their northern brethren, white Baptists now returned to Kingdom-building on their own terms, viewing themselves as benevolent masters whose Christian model of slavery provided both the religious and civic answer to an ordered, harmonious southern society.

The final chapter of this work examines the actions of South Carolina Baptists between 1845 and 1860. In these pivotal years leading to secession and civil war, Lowcountry Baptists succeeded in convincing most churches and associations to join the Baptist State Convention, although some congregations in the Upcountry continued to resist stringently a professionalized ministry and remained open to allowing white women more formal leadership roles. Although vestiges of anti-denominational attitudes remained, churches throughout the state put greater resources into slave evangelization and slave management. They funded missionaries to preach in Lowcountry plantations, created greater denominational expectations for slave conversions throughout the state, and issued more systematic guidelines about the church's role in managing marriages of enslaved people. Enslaved men and women joined churches in greater numbers during these years, finding in conversion and church membership vital ways to affirm their humanity and to find fellowship with others. Yet as more black men and women joined congregations, whites enforced a more rigid system of segregation, separating whites and blacks spatially and in numerous ways reiterating racial difference and black inferiority. Arguing that the Christian model of slavery was nearing perfection, whites congratulated themselves on the growing numbers of enslaved people in their churches, lauding themselves for establishing a model of social harmony that provided benevolence and uplift for the enslaved while also reinforcing white dominance and black subservience. Four long years of bloody battles and the end of the Confederacy ended this white-driven notion of Christian order. Rebuffed by black Baptists who could now reject their racial paternalism and who formed their own independent churches, white Baptists in the postwar years gradually turned their attention away from their black brethren, further cementing the separation of the races that took place so acutely and violently in the nineteenth century and that still largely dominates the social composition of Baptist churches in South Carolina to this day.

CHAPTER ONE

Framing a Christian Order

In the late 1690s, Baptist minister William Screven and his wife Bridget traveled with their church congregation from Kittery, Maine, to Charleston, South Carolina, establishing the first Baptist church in the British southern colonies. The group, which had English as well as Barbadian connections, joined a handful of Baptists who had already settled in the Charleston area.[1] Although they eschewed many of the social customs of the day, early white Baptists established churches that attracted wealthy members and that conformed to the elite white social and racial order that defined Lowcountry society. In the first half of the eighteenth century, these churches grew in fits and spurts, struggled to find ministerial replacements, and divided over degrees of Calvinism. Baptists entered a new phase in the mid-1700s, when Oliver Hart, who came from Pennsylvania to lead the Charleston church, organized existing congregations into an associational model and initiated a program to train new ministers, forging an extra-congregational sense of unity and cooperation and laying the foundation for the growth of a southern Baptist denomination. Throughout this period, white Baptists adapted their religious thinking to the world around them, participating in and accommodating slavery by reconciling the practice with the teachings of the Bible. In the process, they began to develop a Christian model of slavery that recognized the humanity of enslaved people while reinforcing a stark belief in racial difference and African inferiority. By 1760, white Baptists, still relatively small in number, had established an organizational presence in the Lowcountry that stressed the need for inter-church cooperation and a trained ministry. Baptist ministers preached a message of personal salvation to black as well as white listeners, but their actions and practices legitimated a social world based upon white dominance, black inferiority, and the perpetuation of racial slavery.[2]

When William Screven's congregation arrived in South Carolina in the 1690s, they came to a colony dominated economically by planters and merchants, a place where religious diversity was welcomed by the proprietors but where social instability was manifold. Political disunity between English and Barbadian settlers, the threat of naval attack by marauding privateers and by rival European powers, and a growing dependence upon the backbreaking labor of enslaved people led to a heightened sense of volatility among the residents in turn-of-the-century Charleston. Tensions continued throughout the early 1700s, as residents faced Native American hostilities during the calamitous Yamasee War (1715–1718), pirate attacks, yellow fever epidemics, and the potential for revolt among enslaved men and women. This last fear was realized in spring 1739 with the Stono Rebellion, the largest colonial rebellion of enslaved people on the British American mainland.[3] The need to protect settlers from both external and internal disorder became increasingly crucial in the early 1700s, as South Carolina emerged as the wealthiest British American mainland colony, as well as the only mainland colony with an African-majority population. The successful cultivation of rice in the coastal lowlands in the 1690s led to the rapid importation of African enslaved people, so that, by 1708, the number of enslaved Africans surpassed the number of whites in the colony.[4] By 1720 the colony's African population reached roughly two-thirds of the total population. In some Lowcountry parishes, the percentage of black to white settlers was even greater. For most of the remainder of the pre–Civil War years, South Carolina would hold the unique distinction of being the only British American mainland colony, and then the only American state, with a slave majority, positioning its leaders to take radical measures to protect and defend slavery.[5]

William Screven was well acquainted with slavery before arriving in South Carolina, just as he was well acquainted with Baptist beliefs. Screven's early ministry began in Somerton, England, a town in the southwestern part of the island country where religious dissent was strong. Born in 1629, Screven became active in the Somerton church and in Baptist congregations around the area, serving as a lay preacher in the 1640s and 1650s. By the 1660s prohibitive policies against dissenters likely caused Screven, as well as other Baptists in the area, to relocate to the New World. England's Conventicle Act of 1664 made it illegal for dissenters to hold religious meetings. The following year, the Five Mile Act (1665) banned dissenting ministers from preaching within a five-mile radius of towns, cities, or parishes in which they had served.[6] By 1668 Screven had settled in or around Salisbury, Massachusetts, in the northern part of the colony close to New Hampshire. Screven may have joined other Baptists from dissenting counties in western England who moved to this portion of the Bay Colony.[7]

To find employment, Screven apprenticed himself as a shipbuilder for four years and then, in his mid-forties, purchased land in Kittery, Maine. There he met and, in 1674, married seventeen-year-old Bridget Cutt. Bridget's father, Robert, was a local shipbuilder and one of the largest slaveholders in early New England. Cutt had lived in Barbados as well as Maine and owned eight enslaved people, making him a large slaveholder, in comparative terms, in northern New England. When Robert Cutt died in 1674, he deeded his eight enslaved people to his first-born son.[8] Like the Cutts, other leaders in Kittery and nearby Portsmouth also had close ties to Barbados, with some spending their winters on the island. In Kittery, William Screven associated with colonists with intimate ties to Barbados and to slavery; by 1674 he married into a family that knew and accepted slaveholding as part of the social and economic order. Screven's connection with Barbados residents may have also led to his eventual migration to South Carolina.[9]

William and Bridget Screven worshipped with the Baptist congregation in the Boston area, about fifty-five miles from Kittery, in the 1670s and 1680s, becoming members of the church in 1681.[10] Following the habit of Baptist dissenters in England, the congregation shifted from home to home in order to avoid detection and punishment by Massachusetts authorities, but by 1679 Baptists built an official meeting house in Boston.[11] In 1682 Screven and a small group of believers petitioned the Boston congregation to form a new church in Kittery. Baptist elders from Boston traveled to Kittery in September 1682, ordaining Screven as pastor of the Kittery Baptist Church. Ten white men and seven white women comprised the first members of the congregation, which apparently had no African-American members.[12] The formation of the church was not without controversy. Screven was called before both the Court of Pleas and the Massachusetts General Assembly in the spring of 1682—before the church was officially organized or recognized—to face charges of preaching against infant baptism, holding Baptist services, and failing to attend the Congregational church.[13] Although serving jail time in at least one instance, Screven continued to preach in defiance of colonial authority. He appeared in the Court of Sessions in 1683 and was again summoned by the General Assembly in 1684. Colonial turmoil resulting from the establishment of royal control in Massachusetts and other New England colonies in the mid-1680s may account for a lack of further judicial action taken against Screven.[14]

The British settlement of Charles Town (Charleston) in the colony of Carolina presented Screven and other New England Baptists an opportunity to move to a new location where religious dissent was tolerated and where Baptists could worship without fear of repeated colonial reprisal. Although some of the Kittery congregation may have relocated to Carolina in the 1680s, most members of the church remained in Maine until the 1690s, as evidenced by individual appearances on grand juries and in other legal dealings. In 1696 the sixty-seven-year-old Screven, his family, and his congregation, which now numbered around thirty, moved as a body to South Carolina. There, they settled into a colony marked by ethnic and religious diversity as well as extreme disparities of wealth and, within twelve years of their migration, the presence of a colony-wide slave majority.[15] Because the owners of South Carolina, the Lords Proprietors, encouraged dissenting religions, the colony also consisted of a wide assortment of religious sects, ranging from Jews to Huguenots to Screven's Baptists. Baptists, though small in number, were thus part of a broad mix of dissenting religions that found a foothold in Charleston.[16]

Within three years of moving to Charleston, Screven had secured land for the construction of a Baptist meeting house, a sign that people of some wealth were part of the early congregation. In 1699 Baptist planter William Elliott Sr., a General Baptist who had come from England, provided a city lot for the establishment of a church structure on what was later named Church Street.[17] Elliott had earlier purchased the land for twenty pounds after the previous owner, a mariner named Josiah Davis, died. Elliott gave the land "in consideration of the brotherly love which he hath for, and doth bear unto the people of the Church of Christ, baptized on profession of faith, distinguished from all others by the name of Antipaedobaptists, of which Church he professeth himself a member." The gift was intended "to *promote* and encourage so good and pious work as *the building* a place for the said people to meet and worship, &c."[18] The meeting house was completed by January 1701. Aside from Elliot, other wealthy patrons supported the church. Prominent dissenter Lady Elizabeth Axtell Blake, wife of dissenting governor Joseph Blake, likely belonged to the congregation. Lady Blake left twenty pounds each year to supplement the pay of the church's minister, as well paying fifty pounds to help construct a church parsonage.[19]

Although living initially in Charleston, Screven and other family members purchased also land forty miles to the north of Charleston along the Cooper River, in an area which had been named Somerton by prior dissenters from southwestern England. In addition to acreage purchased before 1700, Screven bought roughly three hundred additional acres complete with already built "plantation homes" in the early 1700s, after a fire burned his family's home and belongings in Charleston. Other Baptists affiliated with Screven secured land close to Screven's Somerton settlement. The group may have worshipped together in one another's homes, perhaps using a building on Screven's land, but they probably also voyaged back and forth to the Charleston church.[21]

Intent on spreading God's word to others and lacking a formal organizational plan to expand, William Screven, like other early preachers, traveled from place to place around the Lowcountry to preach the gospel. Congregationalist Joseph Lord in 1699 complained about Screven's proselytizing to residents in Charleston.[22] Screven itinerated, converted, and established new branches or "arms" of the Charleston church throughout the larger settlement. The Baptist minister addressed groups of Baptists living along both the Ashley and Stono Rivers. As a result of Screven's labors, independent churches were established in both areas in the 1730s. Around 1700, Screven baptized a group of believers on Edisto Island, further south of Charleston. Edisto Baptists ultimately migrated further inland, to a settlement called Euhaw, in present-day Jasper County, organizing a separate church in the 1740s.[23] Most of these early congregants, including Screven, identified firmly as Particular Baptists, staunch Calvinists who adhered to the London Confession of Faith. Others, who had come from England, were General Baptists who embraced a milder form of Calvinism that included some degree of human agency. During Screven's ministry, the two factions seem to have coexisted with one another, a situation that would change after the death of the Baptist minister.[24]

In the early 1700s, as they learned of new opportunities to claim land, parts of Screven's congregation made plans to move northward to settle new lands along the Carolina coast. As early as 1704, at least six church members purchased roughly three thousand acres of property (five hundred acres on average) in the Winyah Bay area, home to what would later be the town of Georgetown. Three of Screven's sons, Aaron, Robert, and Permanous, also bought land in the area during this time period. The opportunity to acquire and expand new land must have factored into the decision to relocate from Charleston, but attempts to establish the Church of England as the official church in Carolina may have also played a role in some congregants' decisions. Although Queen Anne overturned establishment legislation in 1704 and 1705, the South Carolina Assembly passed the 1706 Church Act, establishing the Anglican Church as the sole tax-supported church in the colony and formally relegating Baptists to the status of dissenters.[25]

The aging Screven, suffering from bouts of ill health, prepared to move to Winyah after a new minister named White arrived from England in 1706. The minister died soon after arriving in South Carolina. Around this same time, Boston Baptists wrote to Screven, inviting him to serve as minister of the Baptist congregation in that city. Screven declined the invitation in part because of the situation at the Charleston church. Screven could not assume the role, as he "was inclined to do if I could . . . for our Minister that came from England is dead, and I can no means be spared."[26] Screven continued to correspond with Boston Baptists, including his old friend Ellis Callender, to whom he wrote in February 1708 of his hope that the Boston church could find a supply from England, and in another letter from August 1708 that "I have been of late, brought very low by sickness; but I bless the Lord I was helped to preach and administer the communion last Lord's day."[27] Screven also commented on the state of Baptists in the Charleston area, which he estimated at ninety members, making no mention of enslaved versus free members.[28]

By 1710 William Screven had moved to Winyah, where he owned a modest three hundred acres of land.[29] The Screven family added to this landholding legacy in the 1710s and the 1720s. Before his death, the Baptist minister accrued substantially more acreage around Winyah, which he willed to his wife Bridget upon his death in 1713 at the age of eighty-four. Bridget died on June 29, 1717. A memorial from 1732 shows that she willed 1,550 acres, which comprised "half of the land and plantation where she then dwelt at Winyah," to the youngest of her thirteen children, Elisha. In 1729 Elisha created a township plan that included lots for homes, a market, a court, a jail, a grammar school, and several churches, including a church and burial ground designated for "Antipedo Baptists."[30] A disputed land claim led to the loss of almost all the planned lots, although Elisha Screven retained the lot where his parents, and later he, would be buried.[31] Despite initial plans to construct a separate church, Baptists shared a meeting house with other dissenting groups throughout the remainder of the colonial period. An independent Baptist church did not emerge in Georgetown until the 1790s.[32]

William Screven's removal to Winyah Bay left a vacuum of stable and consistent leadership among Baptists in the Charleston church. With no Particular Baptist replacement in the colony, the church turned to its English network to request a supply. A series of ministers from England headed the church over the next few decades (the previously mentioned Mr. White, who died soon after arriving in Carolina, as well as two other preachers, a Mr. Sandiford (or Sanford) and a Mr. Peart).[33] Charleston church members also sent requests to Baptists in the Philadelphia area. In 1723 Thomas Simmons and his family arrived in Charleston from New Jersey, where Simmons had been pastor of the Baptist congregation in Hopewell since 1721. In 1725, the Charleston church called him to be their pastor.[34]

In contrast to the short terms of the ministers immediately before him, Thomas Simmons served as pastor of the Charleston church for almost two decades. However, his leadership was far from stable. Starting in the 1730s, the Charleston congregation fell victim to major theological infighting that erupted into a literal legal battle for control of the meeting house. Simmons initially identified as a Particular Baptist but later aligned with a minority of General Baptists in the congregation. A power struggle ensued, lasting into the 1740s. Renowned Anglican revivalist George Whitefield's visit to Charleston in the early 1740s helped spur renewed growth among Particular Baptists, further alienating those with General Baptist leanings. By the mid-1740s dissent escalated to the point that the two factions of the Charleston congregation battled for control of physical space of the church.[35] In 1745 the South Carolina legislature declared that the opposing groups should share the building, causing Particulars to purchase a nearby lot on Church Street. There, they built a brick meeting house later called the Mariner's Church, which they used on the Sundays when they could not occupy their original building. General Baptists dwindled over the decades, and in 1787 the Particular faction was awarded full control of the original meeting house, where a new church edifice was constructed during the pastorate of Richard Furman.[36]

The rift in the Charleston congregation heightened distinctions between

Particular and General Baptists in surrounding areas. The Ashley River congregation, which became its own separate church in the 1730s, was strongly Particular, while the Stono church, which also became independent in the 1730s, was General in orientation and corresponded regularly with the General Assembly of General Baptists in England, which provided ministers for the church until its demise in the early 1790s.[37] Issac Chanler, an English-born Particular Baptist who came to Charleston around 1733, preached at the Ashley River congregation and later at the Charleston church in the 1730s and 1740s.[38] English-born William Tilly, who had been converted in Charleston in the 1720s, became the Particular preacher for the Edisto Island congregation in the 1730s and 1740s.[39] Additionally, in the late 1730s, a group of thirty Baptists from the Welsh Tract in Delaware settled along the Pee Dee River, where in January 1738 they established what they first called Pee Dee, and later Welsh Neck, church.[40] Additional families from the Welsh Tract in Delaware moved to the community in the late 1730s and early 1740s. Isaac Chanler and Thomas Simmons ordained Welshman Philip James as minister in 1743, and the following year, the congregation erected its first meeting house.[41] Small settlements of German Baptists ("Tunker-baptists") came to South Carolina in the late 1740s, as did a congregation of Seventh-Day Baptists from the middle colonies in the 1750s. Welsh-born Baptist minister Morgan Edwards, who traveled throughout the colonies accumulating information for his history of Baptist churches, noted that by 1770 a distinct variety of Baptists were "to be met with in most parts" of South Carolina. Some Baptists were strongly Calvinistic, others Arminian; "some keep the *seventh* day of the week, and some are *german*."[42]

By the mid-1700s a variety of Baptist groups had settled in South Carolina. They came from different ethnic backgrounds and traditions but were not linked together in any particular connectional way, nor had they developed organized methods to expand church growth or to ensure a line of pastoral succession, instead relying upon traditional evangelical preaching to increase membership and to "plant" new churches. Following the deaths of William Tilly (1744) and Isaac Chanler (1749), Particular Baptists turned again to their wider national and international Baptist network, communicating with Philadelphia and English Baptists about the need for a new minister for the Charleston church.[43] Oliver Hart, who was preparing for the ministry and preaching at a Southampton church, volunteered for the position. Born in Warminster, Pennsylvania, north of the bustling city of Philadelphia, in 1723, Hart grew up in a Baptist home and was baptized at the age of eighteen.[44] Trained as a carpenter, he began preaching at the Baptist church in Southampton, close to Warminster, marrying eighteen-year old Sarah Brees in 1748. After accepting the invitation to preach in Charleston, Hart was ordained at the Southampton church in October 1749. He sailed for Charleston by boat, arriving in early December. Hart's wife Sarah, pregnant with the couple's second child, remained in Pennsylvania until the following year. As Baptist minister Basil Manly Sr. would later attest, Hart's arrival in Charleston seemed divinely timed. The young minister arrived in the city the same day that Isaac Chanler's body was buried. On February 16, 1750, the Charleston church formally called Hart as its pastor.[45] Sarah Hart and her two children arrived by boat in Charleston in late July 1750. Together, the Harts had eight children, four of whom died as infants, before Sarah's death in 1772, soon after the birth of the Harts' last child, a daughter named Sarah.[46]

Almost immediately after arriving in Charleston, Hart initiated organizational changes modeled on Pennsylvania and British Baptist structures. He developed a rigorous preaching schedule and warned about worldly temptations, particularly the sin of dancing in the pleasure-seeking city of Charleston, but he acclimated to the social and racial structure of Lowcountry society without contest.[47] Hart's actions helped instigate a localized revival in 1754. Conversions included Samuel Stillman, who would later join the ministry and serve as pastor of the Boston Baptist Church, and the Englishman Edmund Botsford, who played an integral role in South Carolina Baptist leadership in the late eighteenth and early nineteenth centuries.[48] Like his predecessor William Screven, Hart itinerated to various settlements surrounding Charleston proper. He preached at nearby James Island, where he baptized ten people, many of whom were young women. Hart hoped that the new converts would resist the temptations of the world with Christian fortitude, noting that the women might face more daunting tasks than the men: "Many of them are very Young, and will be Expos'd to many Temptations; most of them are of the female Sex; and therefore their Case is perhaps more Dangerous"[49] Out of this revival developed a new congregation on James Island, where a meeting house was built in 1759.[50]

In addition to full-time preaching, Hart also organized existing churches into an associational model to increase communication and efficiency. Soon after settling in Charleston, he invited delegates from four Particular Baptist churches in the Lowcountry to establish the Charleston Baptist Association. Modeled after the first Baptist association in the United States, the Philadelphia Baptist Association (formed in 1707), the Charleston Baptist Association provided a way for churches to work in concert with one another to evangelize and to train new ministers. In October 1751, delegates from Ashley River, Welsh Neck, and Charleston agreed to establish the association. Representatives from Euhaw could not attend this initial meeting due to high rivers.[51] Sensitive to concerns about extra-congregational decision-making, Hart and the other participating ministers made it clear that an association would not intrude on the congregational governance of churches. A Baptist association "arrogates no higher title than that of advisory council," noted the delegates. It would foster "understanding and fellowship" as well as "harmony and peaceful progress."[52] By November 1752, only months after a highly destructive hurricane hit Charleston, Euhaw delegates convened with representatives from the other three churches for the second annual meeting. White males Oliver Hart, Francis Pelot, John Stephens, John Brown, and Joshua Edwards comprised the five ministers who were part of the early association. James Fowler, William Screven Jr., Richard Bedon, Charles Barker, Benjamin Parmenter, Thomas Harrison, Phillip Douglass, and John Mikell, most likely church deacons, also attended the meeting.[53]

Through the Charleston Association, Hart and other ministers remained in close contact and coordination with Philadelphia Baptists, organizing early missionary endeavors to spread Baptist influence in the southern colonies. In 1755, ministers of the Charleston Association requested the missionary labors of Baptist minister John Gano in the interior portions of North and South Carolina. Gano ministered to a Baptist congregation that had left New Jersey and settled in the "Jersey Settlement" along North Carolina's Yadkin River in the early 1750s. Gano also traveled into South Carolina to fill the pulpit at Cashaway Church, where the regular minister had been suspended for drunkenness. In 1759 the Jersey Settlement congregation joined the Charleston Association, although Native American conflict in the early 1760s caused church operations to cease temporarily. Gano left for the North in 1760 because of the fighting, becoming pastor of the Baptist church in New York City in 1762.[54]

Charleston and Philadelphia ministers also communicated closely about educational initiatives. In 1756 the Philadelphia Baptist Association established Hopewell Academy, the first Baptist secondary school in British North America, located in Hopewell, New Jersey. The school lasted from 1756 to 1767.[55] Under Hart's leadership, the Charleston Association in 1755 organized the Charleston Religious Society in an effort to train aspiring ministers. The society—a separate entity from the Charleston Association—was open to any individual "of good moral character," subject to approval by a majority of members. All members had to pay an admittance fee to help fund a library. Members met weekly, with the goal to "promote the interests of virtue, and cultivate a kind fraternal spirit." Fines could be levied for taking God's name in vain or for coming to a meeting intoxicated (in the latter case, the guilty party was also "ordered out of the society for that meeting"). There was also a spirit of comradery and support: "Upon the death of a member all the others were required to attend his funeral: and if the deceased was in indigent circumstances, his funeral expenses were defrayed by an appropriation from the funds of the society."[56] Although membership in the religious society focused on living a morally cultivated, Christ-like life, its primary focus was ministerial education for the "right" kind of Baptist. As the literature specified, "The principal *end* and *aim* of this Society originally was, and always shall be, to educate such youths, and such *only,* for the ministry, who are of the denomination of Particular Baptists, and who appear to be truly pious, and have promising abilities for the great work of a gospel minister."[57] Future ministers Samuel Stillman and Edmund Botsford received assistance from the Religious Society to study for the ministry.[58]

Hoping to expand financial support for the Religious Society, Hart proposed that the organization be brought under the control of the Charleston Association, allowing the association to assume control of ministerial training. In 1757 he asked, "Whether there could be some method concluded upon, to furnish with suitable degrees of learning, those among us who appear to have promising gifts for the ministry." By 1757, churches in the association raised 133 pounds toward ministerial education.[59] However, questions about whether an association existed solely as an advisory group, instead of a society to extend benevolence, divided these early Baptists. Soon funding for the Religious Society, which remained the main resource for ministerial training, reverted back to separate donations, rather than being channeled through the association.[60] As Baptists created larger and more extensive organizational models in later years, the question of how benevolent efforts would be funded would continue to prove a source of contention.

By 1760, Baptists in South Carolina had established a denominational framework in Lowcountry South Carolina.[61] Through the Charleston Association, they communicated and coordinated with one another about the most effective ways to spread the gospel. Although most of the ministers of this early period, including Oliver Hart, lacked a formal education, church leaders recognized the importance of ministerial training as a means to promote correct theological views and as a way to train and produce new ministers. Early South Carolina Baptists also maintained regular contact with Baptists in Philadelphia, Boston, and England as they developed plans for Baptist leadership and growth, remaining connected to a larger national and international network of Baptists. Simultaneously, South Carolina's early and pronounced dependence upon the labor of enslaved people led white Baptists to develop the beginnings of a sectionalized model of evangelicalism and church growth. From their founding, leading Baptist ministers and lay persons in the Lowcountry participated in slavery and helped it flourish. White ministers in Charleston owned enslaved people, courted white slaveholders, and preached to congregations that included enslaved people. From an early point, these ministers grappled with complex and contradictory questions about slavery and Christianity. Should enslaved people be part of Baptist churches? Did their humanity—the fact that they had souls—counterbalance their enslavement and the distinctly inferior racial status that whites prescribed them? Like other white men and women from religious backgrounds, white Baptists turned to the Bible for guidance, developing a nascent Christian model of slavery that argued that the church as well as individual enslavers had an obligation to treat enslaved people with benevolence, caring for them materially and ensuring their religious instruction. In return, whites believed that enslaved people, as Christians, had an obligation to obey their masters and to live a moral life. This racially grounded interpretation of slavery developed slowly and organically amongst white Baptists, who benefited from its teaching in two primary ways: this interpretation assured ministers that they were performing their duty to preach to all people, slave as well as free, and it reinforced white control in the church, on the plantation, and in larger society. As they accepted Jesus Christ, joined Baptist churches, and claimed a right to Christian citizenship, enslaved people challenged, both subtly and at times overtly, the model of Christian servility that they were expected to obey. But in the collective white mind, Christian enslaved people occupied a distinctly servile position in the church as well as in the larger world.[62]

Enslaved people were not passive participants in white-black religious exchanges. They exercised a significant degree of agency in spiritual matters. More likely than first-generation Africans to embrace Christianity, second- and third-generation Africans found in Baptist churches an institutional framework that allowed them to meld African spiritual beliefs with the belief in the Holy Spirit (these beliefs helped to foster revivalism in the late 1700s in the southern states).[63] Because of Protestantism's emphasis upon personal conversion, enslaved people had the autonomy to decide whether to convert to Christianity. They could often choose which church to join, since most enslavers did not mandate that enslaved people join a particular denomination. Enslaved people showed an active desire to participate in religious sacraments and to help spread the gospel to others. Early European missionaries utilized black leaders fluent in multiple languages to help evangelize to enslaved people; those leaders often assumed the title of elder or deacon in the black community. This tradition continued in the British American colonies and subsequently in the United States, where enslaved people and free blacks, eager to participate fully in congregational life, pressed for leadership roles within white-controlled churches.[64]

In South Carolina, white Protestants, including white Baptists, appear to have preached to and provided religious instruction to enslaved peoples at an early date. Attempts to convert enslaved Africans and Native Americans reflected a larger ideological shift occurring among white Protestants in the early 1700s. In prior centuries, white Protestants had largely excluded enslaved people from Christian conversion, viewing church membership as a right for the freeborn rather than the enslaved. The desire of enslaved peoples to convert to Christianity, along with efforts of Protestant missionaries to preach to the marginalized as well as the elite, eventuated a transition in Protestant practices, so that over time, race, rather than church membership, became the chief way to demarcate freedom versus enslavement.[65] Religious interest among enslaved people, combined with the determination of some whites to preach to nonwhite men and women, was apparent in the first two decades of settlement in Carolina, for in 1691, colonial legislators stipulated in law "that no slave shall be free by becoming a christian."[66] In the early 1700s, Anglican missionaries who came to South Carolina to work for the Society for the Propagation of the Gospel in Foreign Parts (SPG) also provided assurance that conversion did not equate to freedom for the enslaved. SPG missionary Francis Le Jau developed an oath for enslaved people to affirm this position, stating that "You declare in the Presence of God and before this Congregation that you do not ask for the holy baptism out of any design to free yourself from the Duty and Obedience you owe to your Master while you live, but meerly for the good of Your Soul and to partake of the Graces and Blessings promised to the Members of the Church of Jesus Christ."[67] Subsequent laws also addressed the Christianization of enslaved men and women. The 1712 "Act for the Better Ordering and Governing of Negroes and Slaves," for instance, proclaimed the legality of "any negro or Indian slave, or any other slave- . . . to receive and profess the christian faith, and be thereinto baptized" on the condition that "the slave or slaves, with respect to his servitude, shall remain and continue in the same state and condition that he or they was in before the making of this Act."[68] Despite legal statutes, planter acceptance of Christian conversion of enslaved men and women remained gradual at best, even within religious circles. A disciplinary case that severely divided Baptists in 1710 captures the uncertainty white congregants felt about how far they were to go, as Christians, to be humane to enslaved people, particularly when civil law prescribed a far different set of regulations than did Old Testament law.

Responding to the rapid importation of African enslaved people in the 1690s, South Carolina legislators in 1691 and again in 1696 passed a series of wide-ranging laws regulating the behavior of enslaved men and women.[69] Borrowing directly from Barbadian slave laws, these early codes revealed the clear and distinct racism of white settlers, who viewed Africans as an inferior race inclined toward base and inhumane behavior. The laws forbade enslaved people to leave the residence of their masters without written permission; called for slave owners to conduct regular searches of the dwellings of enslaved people for weapons; and provided white patrols authority to break up gatherings of enslaved people on Sundays. More detailed and expansive regulations were added to the slave code in 1701 and 1712, signifying continued white concerns and anxieties about control of a rapidly increasing population of enslaved men and women. The codes required masters, mistresses, or overseers to inflict various levels of punishment, including branding, nose slitting, cutting off the ear, and castration for enslaved men and women who ran away for an extended period of time. Such corporal punishments provoked opposition from Anglican missionary Francis Le Jau because of the law's violations of the Holy Scriptures. "I have had of late an opportunity to oppose with all my might the putting of a very inhumane Law . . . in Relation to run away Negroes," Le Jau wrote. Castrating runaway males and cutting the ears of runaway females ran counter to "Law of God," which in Exodus 21 "setts a slave at liberty if he should loose an Eye or a tooth when he is corrected."[70]

Although Le Jau spoke out against aspects of existing laws about enslaved runaways, noting that portions of the laws contradicted biblical practice, not all white churchgoers shared his opinion in full. Indeed, two years before the passage of the 1712 code, white Baptists in Charleston divided over the corporal punishment of an enslaved person, illustrating that the formulation of a Christian model of slavery was a slow process and one that, in the early eighteenth century, was not endorsed collectively by all religious adherents. The event that propelled the frank discussion about the rights and obligations of a Christian enslaver occurred sometime before November 1710. That month, the Charleston church discussed the fate of a fellow member who had made "an Eunuch of his Slave." By following the law of the land but not of God, had the church member sinned against God? Should he receive church censure? A divided congregation—some believing that the actions of the slave owner were "not becomming [*sic*] a Church"—sought the counsel of leaders of the Baptist Church of South Moulton in Devon, England (a little more than fifty miles from Somerton), suggesting that a strong connection had been maintained between Baptists in the two regions.[73] Devon Baptists discussed the question and sent their response back to their brothers and sisters, some of whom they evidently knew, in Charleston. They lamented the content of the inquiry, noting that it "Occasioned much Sorrow, and heaviness in our hearts, upon information of the low Condition of your Sion, and the difference which, as a root of bitterness, is Sprung up among you, and trouble you." Devon Baptists stated that they had "done our utmost, both by our prayers, and Studys," to provide an opinion that they hoped would repair the divisions in the church and restore its peace and harmony.[72]

So long as he had followed the civil law and he had not injured his slave out of revenge, for obscene reasons, or in an act of attempted murder, Devon

Baptists believed that the Baptist brother had not sinned against the word of God. The civil law in question, they opined, seemed a necessary one, for its intent to prevent "the Vagrancy, theft, robory [*sic*], insurrections, and Outrages of your Slaves" was one of white self-preservation, serving "the common good" and "preserving order." Responding to concerns about the harshness and inequity of slave laws, Devon Baptists underscored their belief that Africans were a heathen race. Mosaic law, they noted, distinguished Jews differently than the "heathenish Servant." "Now if greater mercy was to be shewn to the Jew than to the heathen, Why may it not be thought probable, their penal laws for the punishing of these were more Severe, than for those Jews?" Stricter laws toward enslaved people were also needed because of the inferior nature of African men and women. Weren't "Negroes a Sort of rude, unpolished people, whose Nature requireth a Stricter hand over 'em?" While some might view castration as too severe a punishment, others could view it as necessary to preserve order in society.[73]

Again pointing to the potential vagrancy of African enslaved people, Devon Baptists asked about what would have happened had the enslaved man *not* been punished. Without such severe punishment, would the militant slave have continued to rebel, imperiling his own life but also inflicting damage on the colony? Would the enslaver have lost his enslaved person and as a result not been able to maintain "a comfortable living" for himself and his family? And finally, wasn't it better for a Christian enslaver to punish the enslaved man than for the individual to fall into the hands of a non-Christian? "[M]ay we not se[e] Some mercy mixt with this Brother's Cruelty," they wrote. What if the enslaver had not disciplined the enslaved man "and another had done it for the Sake of filthy lucre, which might have been more Severe and after that have ruled over him with greater rigour"? Better the Christian master, who understood the concept of Christian mercy, than the non-Christian, who may have treated the enslaved person more harshly and with no concern for the individual's humanity.[74]

While they did not believe that the enslaver under question had committed a civil crime, since his action "has been an offence to Some, we think it advisable for him to be laid under admonition, to beware for the future that he do not use his liberty with offence to others; but become a follower of St. Paul, Cor. 8.13 who would not Eat flesh if it 'twas offence to his Brother." They advised that since the action of "our Brother had more good in it, that it had Evill [*sic*]," the church should "labour to bare and forbare, tho, Suffer not sin to rest upon any: but Restore one another in the spirite of meekness. Gall. 6:1."[75]

Devon Baptists closed their letter by reminding Charleston Baptists that theirs was not a final determination, and that they planned to take the question to their next association meeting, where "we hop[e] to have the concurrent Judgment of many able Ministers." A year later, Devon Baptists recounted the judgement of their parent Baptist association, which reinforced the opinion that the enslaver under scrutiny had not committed a crime against either the state or the church. The enslaver had followed the civil law, and because the scriptures recognized both the buying of enslaved people and the existence of civil laws designed to punish enslaved people for running away or "rebelling against their Masters," the church should not punish the white member nor "break communion with him." The association recommended that the Charleston church members attempt to maintain "the Unity of the Spirite [*sic*] in the bond of peace" and to try not to take or give "Offence on light or Indifferent causes." Rather, "in all things," the church should "walk in love one with another To Show their Charity, And to be mercifull, and Compassionate to all men, to Slaves, and beast, as becomes those that profess the doctrine of a mercifull Saviour."[76]

The 1710 dispute over the meaning of being a Christian slaveholder points to two main conclusions. First, even in their early years, white Baptists in South Carolina grappled with the ethical contradictions of human enslavement and began to set the foundations for a Christian model of slavery. They struggled to balance Christian benevolence and care—Christ's mercy and compassion for all, including enslaved people—with a commitment to civil laws designed to protect the white community from slave revolt and rebellion. Over time, as more enslaved people joined biracial churches, white Baptists would argue publicly and more forcefully that the Christian model of slavery was the only way to ensure white protection and social control. In the early 1700s, however, this model of paternalism was still in its developmental stage within individual Baptist congregations. Second, both Charleston and Devon Baptists clearly articulated a belief that African enslaved people were inherently different from and inferior to white men and women, a Eurocentric belief widely shared by whites in the colonies and embraced even more deeply in the slave-majority Lowcountry of South Carolina. The advice of Devon Baptists, evidently accepted by white members of the Charleston church, reinforced the two main tenets of a white model of Christian slavery:

an emphatic belief in white superiority and an understanding that whites, as Christians, had a biblical duty to care for a dependent race of enslaved people.

For white Baptists, Christian paternalism in its developmental stages also included the religious instruction of enslaved men and women. Enslaved people were present in the Ashley River church as early as the 1730s, and most likely were part of the Charleston congregation as well.[77] Some enslaved Baptists attended white-controlled churches, but white ministers also preached separately to enslaved men and women. When Baptist missionary John Gano traveled to Charleston from North Carolina in 1755, Ashley River minister John Stephens asked Gano to help preach at his church. Gano commented that "His congregation, of white people, was small; but the blacks were very numerous." Stephens devoted a great deal of attention to the black members (Gano referred to them as "this latter class") and "was very useful to them." Stephens also informed Gano that Gano "made a very good negro preacher." When Gano left the meeting house, "the negroes stood in two rows, and as I passed, they pronounced many blessings on me, for taking so much care of their souls. This humbled me before God, and I then thought, I would, for the future, take more pains with souls, and especially with negroes; and I now wish I had more strictly adhered to my determination."[78] On another occasion, Gano preached "at the house of a Mr. Bulling; where there was a large congregation of negroes." The enslaved people's attentiveness prompted Gano to "ask them many questions, concerning their souls; and their answers, fully convinced me they had been touched by the spirit of the Lord."[79]

Records of the Charleston Baptist Association show that, by the 1750s, numerous early ministers owned enslaved persons. Additionally, some wealthy patrons deeded not only money and land but also enslaved people to their churches or ministers, showing that, despite its emphasis upon humane treatment, Christian slavery remained, at its base, a system of commodification. Of the five ministers who met in October 1752 to formalize the creation of the Charleston Baptist Association, all migrated to South Carolina from other areas and a majority became slaveholders at some point in their lives. New Jersey–born John Brown moved to Welsh Neck in the late 1730s. Soon after, he had a conversion experience and joined the Welsh Neck church, where by 1750 he became an ordained minister. Brown married in South Carolina and owned eight enslaved people by 1790.[80] Like John Brown,

Oliver Hart owned a small number of enslaved people, although the exact amount is elusive. At least one church member willed Hart an enslaved man upon her death. In 1760 Martha D'Harriette, former wife of James Fowler, on whose land the Particular Baptists had constructed what later became the Mariner's Church, bequeathed her "Negro Boy Slave Named Sampson," two portraits, one of George Whitefield and the other of his wife, and one hundred pounds currency to Hart. D'Harriette also willed one hundred pounds to South Carolina ministers John Stephens (Ashley River), Francis Pelot (Euhaw), Nicholas Bedgegood (Welsh Neck), Samuel Stillman, Martha Stephens (mother of Baptist minister John Stephens), and the famous revivalist George Whitefield himself.[81] In his journal Hart referenced the purchase of a slave, Dinah, and her son in 1771. By 1772 Dinah had delivered a baby girl.[82] Hart's second wife, Anne Marie Sealy Grimball (called Nancy), brought several more enslaved people into the household.[83] Swiss-born Francis Pelot, who came to Carolina with his family as participants in the ill-fated Purrysburg settlement and became minister of Euhaw Baptist Church in January 1752, owned over four thousand acres of land and an unidentified number of enslaved people.[84] Two of the five ministers who helped form the Charleston Baptist Association cannot be identified as slaveholders. John Stephens headed a Baptist congregation in Connecticut before moving to South Carolina. He became minister at Ashley River in June 1750, following Isaac Chanler's death. Although popular, he would leave the church in 1769 because of "an unhappy fondness for strong drink." While records do not indicate that Stephens owned enslaved people, he preached to a wealthy congregation. During Stephen's ministry, a fire destroyed the existing church. Various church members donated land and money for the construction of a new brick meeting house as well as a parsonage; the church also purchased enslaved people to work the land.[85] Joshua Edwards, originally from Wales, moved to the Welsh Tract of Pennsylvania before coming to the Welsh Neck in South Carolina in 1749. Ordained in May 1752, Edwards pastored the Welsh Neck church until the late 1750s. No information exists about whether or not he owned enslaved people.[86]

In addition to the five ministers listed above, seven lay members attended the 1752 meeting of the Charleston Association. Of that seven, at least five were planters who owned more than a handful of enslaved people: Charles Barker, Richard Bedon, James Fowler, Thomas Harrison, John Mikell, and William Screven Jr. (son of William and Bridget Screven).[87] Many of the delegates deeded money to their churches. James Fowler left a fund "for the Support of the Gospel Ministry in that Christian Congrigation [*sic*] where I now stand a Member in full communion in Charles Town."[88] The gifts that were bestowed to various churches were used for the support of the minister but also for the upkeep of the meeting house, or sometimes for the building of a newer, larger worship structure.[89]

As they settled in South Carolina, other Baptist ministers also purchased enslaved people. Born in England in 1731, Nicholas Bedgegood moved to the colonies in the 1750s. After a visit to George Whitefield's Bethesda Orphan House in Georgia, he converted from Anglicanism to the Baptist faith. Classically educated in England, where he had also studied law, Bedgegood held greater formal education than most Baptist ministers at the time, including Oliver Hart. Ordained to the ministry in 1759, Bedgegood preached at James Island and Welsh Neck Church, where at the time of his death he owned sixteen enslaved people.[90] A native of Bristol, England, Edmund Matthews began to preach in the Hilton Head area in the late 1760s.[91] He willed seven enslaved people to his children in 1784.[92] Born in Pennsylvania and raised as a Quaker, Evan Pugh spent part of his youth in Winchester, Virginia, where George Washington instructed him in surveying. Pugh became a Baptist in 1754 while teaching school in North Carolina. By the 1760s he moved to South Carolina, studied with Oliver Hart, Francis Pelot, and other ministers, and became minister of Welsh Neck and, later, Cashaway Church. In 1790 Pugh owned seventeen enslaved people.[93]

Although many early white Baptist ministers were slaveholders, it is less clear how they or the wealthy members in their congregations cared for their enslaved people individually. William Elliott Jr., a planter and the son of the William Elliott Sr. who deeded the lot for the first Charleston church, epitomized in his will the ideological framework of the Christian model of slavery—that so long as enslaver and slave followed biblical teachings, the best would come for both of them. Elliot freed some of his elderly enslaved people upon his death; the others he willed to his children. He included the following testament: "I earnestly desire [that] they would use all my poor Negroes [who] behave well and even tolerably well with great humanity and Mercy and Especially [when] they are old and infirm so I conclude with my Hearty Prayers to Almighty God to send his Blessings to and happiness upon all those both White and Black [who] are mentioned in this Will which I shall leave behind me."[94]

Some ministers specified that their enslaved people remain in the white family. Writing in his journal about the death of his close friend, Euhaw minister Francis Pelot, Oliver Hart remembered that Pelot "not only endeavored to train up his children in the paths of virtue and religion, but . . . also took much pains with his servants to teach them the fear of the Lord and the way of eternal happiness."[95] Pelot's will granted his enslaved people to his wife, sons, and son-in-law "and no other."[96] Yet at least some of the enslaved men and women on Pelot's plantations were eager to trade the Christian model of slavery for freedom. Pelot advertised for runaway enslaved people in the *South Carolina Gazette* at least twice. In February 1774 Pelot sought the recovery of three enslaved men he owned (Friday, Pompey, and Dago) along with two enslaved women who lived on a neighboring plantation. The enslaved people were likely headed to Edisto or James Island with plans to leave the colony by boat.[97] Friday and Pompey must have been caught and returned to Pelot, for they ran away again later the same spring, along with two other enslaved men belonging to the Baptist minister: Tom, "a country born lad" who "used to attend in houses and about horses," and Festus, a cooper of "Eboe" [Igbo] heritage.[98]

Unlike Pelot, some Baptist ministers left the fate of some or all of their enslaved people to their executors. Ashley River minister Isaac Chanler took steps to keep some but not all of his enslaved people in the family. He willed to his wife Elizabeth two enslaved people, Jack and Judy, who were married to one another. He directed his executors to use the remaining enslaved people in the best way possible: "either to keep or Imploy some or all of them on my Plantation abovesaid or otherwise for the use of my Children or else to sell either all or some of them as they shall see meet [fit]." Should the enslaved people be sold, Chanler specified that "my negro man named Lonnon and his wife Pegg and her Sucking child if she has any shall not be parted."[99] William Tilly, who was pastor at Euhaw and who died in 1744, designated all of his enslaved men and women, as well as his land, cattle, horses, household goods, and "Twenty Five Barrells of Rice now in the Barn" to be sold by the executors of his will. The total amount from the sale of his estate was to be divided between Tilly's son, William, and his brother Joseph, a joiner who lived in Warminster in Wiltshire, England. Perhaps Tilly trusted that his executors would not divide enslaved families; his executors were his close Baptist friends Paul Grimball, Joshua Grimball, Isaac Grimball, and John Jenkins.[100]

As late as the mid-1750s, Baptist leaders in South Carolina had yet to develop a public and institutionally accepted model of Christian slavery. But from the start of Baptist settlement, white Baptists participated in and accommodated the buying and selling of African men, women, and children, and no evidence exists to suggest that they overtly challenged the legal underpinnings of the institution. In their churches, white members engaged in conversations about how best, as Christian men and women, to treat enslaved men and women, and ministers evangelized to enslaved people in biracial settings as well as separate settings. While the numbers of enslaved people in early Baptist churches cannot be identified, black Baptists must have gained some form of meaning from organized religion; that some joined churches as early as the 1730s illustrates their active participation in the life of the church. The social, economic, and demographic structure of Lowcountry South Carolina, where extreme disparities of wealth developed earlier than in most southern towns and cities, meant that from the very start of their development, white Baptists had the potential to own enslaved people, to evangelize to enslaved people, and to assure themselves that holding enslaved people was legitimate because it was Christian. From this unique place of wealth, mastery, and a constant need to reinforce racial control, white Baptists were in the vanguard of setting the foundation for a religious proslavery argument that would be widely articulated by white southerners, both secular and religious, by the immediate decades preceding the Civil War.

Between 1696 and 1760, white Baptists from Maine, England, Wales, and Pennsylvania settled in South Carolina, forming by the mid-1700s the beginnings of a denominational model that facilitated inter-church communication and that set in motion a system of religious education for ministers. Although Baptist ministers welcomed converts of different social standing, they catered to the values of the elite, accommodating slavery and reinforcing racial and social hierarchy. In the Lowcountry, many white ministers owned enslaved people, as did lay leaders and other church members. Although they did not yet articulate a cohesive proslavery argument, they began to exhibit a Christian version of slavery, one that called for whites to preach to enslaved men and women and to treat them humanely, and for enslaved people, as a sign of their faith, to respond with loyalty to their enslavers. The Christian version of slavery emphasized salvation for enslaved people but also reinforced a secular racial hierarchy that cast black men and women as inferior and dangerous if their actions weren't controlled by whites. Black men and women responded to the evangelical message of personal salvation, but, as their narratives would reveal, challenged elements of the white-constructed Christian model of slavery. As they established a stable foundation in the Lowcountry, white Baptists grew by preaching widely, organizing together, and espousing a social order that confirmed rather than opposed white power and control. They preached a gospel of Jesus, and they preached a gospel of race.

CHAPTER TWO

Growth, 1760–1790

A Threat to Order

In 1760 Philip Mulkey, a charismatic white preacher in his late twenties, brought a small congregation of Separate Baptists from North Carolina into backcountry South Carolina, where they settled on the Broad River. Soon other Separate leaders, including Shubal Stearns and Daniel and Martha Stearns Marshall, moved into the region, forming what would become a second and notably different Baptist presence in the colony. Passionate, emotional, and subject to a strict interpretation of the Bible, early Separate Baptists proved to be the social antithesis of Lowcountry Baptists, who in turn began to call themselves Regulars to distinguish themselves from their backcountry brethren. Less concerned with social hierarchy and much more removed from elite culture than Lowcountry Baptists, Separate Baptists often eschewed pastoral education and allowed women and sometimes enslaved people to preach. Although many Separate congregations disappeared during the revolution, they exerted a tangible influence on new Baptist settlers who migrated to the backcountry from the Great Wagon Road and established churches in the region.[1]

In the 1770s many white Lowcountry Baptists became primary actors in the American Revolution, promoting independence and campaigning for religious as well as political liberty. They played a significant role in the disestablishment of the Anglican Church in South Carolina, legally incorporating their churches in the years after the revolution. In a state where slavery was more centrally tied to society and economy than any other, white Baptists also helped shape a southern response to the Revolutionary contradictions of slavery and liberty. In the immediate years after the revolution, a few ministers who had come from England or from northern colonies publicly questioned the legitimacy of slavery. Most white ministers, however, embraced Christian slavery as the only viable way to manage white-black relations in South Carolina. Viewing black men and women as a fundamentally different "class" from whites, white Baptists articulated more clearly a view of racial paternalism within their churches, collectively asserting that Christian slavery fulfilled God's wishes for the establishment of a Christian social order by benefiting both enslaved and enslaver. Some black Baptists, by contrast, promoted freedom by running away or aligning with Loyalists during the revolution.[2] For the majority of enslaved Baptists who remained in South Carolina, Baptist churches offered opportunities for spiritual affirmation and religious community, even though the experience of going to church remained racially segregated and stratified. By claiming a role within the fellowship of Baptist believers, black Baptists negotiated with whites their humanity and their religious rights, constantly challenging the white Christian model of slavery's emphasis upon racial subordination and prescribed servility.

Separate Baptists originated in New England, where, in the midst of the First Great Awakening, they literally separated from Congregationalist churches to create new congregations. While some Separates remained Congregationalists who practiced infant baptism, others embraced believer's baptism and formed congregations of Separate Baptists. Isaac Backus of Norwich, Connecticut, was an early Separate Baptist, as was a young minister named Shubal Stearns, a resident of Tolland, Connecticut. Stearns, who underwent a spiritual awakening after hearing George Whitefield's preaching, organized a Separate Congregational church in Tolland in the 1740s before converting to the Baptist faith in the early 1750s.[3] After being ordained to the ministry, Stearns and his family migrated south in 1754, traveling first to Virginia and then, by 1755, to Sandy Creek, North Carolina. Stearns's sister Martha and her husband, Daniel Marshall, who had been serving as missionaries to Mohawk Indians in Pennsylvania, also converted to the Baptist faith and joined the Stearns family in Virginia before moving with them to Sandy Creek.[4]

Early Separates endorsed a radically different preaching style and church order than the more established churches from which they had separated. Defining their religious experience by the "new birth," the momentous occasion when they received the Holy Spirit and became followers of Christ, Separates engaged in a distinctive and often emotional worship experience that centered upon the Holy Spirit. The conversion experience was frequently animated and demonstrative, as was Separate preaching, which was passionate, emotional, and often characterized as loud or "high-pitched." Adamantly opposed to creeds, Separates used the Bible as their only guide for worship and for living. In addition to believer's baptism and the Lord's Supper, which Lowcountry Baptists practiced, Separates observed seven additional biblical rites, including foot-washing.[5] Separates were also more egalitarian than the more hierarchical and elite-leaning Baptists of the Lowcountry. Early Separate Baptist ministers did not have formal ministerial training, although some clearly valued learning. They allowed women more roles in church governance, in some cases authorizing women to preach and to serve as eldresses and deaconesses. They may have also given enslaved people greater preaching autonomy. The practices of the Separates drew concern from the hierarchical Lowcountry Baptists, who viewed them as a disorderly group and were particularly concerned about their style of preaching and allowing women to preach.[6]

The Sandy Creek Church grew extremely rapidly, increasing from sixteen to over six hundred members soon after its establishment. Separates also developed new congregations in colonies including North Carolina, Virginia, South Carolina, and Georgia—forty-two within a seventeen-year period—prompting the formation of the Sandy Creek Association as early as 1758 to facilitate communication among the churches.[7] Stearns's preaching soon became legendary. Stearns was best known for his "zealous, animating manner," which characterized many of the New England New Lights.[8] Although not formally educated, the minister "was pretty well acquainted with books," according to the early Baptist historian Morgan Edwards. His delivery was noteworthy: "His voice was musical and strong, which he managed in such a manner as, one while, to make soft impressions on the heart, and fetch tears from the eyes in a mechanical way; and anon, to shake the very nerves and throw the animal system into tumults and perturbations."[9] Stearns also served as a model for other Separate preachers. "All the Separate ministers copy him in tones of voice and actions of body," Edwards wrote, with a small number surpassing his impact. Stearns died at Sandy Creek in 1771 at the age of sixty-five, after leading the church for sixteen years.[10]

South Carolina's first Separate minister, Philip Mulkey, was baptized around Christmas Day in 1756.[11] Mulkey's vivid conversion story gives readers a glimpse of what his preaching may have encompassed, showing a belief in supernatural intervention shared in varying degrees by many ministers in the eighteenth century.[12] Mulkey recounted leaving a dancing party where he had been fiddle playing and being confronted by a "hideous specter" that he soon determined to be the devil. The experience left Mulkey with a dread he could not shake. For days, he could neither sleep nor eat. He sought the help of his wife, but she could not help him purge the feeling of being damned and that he "shall soon be in Hell!" Only after a Baptist minister visited him and shared with him the news of salvation did Mulkey experience a spiritual renewal. He began preaching, first to his wife and a begrudging neighbor, who initially challenged Mulkey to a fight and then began to cry alongside Mulkey, although Mulkey's "talk of the new birth was not understood by [the neighbor] any more than by [his wife]." Mulkey soon "made myself known to Shubal Stearns and church, and was surprised to find that they understood the new birth, and had knowledge of the tribulations attending it which I had fancied were peculiar to my own case." After joining Sandy Creek church, Stearns was ordained a minister in 1757.[13]

Mulkey and a small band of followers moved into South Carolina around 1760, founding Fairforest Church in 1762, Congaree Church in 1766, and High Hills of Santee Church in 1772.[14] Like other Separate ministers, Mulkey had the capacity to influence his congregations emotionally. Morgan Edwards found nothing "extraordinary in his [Mulkey's] natural endowments, except a very sweet voice, and a smiling aspect." However, Edwards reported that Mulkey's cadence "manages in such a manner as to make soft impressions on the heart and fetch tears from the eyes in a mechanical way."[15] Anglican missionary Charles Woodmason, who criticized the backcountry Baptists and Presbyterians he observed during his travels liberally, lamented Mulkey's ability to draw a crowd: "Would any Mortal. . .have dreamd or imagin'd that such a Person as the infamous *Mulchey*, who came here lately in Rags, hungry, and bare foot can now, at his beck, or Nod, or Motion of his finger lead out four hundred Men into the Wilderness."[16]

Despite Mulkey's achievements in founding new churches in South Carolina, the minister's personal behavior came under scrutiny in the late 1760s, when he ostensibly fathered a child with a widow who held membership in one of his churches. Morgan Edwards wrote in 1772 about Mulkey that "His success has been such as to hazard being exalted above measure in his own esteem and in the esteem of his converts; but a thorn was put in his flesh about 4 years ago which will keep him humble when he lives, and teach his votaries that he is but man."[17] Mulkey's illicit behavior apparently continued, for in 1790 the Charleston Association warned against the minister for his "enormous crimes; such as adultery, perfidy and falsehood, which have been attended with very aggravating circumstances, often repeated and continued in for years; and part of the time, united with his highest pretensions of zeal and piety."[18] In 1795 Baptist leaders again warned against Mulkey for "Practice of Crimes and Enormities at which humanity Shudders." The minister probably relocated to east Tennessee, where his son Jonathan Mulkey served as minister at Buffalo Ridge Church in the early 1800s.[19]

In 1759 or 1760, not long after Phillip Mulkey settled in South Carolina, Daniel and Martha Stearns Marshall led a second group of Separates to the state.[20] They established a church that year on Beaver Creek, close to the Broad River. In 1762 the Marshalls and some of their congregation migrated west to a locale close to Augusta, Georgia, establishing Stevens Creek Church along the Savannah River. The Marshalls personified the idea of itinerant evangelicalism. Nineteenth-century Baptist historian David Benedict noted that "'tho not possessed of great talents," Marshall was "indefatigable in his efforts." Another Baptist remarked upon Marshall's "bold and independent method of procedure." Not attached to specific locations, Marshall "went from place to place, instructing, exhorting, and praying for individuals, families, and congregations; whether at a muster, a race, a public market, the open field, an army, or a house of worship; wherever he was able to command attention."[21] The Marshall family itinerated on both the South Carolina and the Georgia side of the Savannah River, beginning a legacy of churches in Georgia.[22] The work of Philip Mulkey and the Marshalls resulted in a wider span of Separate churches in the South. As a result of this geographic expansion, in 1771 South Carolina's Separate churches were dismissed from the Sandy Creek Separate Baptist Association, which had become large and unwieldy, to form the Congaree Baptist Association.[23]

The relationship of early Separate Baptists to slavery suggests that they did not overtly oppose the practice. While the most prominent early Separate ministers—Stearns, Mulkey, and the Marshalls—did not own enslaved people, other Separates did, and some enslaved people belonged to Separate churches in the 1760s. When Mulkey and his small group of Separates moved from the Haw River settlement of North Carolina (where eldresses were present) into South Carolina, others from the congregation stayed behind, including "Sharper and Cates (negroes)."[24] Some Separate ministers also owned enslaved people. Timothy Dargan, an early convert of Philip Mulkey in South Carolina who was licensed to preach in 1769, grew up in a household that included enslaved people and owned enslaved people as an adult.[25] Overall, though, few enslaved people were present in the earliest Separate churches. Early commentators critiqued not the roles of enslaved people in Separate congregations but the roles of white women, lamenting that white women were given authority to preach to mixed audiences. Morgan Edwards described deaconesses who cared for "the sick, miserable, and distressed poor" and eldresses who prayed with, taught, baptized, and watched over the behavior of women in a number of Separate congregations in the early 1770s. Edwards wrote that women were expected to "be veiled when they preach or pray, especially if men be sent to their assemblies."[26] Martha Stearns Marshall, Shubal Stearns's sister and the wife of Separate leader Daniel Marshall, exhorted to women and likely to mixed audiences. Robert Semple, noting Marshall's "surprising elocution," recounted that she had "melted a whole concourse into tears, by her prayers and exhortations!"[27] In the 1790s Richard Furman's mother-in-law Mary Burn McDonald wrote about churches in interior regions of Georgia, where Separates were bountiful, permitting "their women to exhort."[28] Early Separates were thus unique—and, to Lowcountry Baptists, greatly in error both theologically and socially—in that they allowed women to preach to gender-specific audiences and, likely, to mixed audiences.[29]

When Separates first arrived in South Carolina, despite the differences between the two groups, ministers from both networks were open to the possibility of unification. Oliver Hart and Evan Pugh, a young ministerial student of Hart's, served as delegates from the Charleston Association at a meeting at Sandy Creek in North Carolina in the early 1760s, ostensibly for the two groups to work together. Likewise, Philip Mulkey attended the meeting of the Charleston Association in 1762.[30] However, the differences between the two groups prevented early integration. Separates refused to share in the Lord's Supper with those who did not observe the same sacraments as they. Alternately, Lowcountry Baptists, who firmly emphasized patriarchal and elite governance, disagreed strongly with Separates' willingness to allow untrained men to serve as preachers, as well as their proclivity to let women into roles of authority. The Regular Baptist minister in the Pee Dee River area, most likely Nicholas Bedgegood, "sternly refused" to participate in the ordination process of Daniel Marshall, "declaring that he held no fellowship with Stearns' party: that he believed them to be a disorderly set: suffering women to pray in public, and permitting every ignorant man to preach that chose: that they encouraged noise and confusion in their meetings."[31] Regulars were not the only faction to be exclusionary. Separate Baptist John Newton, who moved from North to South Carolina in 1765, was ordained in 1768 by Regular ministers Oliver Hart and Evan Pugh. Congaree Church (Richland County), having sought guidance from the Sandy Creek Baptist Association, banned Newton from preaching because he had been ordained by Regular ministers.[32]

By the 1770s some Separate Baptists in the central portions of the state, close to the more established Lowcountry area, had begun to adopt the social and theological practices of Lowcountry Baptists, shifting and leaning toward a Lowcountry (Regular) Baptist orientation. Joseph Reese and his protégé Richard Furman illustrate this shift. Reese in many ways developed a hybrid model of Separate and Regular Baptist sensibilities, never relenting from some Separate beliefs, though by the late 1780s and 1790s Richard Furman had fully transitioned to a Lowcountry Baptist culture. Born in Kent County, Pennsylvania, Reese (originally Rees) and his family moved to the Congaree area of South Carolina in the 1740s. Joseph was an Anglican by birth but in the mid-1760s converted to the Separate faith after hearing the preaching of Philip Mulkey. Reese was one of the original members of the Congaree Church, of which he became pastor in 1771. Along with other Separate preachers, Reese, whose "natural eloquence, and command of the passions of his hearers were extraordinary," helped establish four additional branches of Congaree Church. One of those branches was High Hills of Santee, to the east of present-day Columbia. Though High Hills was deemed a "wicked, wicked" place by a visitor in 1769, Reese's preaching there sparked a revival in the early 1770s; one of Reese's converts was fifteen-year-old Richard Furman, who began exhorting at the church in 1772, the same year the church became an independent entity, with about seventy families holding membership. Although Reese was converted as a Separate Baptist and held some Separate practices close to his heart, in wealth and social position he fit easily with Lowcountry culture, and his preaching style

High Hills Baptist Church, Stateburg, South Carolina, established in 1770. Library of Congress.

was probably more comparable to Lowcountry delivery. As a sign of the changing orientation of Joseph Reese, both Reese and Regular Baptist Evan Pugh ordained Furman to the ministry in 1774.[33]

Joseph Reese's protégé, Richard Furman, shifted more distinctly from the Separate to the Regular model. Furman was born in 1755 in Esopus, New York, to Wood and Rachel Furman, who moved their family to South Carolina when Richard was ten months old, settling originally High Hills of Santee.[34] The Furman family moved to different locations around Charleston during Furman's youth, and Wood Furman held various jobs, including schoolmaster and justice of the peace. Tutored by his father, Furman thrived on knowledge and learning. Through his studies he acquired the foundation of a classical education as well as a broad knowledge of medicine. In 1770 the family returned to High Hills, where his father engaged in planting. Wood Furman died in 1783 with three enslaved people—Sirrah, Glasgow, and Jinny—willed to his wife Rachel Furman. He deeded 250 acres of land to his wife and roughly 500 acres of land to each of his three children, Josiah, Richard, and Sarah.[35]

In 1771, fifteen-year-old Richard Furman attended a revival service preached by Joseph Reese and converted to the Baptist faith.[36] By 1774 Furman had been ordained as minister and taken charge of High Hills Church. He interacted regularly with Oliver Hart and other Charleston Baptists. In contrast to Separates further inland, both Furman and Joseph Reese engaged actively in the Patriot cause during the revolution. In 1778, Furman persuaded his church—of Separate origin—to join the Charleston Baptist Association, to present a more unified Baptist front, and one more friendly to the new state constitution that promoted religious liberty.[37] Reese, by contrast, held firm to this aspect of his Separate background, refusing to guide his church into the (Regular) Charleston Association even after Furman's church at High Hills joined the group. Only after Reese's death did his church join the association.[38]

The assimilation of Separate Baptist ministers such as Reese and Furman into the Regular Baptist social order helped diffuse some of the doctrinal differences between the two groups. Oliver Hart seemed particularly willing to interact with and welcome Separates into his company, and most likely helped meld the two traditions together by bringing Richard Furman into his circle. In addition to Furman, Abraham Marshall (son of Daniel and Marsha Stearns Marshall), Philip Mulkey, and Joseph Reese all preached as guests at the Charleston church. Hart also shared his pulpit with ministers from other denominations and built a close relationship with Charleston minister William Tennent, with whom he would travel into the backcountry during the American Revolution politicking for civic and religious freedom from Great Britain.[39] Yet formal unification continued to meet roadblocks in the 1770s, a decade after Separates established their presence in South Carolina. Separate ministers Daniel Marshall, Joseph Reese, and Samuel Newman attended the Charleston Association meeting in 1773 to discuss "union," but "as the Separates were tenacious of their peculiarities nothing was accomplished." Two years later, in 1775, Philip Mulkey attended the Charleston Association again with a plan from the Congaree Association to combine "the several Associations in this Province into one," but the two groups could not agree upon terms of unity. Both sides attempted unification at different times, usually on friendly terms.[40]

Concerned about the perceived disorder of Separate Baptist practices,

Lowcountry Baptists produced a publication detailing how churches should be properly ordered and designed. In 1767, ministers of the Charleston Baptist Association appointed Oliver Hart and Francis Pelot to "draw up a system of Discipline agreeable to Scripture, to be used by the Churches." Baptist ministers Morgan Edwards and David Williams also helped with the document, which was adopted by the association in 1773 and published as *Summary of Church Discipline* in 1774.[41] This short treatise was written "chiefly for the benefit of the poor and unlearned," with the purpose of lessening "the ignorance of but too many church members, about discipline." The summary provided information about "the right understanding of God's Word" and welcomed readers to refer to relevant scriptural passages supporting their suggestions. Six main areas of biblical instruction were included: what constituted a "true and orderly gospel church"; its church officers; procedures for church membership; the duties of church members; church censures; and church associations.[42] The Philadelphia Baptist Association had published a similar set of instructions and guidelines in 1743 called *A Short Treatise Concerning a True and Orderly Gospel Church*. The Charleston Association's *Summary* was similar to the Philadelphia *Treatise* in most regards, although the two differed in at least four ways. While the Philadelphia *Treatise* specified plural eldership and also specified that elders should lay hands on newly baptized converts (the Charleston *Summary* made no mention of either point), the Charleston *Summary* specified the need for a written church covenant and stipulated that women could not vote in church (the Philadelphia *Treatise* made mention of neither).[43]

Intended to provide guidance for Baptist churches in South Carolina, the *Summary of Church Discipline* served as a detailed reminder of both theological and social expectations of white Lowcountry ministers and as a blueprint to avoid the gendered and classless "disorder" of Separate congregations, who allowed uneducated men and sometimes women to exhort and to preach. A patriarchal church with properly trained ministers, essential to the stability of a hierarchical Lowcountry society, barred white women from any governing role in church polity, a stark contrast to the egalitarian openness of more radical Separate churches in the interior. Neither the Philadelphia *Treatise* nor the Charleston *Summary* mentioned slavery, a strategic silence in a complicated biracial narrative. Enslaved people's roles, in any formal capacity, were erased in both networks because of race.

As they preached the gospel and engaged in distinctly different models of worship, Separates and Regulars became increasingly absorbed in the political unrest that led to the American Revolution. Political protests before the revolution, followed by the outbreak of the Revolutionary War, drew further attention to the divide between Separates in the far interior and Regulars and Separates in the plantation areas of South Carolina. Ministers on both sides of the war assumed political roles in their communities. Like most Charleston Regular Baptists, Separates who had closer commercial ties to the Lowcountry, such as Joseph Reese and his protégé Richard Furman, were Patriots.[44] In 1776 Richard Furman tried to join colonial military forces but was persuaded by Patriot leaders to maintain his civilian role; he preached to soldiers in the name of political and religious rights, drawing ire from the Crown.[45] Early Separate founder Daniel Marshall, who in the early 1770s had relocated to Georgia to establish churches, was imprisoned for his support of the Patriot cause; Daniel's son Abraham also supported the Patriots.[46] Further in the backcountry, Separate leader Philip Mulkey remained a Loyalist, while still other Separates were neutral. Much fighting took place in the backcountry, dispersing the population. Skirmishes and battles occurred close to Separate congregations of Steven's Creek (close to Augusta, Georgia), Goucher (close to Anderson Fort), and Fairforest (north of the Enoree River).[47] After the revolution, some Separate congregations no longer existed. Those that remained, supplemented by additional churches formed by settlers moving into the region from North Carolina, Virginia, and states further north, became doctrinally closer to Particular (Regular) beliefs but often retained an anti-educational and anti-institutional culture. These churches played a significant role in resisting the denominational reach of Charleston Baptists in the early nineteenth century.[48]

While backcountry Baptists took varying political positions toward the revolution, many Lowcountry Baptist ministers, eager to promote religious as well as civic freedom from Great Britain, became heavily invested in the Patriot cause. Edmund Botsford, a protégé of Hart's who had immigrated from England in 1766 and was ordained a Baptist minister in the early 1770s, publicly advocated against British policies.[49] But it was Hart, the most well-known Baptist leader in South Carolina, who also held the most visible political role in resistance to British measures. Hart had gone through hard personal times in the early 1770s. In October 1772, his wife Sarah died just days after the death of the couple's infant daughter.[50] The following year,

Hart began courting Anne Maria Sealy Grimball (1741–1813), widow of Charleston planter Charles Grimball. Hart had baptized Anne, seventeen years younger than he, in 1770. The two married on April 5, 1774.[51] Hart praised Anne, whom he called Nancy, for her "unsullied character," noting that "as a maid, a wife, and a widow," she served as "a pattern and ornament to her sex." Nancy viewed Oliver Hart, her "most affectionate and loving husband," as her "counselor—guide—friend."[52] The two had one child who lived to adulthood, William Rogers Hart, named for Hart's close friend, New Jersey minister William Rogers.[53]

Hart's prominence as a minister in Charleston, his vocal stance against British measures, and his interaction with Separate Baptists led Lowcountry political leaders to seek Hart's help in persuading Separates to support the Patriot cause. In July 1775 Henry Laurens, president of South Carolina's thirteen-person executive association called the Council of Safety, asked Hart to join planter and lawyer William Henry Drayton and New Jersey–born William Tennent, grandson of Log Cabin minister William Tennent and minister of Charleston's Independent Church, to travel into the backcountry to convince loyalist citizens to support the Revolutionary Provincial Congress.[54] Laurens noted that the three delegates' "compliance will be esteemed by the Council of Safety as an instance of your zeal and in the public service, when the aid of every freeman and lover of constitutional liberty is loudly called for."[55]

During his travels into the backcountry, which began in July 1775, Hart spent time with Separate Baptist Joseph Reese, who traveled with Hart on part of his journey. Hart also visited Separate Baptist Philip Mulkey, with whom he had shared past meetings and who at the time was minister of Fairforest Baptist Church, located in present-day Union County. Mulkey and his congregation refused to pledge support to the Patriots; Hart commented that the settlers were "irritated in the extreme."[56] Further to the northwest, close to Spartanburg, a threatened clash between Loyalists and Patriots—roughly 270 men in all—turned peaceful, with some, though not all, of the party reversing their allegiance and supporting the Revolutionary South Carolina government. Hart also journeyed through portions of present-day Richland, Newberry, and Laurens Counties citing scriptural references to spiritual liberty. He returned to Charleston in early September to greet a new son, Silas, to whom Nancy had given birth on August 30. Silas died within weeks of Hart's return, prompting Hart to note the "heavy trial to my dear Nancy."[57]

As fighting continued in portions of the state, South Carolina's Provincial Congress passed a new state constitution in March 1776 that recognized the Church of England as the official state religion. Anxious to disestablish South Carolina's Anglican Church, Welsh Neck Church minister Elhanan Winchester proposed an interdenominational meeting be held for dissenting ministers. The meeting convened in April 1776, at High Hills of Santee. Ministers drafted a petition calling for the disestablishment of the Anglican Church and stating that "all Protestants demeaning themselves peaceably under the government established under the constitution shall enjoy free and equal privileges, both religious and civil."[58] They chose William Tennent to present the petition to the General Assembly, which he did in January 1777. Some representatives proposed to maintain civil support for the Church of England because of its work with the poor, but ultimately delegates voted unanimously for disestablishment.[59] Dissenting ministers, Baptists amongst them, had achieved the goal that "no Protestant inhabitant of this State shall, by law, be obliged to pay towards the maintenance and support of a religious worship that he does not freely join in or has not voluntarily engaged to support, nor to be denied the enjoyment of any civil right merely on account of his religious principles."[60] Christian churches could apply for incorporation, becoming their own legal entities. The Charleston church applied for and received incorporation from the state the following year, in 1778.[61] That year, as the war progressed, Hart wrote to his brother in New Jersey of his hopes that out of the war would emerge a religious and morally cultivated society. He looked forward to a time when "Peace, like the swelling Tide, shall flow over the Mountains and cover the whole Land," when "Religion, freed from its Shackles—Learning and Virtue, encouraged and promoted, shall spread far and wide," and when "Wisdom and Knowledge shall increase, and every Pesant [*sic*] be qualified for a Senator." The outcome of the war with Britain, Hart hoped, would be an independent, Christian nation where "Every Man shall sit down peaceably under his own Vine, and under his own Figtree; and the Trade, Favour and Protection of America will be courted by all Nations under Heaven."[62]

But peace was still years ahead. In 1778 British troops occupied Savannah; by May 1780 British forces under the command of Sir Henry Clinton had captured Charleston. Many Baptist ministers who took an active role in promoting the Patriot cause fled the colony. Richard Furman and his family found sanctuary in North Carolina and Virginia, with the exception of two trips back to Society Hill, home of Welsh Neck Church.[63] In 1780 Oliver Hart rendezvoused with one of his protégés, Edmund Botsford—who had fled Georgia in 1779—and the two traveled north, preaching in North Carolina and Virginia en route to Pennsylvania. The pair separated in Virginia, where Botsford remained temporarily. Hart traveled on to Pennsylvania, arriving in his home town of Warminster on October 12, 1780.[64] In December, Hart accepted a call to supply the Hopewell Baptist Church in New Jersey. Nancy had relocated to Edisto Island to live with her sister during Hart's absence and "opened school . . . to get my living" but joined Hart in New Jersey in September 1781. Hart wrote in his diary that, with Nancy's arrival, God had "answered my prayers in restoring to me the joy of my heart." Nancy's arrival doubtless made it easier for Hart to remain at Hopewell, where, in addition to serving his home church, he itinerated in Maryland, Pennsylvania, New Jersey, and New York.[65] Hart continued to entertain thoughts of returning to the Charleston church—members eagerly sought his return—but ultimately remained in New Jersey, leaving the Charleston church without a full-time minister for much of the 1780s.

Just as the American Revolution divided Baptists in South Carolina, it generated questions about the future of slavery. A dearth of ministers in the colony forced congregations to turn to a wider national and international network to secure new pastors, some of whom held different views about slavery. During the Revolutionary era, a few white ministers in South Carolina questioned slavery outwardly, but most, even those initially uncertain about its permanence, adapted to and accommodated the institution, agreeing that a Christian model of slavery was the best way to ensure the moral regulation of black men and women. Through this model, whites would provide religious instruction and humane care to enslaved men and women, with the expectation that enslaved men and women would obey and support the will of their benevolent enslavers. In the eyes of white Baptists, by emphasizing both the humanity and the racial subordination of enslaved people, Christian slavery thus benefited whites and blacks alike. As the number of enslaved Baptists increased in the post-Revolutionary years and as black members sought opportunities to preach the gospel to others, the model of Christian slavery assumed subtle but significant locational differences. In Charleston and surrounding Lowcountry areas, whites specifically prohibited the establishment of independent black churches. In western South Carolina and eastern Georgia, however, where Separate influence remained stronger, whites sometimes permitted enslaved people to serve as preachers of independent congregations. In these locations, enslaved people such as George Liele, David George, and Andrew Bryan established remarkable preaching careers that had implications for the global world.[66]

George Liele, converted in a Baptist church in Burke County, Georgia, began preaching to enslaved people and free blacks in the 1770s. Swayed by the words of a white preacher, Liele realized that his life "hung by a slender thread, and it was the will of God to cut me off at any time, and I was sure I should be found in hell, as sure as God was in Heaven." Recognizing that he could be saved only through "the merits of my dying Lord and Saviour Jesus Christ," Liele asked for Christ to come into his heart. He then "felt such love and joy as my tongue was not able to express." Following his conversion, Liele "declared before the congregation of believers the work which God had done for my soul."[67] After he was baptized, white members licensed Liele to preach. With both the church's and his enslaver's permission, Liele preached at different plantations on the Georgia and South Carolina sides of the Savannah River, including Yamacraw, close to Savannah.[68] The literate Liele lined hymns for enslaved people to sing, explaining portions of the hymns as well as instructing them about the gospel.[69] Freed by his Loyalist owner during the revolution, Liele helped organize a Baptist congregation in Savannah before moving to Kingston, Jamaica, where by 1790 he had baptized over four hundred converts and where he also helped establish a school for free and slave children.[70]

While in Georgia, Liele met and baptized not only his wife, with whom he raised four children in Jamaica, but other enslaved people who left a preaching legacy in plantations and communities along the Savannah River. David George, an enslaved man converted by Liele, preached and exhorted at the Silver Bluff plantation in western South Carolina starting around 1773. When the revolution ended, George fled with other British settlers to Nova Scotia, where he established a biracial congregation before moving with his congregation to Liberia.[71] Another convert of Liele's, freed slave Jesse Peters, also preached at Silver Bluff. In the 1780s Peters and followers established the Springfield African Baptist Church in Augusta, Georgia; Abraham Marshall and David Tinsley, white Baptist ministers, "constituted" the church.[72] A third convert of Liele's was Andrew Bryan, an enslaved man belonging to

Silver Bluff Church, the first African American congregation established in South Carolina. It was founded on the Galphin Plantation near Augusta, Georgia, in 1773. Public Domain.

evangelical planter Jonathan Bryan. Andrew Bryan replaced George Liele as the pastor of what became Savannah's First African Church after Liele left for Jamaica. Jesse Peters and white Baptist Abraham Marshall ordained Bryan to the ministry in 1788, baptizing forty-five black members in the same visit. By 1790 the Georgia Baptist Association (comprised of white-controlled biracial churches) admitted the Savannah church to its organization. The congregation was repeatedly threatened by white authorities in the early 1790s, but over time the First African Baptist Church came to be accepted by the white community and survived throughout the antebellum years, with portions of the congregation forming two additional churches, the Second and the Third African Baptist Church.[73]

In contrast to the more flexible roles held by African American Baptists in westernmost portions of South Carolina (and across the line in Georgia), enslaved men and women in the Charleston area faced white opposition to the establishment of independent African and African American churches. In these areas, where white racial control had been paramount from early settlement, enslaved men and women participated in semi-autonomous congregational leadership positions, usually with white oversight. Many enslaved members of the Charleston church, for instance, enjoyed regular worship on their own plantations but also traveled to town to participate in services on a monthly basis. Just as organized religious opportunities for African Americans varied, white ministers in the Revolutionary and post-Revolutionary years, many of them non-natives of South Carolina, exhibited varying thoughts about the permanence of slavery. A brief look at the views toward slavery of three Lowcountry ministers—Elhanan Winchester, Edmund Botsford, and Oliver Hart—shows the range of thought that proliferated among white Baptist leaders during and immediately after the American Revolution. Winchester, born in Massachusetts and a vocal opponent of the slave trade, moved to South Carolina in the 1770s. Edmund Botsford immigrated from England to South Carolina, over time becoming a public advocate of Christian paternalism. Oliver Hart, born in Pennsylvania, became an owner of enslaved people once he moved to South Carolina. Hart returned to Pennsylvania during the revolution, where at the time of his death he and his wife set forth the gradual emancipation of the men, women, and children that he legally owned.

Elhanan Winchester, a Separate Congregationalist turned Baptist, preached in Massachusetts before coming to Welsh Neck Church in late 1775, where he served as minister until 1779. Earlier in 1774, Winchester had delivered a public discourse in Fairfax County, Virginia, against the slave trade; the sermon was published in 1778 in England and touted by prominent Baptists Caleb Evans and John Rippon.[74] At Welsh Neck, Winchester likely expressed his views about the slave trade. He probably also acted on his evolving beliefs about universal salvation, a stance that he embraced in full by the early 1780s. The church underwent a major revival in 1779. Winchester preached to up to 1,000 spectators on some Sundays, and by the end of the year, 240 new members had joined the church.[75] Winchester tailored portions of his preaching specifically to enslaved people, organizing them into a separate congregation. Ninety-eight black men and women joined the church in 1779 (sixty-five of the ninety-eight, many from the same plantations, joined the church within a three-week period).[76] Winchester's support for gradual emancipation may have attracted many enslaved people to his church, but his views about slavery as well as about universal salvation probably left some white church members uneasy. The congregation discussed calling other ministers at different times, but Winchester remained at the church until 1779, when he left for the North, having accepted the pastorate of the Philadelphia Baptist Church. In Pennsylvania, Winchester advocated more strongly against slavery and the slave trade; he also shifted fully to a universalist position regarding salvation.[77]

More typical of Baptist ministers in the Revolutionary years was Edmund Botsford, who became pastor of Welsh Neck Church in 1779, after Elhanan Winchester's departure. Upon assuming leadership of the congregation, Botsford excluded many members, both white and black, who had been admitted by Winchester. He noted that "upon examination" the black members, particularly, "appeared to be very ignorant of the nature of true religion." Botsford dismantled the separate congregation of enslaved people, bringing those who remained members back into a biracial—but segregated—setting.[78] As he became immersed in ministry, Botsford found that he had a strong aptitude for preaching to enslaved people. With the approval of the Welsh Neck congregation, the minister took a two-month hiatus to preach at the Charleston church in spring 1785, which remained without a regular minister after the departure of Oliver Hart. Religious interest was on the rise in Charleston: in January 1785 Richard Furman, who was among a number of young ministers who preached at the church during Hart's absence, wrote to Botsford of "concern about Religion in the Minds of several, especially the Negroes." While in Charleston, Botsford preached forty-one sermons and paid numerous visits to the homes of various city residents. Noting that he had "hardly enjoyed an hour to myself since I have been in town," the visiting minister wrote about the many black men and women who came to see him, as well as some whites, while many others he "must go and see." Pleased with the religious responses he received, Botsford believed that "there would soon be a flourishing Church," should a regular minister become available. Botsford also gained confidence in his preaching in this urban setting: "Who would have thought that your poor son Botsford would have been owned as an instrument to bring souls to the Charleston Church?" he asked, noting that "the heart is the same in Charleston, as in the country."[79]

Returning to Welsh Neck Baptist Church in late spring of 1785, Botsford encouraged his church to make a more deliberate commitment to Christian slavery. Possibly influenced by a similar stance among white Baptists in

Charleston, Botsford's Welsh Neck congregation in June 1785 revised their congregational covenant, agreeing with one another that "that if we should be possessed of negro or other slaves, that we will act a truly christian part by them; by giving them good advice, laying our commands on them to attend the worship of God in public on Lords day & in private in our families when convenient." Agreeing that they had a collective duty to be benevolent masters, white churchgoers pledged not to be cruel to their enslaved people, "nor prevent their obtaining religious knowledge, & will endeavor to prevent their rambling and will encourage those who can read, at proper times to instruct others; & in all things endeavor to act in our families, as to obtain the blessing of God."[80]

Welsh Neck Baptists' congregational promise to enforce a Christian model of slavery did not signal a concession to social egalitarianism. As white members pledged to care for their enslaved people in a Christian manner, they also reminded enslaved people of their secondary and servile status. Welsh Neck, like other biracial churches, separated enslaved people spatially. In 1790 the church replaced the slave seating from the gallery with the addition of a "shed the length of the House . . . for the use of the negroes."[81] Botsford preached to enslaved people in the church but also at surrounding plantations, where loyal and pious enslaved people were given multiple leadership roles. From Welsh Neck in 1790 Botsford wrote to English Baptist John Rippon that he was "very fond" of teaching enslaved people. He had preached "to 300 of them at a time, and not one *white* present but myself"—a telling point given laws from 1740 prohibiting large meetings of enslaved people for religious gatherings. Botsford believed that enslaved people could embrace Christianity just as wholeheartedly as whites, and that they often exerted more Christian compassion to one another: "those who are truly religious," he noted, "in general far exceed the *whites* in love to each other, and in most other duties." Many of the enslaved people he preached to at Welsh Neck were literate and loved to sing hymns (they "sing delightfully," Botsford remarked). At Welsh Neck, some black leaders "go to the plantations, and preach to their own colour on Lord's-day evenings, and at other times when we have no service in the meeting-house."[82] Yet, despite the leadership roles claimed by black Baptists, whites retained ultimate oversight. In the midst of a revival in 1790, Botsford and a number of white male members formed a committee to examine enslaved people who wished to join the church and to oversee discipline amongst the members.[83] White-constructed

Christian slavery underscored benevolence to enslaved people, but always in the context of white order and control.

While Edmund Botsford labored among enslaved people and whites at Welsh Neck in the 1780s, the most significant Baptist minister in eighteenth-century South Carolina, Oliver Hart, remained in New Jersey, despite repeated calls to return to the Charleston church. Hart's reason for staying in New Jersey may well have hinged on the issue of slavery. Opposition to the slave trade and to slaveholding was on the increase in New Jersey, Pennsylvania, and other northern states, where Baptists became involved in antislavery societies in the 1780s and 1790s. William Rogers, one of Oliver Hart's closest friends, in 1790 became vice president of the Pennsylvania Society for Promoting the Gradual Emancipation of Slavery, an organization that included Benjamin Franklin and Benjamin Rush. Samuel Stillman and James Manning, both of whom had South Carolina connections and both of whom were friends of Hart, participated in abolitionist activities in Providence, Rhode Island, in the early 1790s.[84]

Hart's interaction with his close ministerial friends—Rogers, Manning, and Stillman—must have influenced his changing views about slavery. In his published eulogy for Hart following Hart's death in 1795, William Rogers described Hart's transition from owning enslaved men and women to serving as "an advocate for universal liberty." In 1780, when he became minister of Hopewell, Hart "laboured under some prejudices in favor of the slavery of the poor Africans and their descendants." However, the minister was "soon brought to contemplate the whole with horror—and to *wish*, yea more, *fervently to pray* for success to attend the endeavours of those individuals or societies who are laudably engaged in promoting the happiness of the great human family!"[85] In his will, Hart had granted gradual freedom to an enslaved man; Hart's wife, "since the death of her husband, has liberated a Negro Woman, with her youngest child, and disposed of her two other children, each until the age of 25—when they are to be free also."[86]

William Rogers was not the only person who eulogized Hart in 1795. Richard Furman, a close protégé of Hart, did so in South Carolina, where, in contrast to Rogers, he mentioned nothing about slavery. In his tribute to Hart, delivered on February 7, 1796, and called *Rewards of Grace Conferred on Christ's Faithful People*, Furman portrayed Oliver Hart as a man who loved his church and who loved his white family.[87] He said nothing about slavery in his memorial to his close friend and mentor, choosing a strategic silence about Hart's ultimate decision to liberate his enslaved people. For Richard Furman, Christian slavery, not emancipation, was the only feasible way to promote order between whites and blacks in South Carolina.

Between 1760 and 1790, white Baptists experienced dramatic changes in South Carolina. A new network of Baptists, the Separate Baptists, emerged in the backcountry, challenging both the doctrinal and the social order of Lowcountry Baptists. The two groups initiated attempts to work together, but both cultural and theological differences punctuated their efforts. The American Revolution further separated the two groups. The revolution also politicized religion, especially in the Lowcountry, where Baptist ministers blended religious goals with civic ones to fight for freedom from British authority. This mixture of church and state would influence the actions of some ministers in the postwar years. Finally, the revolution brought greater scrutiny to the moral and philosophical meanings of slavery and freedom. Responding to the desires of black Baptists to preach and to share the gospel with others, some white Baptist ministers granted black men flexibility to lead congregations in portions of South Carolina, and at least one minister who came to South Carolina in the 1770s voiced antislavery sentiments. The majority of white ministers, however, both Separates and Regulars, legitimized the institution by further refining a Christian model of slavery that recognized the humanity and the spirituality of enslaved people and that granted enslaved people varying degrees of religious autonomy, but that simultaneously reinforced racial subordination in an effort to protect white authority. For white Baptists who remained in South Carolina, the Christian model of slavery—one that, in white eyes, benefited both whites and enslaved people—increasingly became the only commonplace and viable solution to Revolutionary demands for freedom.

CHAPTER THREE

National Denominationalism, 1790–1830

In the decades following the American Revolution, Charleston Baptist ministers retained a highly visible role in forging a national as well as state denominational presence. Much of their incentive came from the leadership of Richard Furman, who became pastor of the Baptist church in Charleston in 1787. A forceful presence in the Baptist world as well as in Charleston society, Furman believed his role was to be a religious statesman who, if necessary, could step into the political world to promote and defend a moral, virtuous, and orderly society steeped in Christian and republican goals. Under Furman's watch, Lowcountry Baptists aggressively expanded their organizational network. Dedicated to spreading "the general interests of the Redeemer's kingdom, by united and common efforts" Charleston ministers played a chief role in establishing a national denomination committed to the burgeoning foreign mission movement. They engineered the first state convention in the South, the South Carolina Baptist State Convention, to oversee missionary and educational efforts at home and abroad, in coordination with the national Triennial Convention. In 1826 Lowcountry Baptists created the Furman Academy and Theological Institution, which opened its doors to students in 1827. Significantly, they were committed to producing ministers and congregants that replicated the Lowcountry model of hierarchy and order. Lowcountry Baptists' support for a professionalized ministry, trained missionaries, and denominational education aligned with middle- and upper-class cultural values that prized intellectual and educational uplift. The creation of a denomination committed to "the pursuits of religion and virtue," one that spread "evangelical and useful knowledge," was designed to create a moral, virtuous, and orderly Christian citizenry that not only spoke to the importance of individual salvation but would ensure peace and harmony in society.[1]

Efforts to build an elite-controlled denomination that was both state and national in scope drew sharp dissension from Baptists in the Upcountry, who refused to join a state convention dedicated to missions and education. Nowhere in the Bible, Upcountry Baptists claimed, were Christians instructed to support foreign missions, much less a trained, professionalized ministry. Rather, the Bible told believers that any man who felt called to preach should do so and did not need formal educational training, and the Bible certainly did not mandate that congregations send money to finance missionaries in foreign lands. Upcountry Baptists also remained more open to white women serving in governing roles. As Lowcountry Baptists affirmed and promoted middle- and upper-class values centering on education, uplift, and strictly defined social roles within as well as outside of the church, numerous Upcountry Baptists retained a strong folk tradition that allowed for more flexible gender roles and that exercised hostility to educated, professionalized ministers. Although Baptist growth increased dramatically in both the Upcountry and the Lowcountry—from roughly 4.7 percent of the overall population in 1800 to 10.1 percent of the overall population in 1830, white Baptists were no means united. The determined efforts of Lowcountry Baptists to spread a denominational vision into the South Carolina Upcountry produced strong dissension between the two groups of Baptists, leading to an intrastate culture war that resonated in South Carolina for years to come.

In the fall of 1787 thirty-two-year-old Richard Furman accepted the call to serve as pastor of the Baptist Church in Charleston, the state's landmark Baptist church. Holding the position until his death in 1825, Furman rose to become the uncontested leader of the Lowcountry Baptists and one of the most influential religious statesmen of his time. When Furman accepted the call to serve the church, he had just lost his first wife, Elizabeth Haynsworth Furman, who died in June 1787, at the age of thirty-two.[2] Furman moved with his three children (Rachel, ten; Wood, eight; and Richard, five), his widowed mother, and his enslaved men and women, who by 1790 numbered six, to the parsonage on Church Street in November 1787.[3] Two years later, in May 1789, Richard Furman wed again, this time to Dorothea Maria Burn.

Burn, born around 1773, was only sixteen years old at the time of her marriage to the thirty-three-year-old Furman. The couple raised to adulthood eleven children, including ministers James Clement Furman and Samuel Furman. Dorothea, whom Furman called Dolly, and Richard had their last child, William, in 1817. William died the following year, and Dolly died in 1819, at the age of forty-six.[4]

Richard Furman settled into Charleston life with enthusiasm, adapting both his dress and his religious vision to a more cultured group of elites. Significantly, he began wearing clothing associated with the Lowcountry gentry, a Revolutionary style that included "a coat with pockets in the skirts opening outwardly under a lapel, waistcoat reaching the hips, knee-breeches and long stockings, the latter protected in foul weather or a journey by high-topped boots." Irritated that Furman had changed his attire to fit with elite fashion in the Lowcountry, High Hills Baptists lodged a complaint at the 1788 meeting of the Charleston Association, querying, "What rule are we to observe respecting the strange fashion of apparel which come up among us?"[5] Furman wrote to his sister Sarah Haynsworth that "considerable offense has been taken at the Hills on account of my dress and appearance in Charleston." The minister felt some duty to "conform in a moderate degree to the prevailing customs in the place where we live." Just as he had adapted to the coarser, homespun dress style of residents of High Hills, he modified his clothing in Charleston to fit the city's customs. Furman believed that it was natural to shape one's behavior "in a moderate degree to the prevailing customs in the place where we live . . . the reason is obvious, as it is the means of avoiding an odious singularity, and of conciliating the minds of associates to a free and familiar intercourse."[6] Placed in the difficult situation of having to answer to charges against their moderator, the Charleston Association settled on a middle ground. "We think . . . that both extravagance and neglect should be avoided, that due respect be paid to the age, circumstances, and stations of persons, and to the customs of the place where we reside," the Association found; "also our income should not be exceeded, as we are under moral obligations to improve our substance for necessary and useful purposes."[7]

Furman did more than "fit in" to Lowcountry society—he worked actively to promote and enlarge Christian morals and elite values within and outside the walls of the church. In Furman's view, ministers should play an active role in politics in order to shape and influence a moral society, just as

Furman and other religious leaders had exercised their religious influence to promote political goals during the American Revolution. Along with other ministers, including Baptist Evan Pugh, Furman was chosen to be a delegate to the 1790 state constitutional convention, which met to address various issues including greater backcountry representation. Delegates also discussed whether ministers should be allowed to serve as legislators, with Furman maintaining that ministers, who wielded significant moral and intellectual influence in their communities, should be able to serve in such a capacity. While Furman's position did not hold sway, the Charleston minister found other ways to exercise civic and political influence, joining with both politicians and community leaders to advance moral literacy and education and to shape a more virtuous society in very public ways.[8] "Our Liberty religious as well as civil is unrestrained," Furman wrote to a Baptist minister in 1791, "and those who have Ability and Worth of every Denomination are eligible to Places of civil Trust."[9]

Furman's alliance with statesmen and leading elites in the community remained strong throughout his years in Charleston. The Baptist minister collaborated closely with Revolutionary War veteran and eminent statesman Charles Cotesworth Pinckney, an Episcopalian who ran as Federalist candidate for the United States presidency in 1804 and 1808. In 1795 Furman and Pinckney created a society of Charleston leaders to promote "Emigration of virtuous citizens from other Countries."[10] Furman also preached to and helped organize various civic and benevolent causes. In the early 1800s, Furman and Congregationalist minister Isaac Keith co-founded the Charleston Tract Society, of which Furman served as early president. The Charleston minister delivered an address on the anniversary of the Charleston Orphan House, which had been founded in the 1780s and which he argued brought together "good men of every denomination in vigorous, and common efforts, to promote the best of causes" and to uplift and improve civil society.[11] In 1802 the Society of the Cincinnati and the American Revolution Society invited Furman to present an address on the Fourth of July. Titling his speech "America's Deliverance and Duty," the well-known minister compared America's independence with the Israelites' exodus from Egypt. God had intervened in both causes to bring liberation to his chosen people.[12] Furman also preached to the Cincinnati and American Revolution societies upon the death of George Washington in 1799 and Alexander Hamilton in 1804. Lauding Hamilton as "a man of transcendent genius,"

Furman called South Carolinians to employ "patriotism and religion" to end the "barbarous practice" of dueling.[13] Later in 1804, at the request of the Cincinnati and Revolution Societies, Furman drafted a petition to the legislature calling for a law to end dueling. When ministers met for the annual meeting of the Charleston Association in November 1804, delegates passed a resolution of support for the memorial, noting that "this Association will unite with their fellow citizens in the petition of the Legislature of this State for an Act to abolish the bloody practice of dueling."[14]

Furman's belief in the importance of civic morality translated to full-fledged political support for Charles Cotesworth Pinckney in 1808, when Pinckney accepted the Federalist nomination for president of the United States. Furman politicked openly for his close friend, noting Pinckney's strong support of disestablishment during the revolution. Furman wrote: "To me it appears just and requisite that our Citizens at large and those of South Carolina, in particular, should know and at this time remember that General Pinckney was in the American Revolution an early and influential Advocate of religious as well as Civil Liberty."[15] Closely tied to a vision of a moral and pious citizenry, Furman and Pinckney continued to promote religious and civic improvement into the 1810s and 1820s. They participated actively in the Bible Society of Charleston, formed in 1810 as an auxiliary of the British and Foreign Bible Society and later the American Bible Society. The goal of the Bible Society was to distribute Bibles free of charge to those destitute of religion. Bible societies spread into other towns and cities throughout the state, just as they did throughout the nation. The society was non-denominational, but its leaders were primarily Federalists. Pinckney served as president of the society, with Furman serving as vice-president until his death.[16]

Although an avid leader in Lowcountry civic life, Richard Furman's primary focus remained the creation of a professional, educated class of Baptists throughout South Carolina. Lowcountry Baptists were painfully aware of the illiteracy of many Baptist ministers and members in rural South Carolina churches, particularly in the Upcountry. Furman wrote to a Baptist minister in England that "a great part of our ministers as well as members are illiterate," an issue that proved a "great hindrance" to the Baptist cause.[17] In an effort to increase and to formalize ministerial training, Furman and other leaders replaced Oliver Hart's "Religious Society" model, which had lost momentum during the revolution, with a "General Fund" of monies closely tied to the Charleston Association. Money would be raised through charity sermons preached to individual congregations, as well as through personal contributions.[18] In 1791, association delegates created a General Committee of ministers to administer monies raised through the General Fund; incorporated the following year (1792), the General Committee was comprised of one delegate from each church in the Charleston Association. Richard Furman served as president of the committee until his death in 1825.[19] The General Committee, which met during each annual association meeting, placed students with ministers for mentoring and sent some students to local South Carolina academies, as well as two of its earliest students, Joseph B. Cook and John M. Roberts, to Rhode Island College (Brown University).[20] By 1800 Roberts, who had returned to South Carolina to become minister of the High Hills church, established a private academy at High Hills, boarding students in his home. In 1802 the Charleston Association's General Committee agreed to equip "a complete theological library" for students of the academy. The school most likely lasted until 1809 or 1810. Along with Baptist divines, prominent Methodist minister William Capers was educated here.[21]

In addition to educational endeavors, the General Committee—the guiding force in driving denominational growth in South Carolina—discussed in 1800 whether the Charleston Baptist Association should support domestic and foreign missions "in union with other Christians of various denominations." Shouldn't Baptists engage in efforts "to send the gospel among the heathen; or to such people who, though living in countries where the gospel revelation is known, do not enjoy a standing ministry, and the regular administration of the divine ordinances among them?"[22] The association took its first step in the area of organized missions in 1803, when delegates granted the General Committee the authority to appoint a missionary, John Rooker, to preach the gospel to the Catawba Indians in the South Carolina backcountry. A school for Native Americans was established around 1805 but struggled to remain open due to poor funding. Rooker remained in his post as domestic missionary until 1817, when "from the diminution of the tribes, their being so entirely surrounded by the habitations and churches of the whites, and their own wandering habits," the General Committee ended the mission.[23]

While Lowcountry Baptists in the early 1800s accelerated their plans for educational and denominational growth, Upcountry Baptists (as well as Methodists and Presbyterians) experienced a major revival that greatly strengthened their presence in the piedmont and mountains. Fueled by Presbyterian James McGready's phenomenal revival in Kentucky in the late 1700s, Baptists, Methodists, and Presbyterians worked together at the turn of the century to foster interdenominational camp meetings throughout the Southeast. Religious interest increased through the Upcountry as news spread of the camp meetings. The 1800 annual meeting of the Upcountry Bethel Association, held at Bethlehem church in Spartanburg District, drew almost 3,500 people to hear ministers preach and exhort.[24] By May 1802 the first major interdenominational camp meeting occurred in South Carolina, at the Waxhaw settlement in Lancaster District. A total of twenty-one preachers (five Methodists, five Baptists, and eleven Presbyterians) attended the meeting. Ministers took turns preaching at the two main stands; in between sermons, they also traveled from tent to tent praying and exhorting. The preaching was electric. Estimates of crowd attendance ranged from three to eight thousand people.[25]

Other camp meetings followed in Upcountry South Carolina. Presbyterians initiated, and Baptist and Methodists joined, a camp meeting at Nazareth Church in Spartanburg District that attracted between 5,000 and 6,000 people. Individual churches and associations experienced revival as well. A reported 2,000 people gathered at Woodruff Baptist Church in Greenville District in the summer of 1802, where 36 people were baptized in one day.[26] 1802 and 1803 proved particularly fruitful years, with additions by baptism ranging from 100 to 400 in some churches. Between 1802 and 1803, an overwhelming 420 members were baptized at Padgett's Creek in Union District. Bethel and Fairforest recorded 247 and 216 new members, respectively. Additional churches received over 100 new members during this time period. Enslaved people as well as whites took part in the revival, although their numbers were still minimal in the far northern and western portions of the state, where the revival had its greatest impact.[27] Overall, the Great Revival significantly increased Baptist strength and influence in the Upcountry. By 1803 roughly 10,000 whites and blacks belonged to South Carolina Baptist churches, representing an 80 percent increase in membership over a three-year period.[28]

Although the Great Revival affected Upcountry churches primarily, a more limited form of revivalism also occurred in other parts of South Carolina. At the Waxhaw meeting, Richard Furman observed many people "from the lower part of this state" in attendance, some of whom "came under

. . . impressions."[29] Their experiences created religious excitement in some Lowcountry churches. A major revival occurred in the Beaufort area between 1803 and 1804, assisted partially by Baptist preachers from nearby Savannah, Georgia. At Black Swamp Church outside of Beaufort, roughly 1,200 people participated in a three-day camp meeting in December 1803. Organizers constructed a large stage connected to two rows of tents, "from which there were five or six sermons delivered on each day and night, besides exhortations in different parts of the camp." The Charleston *City Gazette and Daily Advertiser* remarked on the high percentage of female converts, while "a very small proportion" of enslaved people and free blacks attended the gathering.[30] In the town of Beaufort, white men also were drawn to the revival. Future leader William Bullein Johnson was converted at this revival in 1804 (at the age of twenty-two). Thomas Fuller, father of future Baptist minister Richard Fuller, was baptized along with several enslaved people who had been converted during the revival. Fuller noted that his conversion caused "some estrangement between my friends and myself," but that he felt "cause to rejoice that the blessed Lord my God led me in this way, and plucked me as a brand from the burning."[31]

The Great Revival generated tremendous religious excitement and growth in the Upcountry, leading to many new churches and instilling a Baptist presence that was much stronger than it had been in the past. However, it did not forge a unified white Baptist culture in South Carolina; instead, it widened rather than narrowed the gap between denominational and congregational Baptists. The emotionalism of Upcountry camp meetings drew criticism from Lowcountry Baptists, who believed that ministers should preach formally and eruditely to their audiences and that church members should understand and follow correct lines of hierarchy and patriarchy. Richard Furman, for instance, voiced concerns about the "enthusiasm" of the camp meeting and the "too free intercourse between the sexes in such an encampment."[32] For Lowcountry Baptists in Furman's circle, the Upcountry revival was not the way to spread religious growth. Instead, organized religious efforts—properly trained ministers who could take the word of God to the heathen—represented the proper process of spreading God's kingdom on Earth. In terms of denomination building, God's work went on in distinctively different ways for these two networks of Baptists.

In 1812 Boston Congregationalist missionaries Luther Rice, Adoniram Judson, and Ann Judson converted to the Baptist faith while traveling to India. While the Judsons remained in India, Luther Rice returned to the United States to seek support among Baptists for, in William Johnson's words, "the great work of Foreign Missions."[33] With the backing of Boston Baptists, Rice traveled throughout the eastern coast encouraging the formation of foreign mission societies. From his travels a plan emerged for delegates for the various societies to meet in Philadelphia in 1814 to form a central missionary organization, the Baptist Foreign Missionary Society for the United States. Rice spent time with Richard Furman of the Charleston Baptist Association and with William Bullein Johnson, who had moved to Savannah in 1811 to preach at the Baptist church in that city. Learning of Rice's proposal, the Savannah River Association, which encompassed churches in Georgia and western South Carolina, established the Savannah Society for Foreign Missions "without delay, to make the necessary preparations for the meeting in May 1814 in the city of Philadelphia."[34]

At their first meeting in 1814, thirty-three delegates representing twenty foreign missionary societies, including the Savannah Society for Foreign Missions, convened in Philadelphia to form the "General Missionary Convention of the Baptist Denomination in the United States of America for Foreign Missions," which earned the name "Triennial Convention" because the group met every three years.[35] Delegates came from eleven states, as well as the District of Columbia. Although northerners dominated numerically, the convention elected as president the South's most well-known Baptist leader, Richard Furman. Connecticut-born Thomas Baldwin, pastor of Second Baptist church in Boston, Massachusetts, was chosen to be secretary.[36] During the inaugural meeting of the Triennial Convention, delegates also created an executive governing board called the Baptist Board of Foreign Missions for the United States, which came to be called Governing Board. Furman, chosen president of the Governing Board, declined the position because of South Carolina's lack of proximity to Philadelphia; instead, Thomas Baldwin became president.[37] Still, as president of the larger convention, Furman's forceful leadership gave the national organization important shape. Furman held the position of president of the convention at each meeting—in 1817, 1821, and 1824—until his death in 1825, signaling his national influence in Baptist circles and revealing the importance of South Carolina as a driving force in the building and shaping of an American Baptist denomination.

Baptists both north and south were energized by the formation of the Triennial Convention. Leaders agreed that combining various benevolent institutions into a national convention channeled "the Energies of the whole Denomination in one sacred effort, for sending the glad tidings of Salvation to the Heathen, and to nations destitute of the pure Gospel-light."[38] In his introductory sermon to the convention, Richard Furman captured the millennial hopes of the group. "The Nations are convulsed," Furman preached, "and great events with respect to the Kingdom of Christ appear to be drawing near."[39] Johnson later remembered that the "organization of this convention formed an epoch in the history of the Baptists of the United States, that was followed by a most blessed era of successful benevolent effort in various departments of the Kingdom of Christ, that spread the unspeakable blessings of literature & salvation throughout millions of our race in these & in foreign lands."[40]

In addition to foreign missions, the Triennial Convention adopted a vision for Baptist education. Pennsylvania and New England Baptists had established Rhode Island College in 1764 and in 1804 renamed the institution Brown University, in honor of alumni and benefactor Nicholas Brown, but at the founding of the Triennial Convention, no other Baptist college was in existence.[41] At the 1814 convention, Richard Furman in his presidential address called for the creation of education societies and suggested the idea of a "general theological seminary." In 1817, members added to the constitution of the Triennial Convention a plan to establish a "national seminary of learning" to train aspiring ministers in classical and theological education.[42] Funds not earmarked specifically for missions would be directed toward the seminary.[43] By 1818, Baptists opened a theological seminary in Philadelphia; struggling for money, it was combined with the newly instituted Columbian College (later George Washington University) in Washington, DC, in 1821.[44] The formation of a national Baptist seminary ran into roadblocks, however. Columbian College struggled financially, and in 1825 its theology department moved to the newly formed Newton Theological Institution in Newton, Massachusetts.[45] Undeterred, Baptists engaged in efforts to establish state and regional institutions, creating Hamilton Theological Seminary (New York), Waterville (Maine), and Georgetown College (Kentucky).[46] South Carolina leaders worked closely with Georgia Baptists to establish a seminary; ultimately the two states created separate academies and theological seminaries, the Furman Academy and Theological Institution in South

Carolina (1826) and Mercer Institute (1833).[47] An energetic vision for Baptist national and international outreach was now underway, with a strong national focus on a professionalized ministry, denominational education, and missionary societies.

In Lowcountry churches, support for the new missionary movement abounded. Ministers encouraged all church members, including children, to support the Triennial Convention's goal to bring salvation to people throughout the world. White women such as Hepzibah Townsend of Edisto Island became involved in foreign missions. Townsend formed the Edisto Female Mite Society in 1812; in 1822, the society raised $122.50.[48] Other churches followed in line. In the 1830s three female domestic missionary societies, all auxiliaries of the Edgefield Domestic Missionary Society, were in existence in the Edgefield Baptist Association.[49] Believing that Baptists of all ages should support the missions effort, Richard Furman organized a Juvenile Missionary and Educational Society and held a "children's time" at the Charleston church.[50] The buy-in was to be complete—whites of all ages, as well as enslaved people, were encouraged to support the grand missionary enterprise of spreading the gospel to the heathen.[51]

In the late 1810s, white Lowcountry Baptists, driven by a desire to educate and uplift illiterate Baptists in the Upcountry and to unite them behind national missionary purposes, proposed the formation of a state Baptist convention.[52] Establishing a state convention was a clear effort by Lowcountry Baptists to mold Upcountry congregations in their own image. Membership in the Charleston church more than doubled between 1787 and 1805—increasing from 152 to 331. The size and growing wealth of the congregation, driven by the leadership of Richard Furman, led to the commissioning of a new, elegant meeting house in the late 1810s, designed by well-known architect Robert Mills and completed in 1822.[53] In other parts of the state, however, hurdles remained. To Lowcountry Baptists, most Upcountry congregations seemed unpolished. Many Upcountry ministers lacked formal education and training. Upcountry suspicion about funding for missions was strong. A state convention, Lowcountry Baptists hoped, would draw interest from the more educated Baptists in the Upcountry. Associations would be asked to send "their most enlightened and influential members, men who are governed by the fear and love of God, to concert measures in favor of these general interests . . . and particularly with a view of the work of collecting and establishing funds in favor of educating ministers, and of sending the gospel to the destitute."[54]

Charleston Baptists first publicly discussed the creation of a state Baptist organization in 1819 and 1820. Unsurprisingly, they received little support from backcountry associations. Furman and other leaders, including John Roberts and Joseph B. Cook (who both studied at Rhode Island College) wrote to the associations about the need for greater educational preparation. Ministerial training was "a subject of the first importance . . . ministers who have failed to obtain some share of education are not fitted to take that station in society, or exert that influence which would properly belong to them if they had," Furman wrote. Preachers with "little fluency of speech" were an embarrassment to the denomination. "Is not this apparent to persons of common discernment; and are not their defects in language and knowledge, lamented by their friends, while they become the matter of scoff and derision to their enemies?" Furman asked. Even children who had been provided some form of education could "see these defects" and feel embarrassed by improperly trained and uneducated ministers. Ministerial training was imperative to enlighten Baptists and to create a better, more improved society for both the current and future generations of South Carolinians.[55]

Upcountry associations, unpersuaded by the appeals of Charleston Baptist leaders, declined to send delegates to a state convention. Nevertheless, Charleston Baptists in 1821 moved forward with their plan, meeting at the Baptist church in Columbia on December 4, 1821, to establish "a Convention of the Baptists in the State of South Carolina." Of the seven Baptist associations in the state, the three most connected to the Charleston Association's vision—the Charleston, Edgefield, and Savannah River associations—agreed to the new organization. The other four—Bethel, Saluda, Broad River, and Moriah—remained independent associations.[56] After prayer and "an appropriate address" by Richard Furman, the delegates constituted themselves a regular body, electing Furman their president and Abner Blocker of Edgefield their secretary. Agreeing that their "direct object" was "the promotion of the cause and interest of the Redeemer," members approved a constitution that set forth their denominational vision.[57] Their body would be called formally the "State Convention of the Baptist Denomination in South Carolina" and would be comprised of "a coalition of Associations." The main goals of the convention were to be "the promotion of evangelical and useful knowledge, by means of religious education; the support of missionary service among the destitute; and the cultivation of measures promotive of the true interest of the churches of Christ in general, and of their union, love, and harmony in particular." The constitution called for the creation of a state seminary "for the gratuitous education of indigent, pious young men for the Gospel ministry, on a plan of accordance with the interests of that established by the denomination at large, in the United States." The seminary would allow paying students to attend, "it being distinctly understood, that the course of education and government, shall be conducted with a sacred regard to the interests of morality and religion." The most "able, pious, and suitable" ministers should be selected to promote the convention's "important design" of "missionary service." Additionally, the constitution called for the "establishment of Sunday Schools, as well as the religious education of children in families." [58] Delegates described the means of funding the convention in 1821 and in more detail in 1822. Churches were to provide "regular, yearly contributions" to the state convention to help achieve its grand missionary goals, but founding delegates pledged not to intrude upon the "spiritual, or temporal interests or rights" of individual churches. Churches were encouraged to hold annual charity sermons to raise money for the state convention and to form auxiliary societies to raise additional money for this purpose. Rules for the auxiliary organizations, which were to be called "Education and Missionary Societies," were uniform: church members could join for two dollars, contribute at least one dollar each year after the first year's membership, and become a lifetime member for fifty dollars.[59]

With its establishment in 1821, the South Carolina Baptist State Convention became the first statewide Baptist convention in the South, showing again the leading role that South Carolina Baptists took in forging denominational growth. Georgia Baptists followed suit in 1822.[60] Lowcountry leaders continued to appeal to Upcountry Baptists to join the convention. They visited Upcountry associations and sent written and impassioned pleas for their cause, assuring white Upcountry Baptists that joining the convention was not an infringement of individual liberty or congregational authority, that religious seminaries were biblical—after all, Jesus taught his disciples—and that foreign and home missions were necessary. White Baptists throughout the state were "co-workers with God," they argued, who had a duty to work together toward "the diffusion of the glorious Gospel of the Son of God, by missionary service; the suitable preparation of faithful men, called into the ministry; the right-instruction of the rising generation; the promotion of union, love and harmony, among brethren of the same family, and zeal for God according to knowledge."[61] Baptists throughout the state, Lowcountry leaders contended, had a Christian responsibility to spread the Kingdom of God through educational and missional activity.

Baptists also attempted to win support for their denominational vision by sending formally trained ministers into areas without a strong Baptist presence, or where existing Baptists had little connection to the Baptist State Convention. They found immediate success in Edgefield District in the western part of the state. The Baptist State Convention paid the twenty-four-year-old Baptist minister Basil Manly $800 to evangelize the area in 1822. Joining Edgefield's Big Steven's Creek Church, Manly was ordained in March 1822. The following month, he helped establish a Baptist congregation in the village of Edgefield.[62] As he surveyed the territory the year before, Manly informed his close friend and Baptist minister Iveson Brookes that of the roughly thirty-seven or thirty-eight churches in the district (most of which had a great deal of wealth), fewer than ten had ministers, "and not one of those ministers can write a sentence fit to appear even in the minutes." Manly counted at least three churches worth "at least $500,000," with others boasting lesser but still significant wealth. Such possibilities for pastoral support, and the need for educated Baptists ministers, provided a fertile ground for Lowcountry Baptists to send additional preachers into the area for explicitly denominational reasons, "not to undo them and make Methodists and Presbyterians out of them, but to build them up and rescue the sinking Baptist name."[63] Manly remained at the Edgefield church, where he led a significant revival in 1822, until 1826, when he relocated to Charleston to assume the role of minister of the Charleston church following the death of Richard Furman.[64]

Like Manly, William Bullein Johnson hoped to instill support for Lowcountry Baptist denominational efforts among Upcountry Baptists. In 1822 Johnson moved with his family to Greenville for health reasons and to serve as principal of the newly established Greenville Female Academy.[65] Like other nearby towns and villages, mountainous Greenville served as a resort town for Lowcountry elites from both South Carolina and Georgia, who resided there in the late summer and early fall, but locals, many with much less wealth, also inhabited the area.[66] Wealthy residents proposed the establishment of the male and female academies: as Johnson wrote in his

"Reminiscences," "A few families of wealth & refinement made it their abode for several months of the year, at whose suggestion the citizens determined to erect two academies of brick for male & female students."[67] Johnson determined the curriculum and taught courses for female pupils, whose ages ranged from ten to fifteen. On the elementary level, the pupils studied reading, spelling, and writing before advancing in the second year to geography, arithmetic, and English grammar. By their fourth year, female students learned natural philosophy, chemistry, logic, moral philosophy, Latin, and Greek.[68] Some of these disciplines were unusual for women, but for Johnson, like Furman, an educated citizenry was the ultimate civic and religious goal. In keeping with the tradition of providing moral and intellectual uplift to the community, Johnson also began a Bible Society, and his oldest daughter, Mary, established a Female Library Society."[69] In nearby Pendleton, Johnson remembered, "the society was larger and more improved, in consequence of a larger number of inhabitants from the low country who were possessed of wealth & learning, and made it their permanent place of learning. A Bible Society, Library, & Schools for both sexes had also been for some time in operation."[70]

No Baptist church existed in Greenville in 1822, so Johnson joined the closest church, Brushy Creek Baptist Church, "7 miles out of the Village." The churches of the region "consisted of good & substantial members," Johnson wrote, and the ministers were effective but not well-educated: "The ministry of the churches was destitute of scholastic education; but they were sincere, laborious, & earnest in their labors, & their work was blessed by the Great Master."[71] Since there was no church in Greenville, Johnson began regular preaching at the courthouse, soon starting a Sunday school "Requiring several Teachers."[72] As his followers grew, the Baptist minister began a subscription for the building of a church on land donated by Greenville's biggest benefactor, Vardry McBee. The first Baptist meeting house in Greenville was completed and the church constituted in 1831.[73]

Eager to promote the virtues of the Baptist State Convention to Upcountry Baptists, Johnson and Basil Manly, who had traveled from Edgefield, spoke in 1823 to delegates of the Saluda Baptist Association (of which Greenville was a member church) about the benefits of foreign missions. Their message was powerful enough that a majority of ministers approved a resolution to join the state convention. The vote quickly caused backlash within member congregations, however. According to Johnson, "many of the churches sent up an expression of their unwillingness to continue in the Convention, & the Association discontinued their union with that Body."[74] Anti-convention ministers also voted to rescind the circular letter written by Johnson the prior year, which discussed the positive work of the convention. Johnson responded by writing and publishing a circular called "The Alarming Condition of the Churches," which lamented the choice of many churches in the Saluda Association to reject the convention's "enlarged views of the Divine glory, character and designs."[75]

Experiencing both progress and setbacks, Charleston Baptists continued to pursue an aggressive denominational vision. No task assumed greater attention in the convention than the founding of a statewide Baptist seminary and academy. Initially, leaders conversed with Georgia Baptists to establish a seminary together, possibly in the growing town of Augusta, along the Savannah River. An economic downturn, coupled with drought and a bad crop year in 1824, may have shifted Georgia Baptists' interest in such a venture. Solo efforts among South Carolina Baptists continued, with Richard Furman, as always, the driving force. Plans for the school stalled in the summer of 1825, however, when Furman, South Carolina's most visible and most visionary Baptist leader, died in late August at the age of seventy. Befitting his public image, an elaborate funeral ensued in Charleston, complete with a funeral procession that included ministers from churches throughout the city, members of Furman's household (white family members first, followed by Furman's enslaved people), white church members, members of the Charleston Bible Society, members of the Charleston Religious Tract Society, Revolutionary Society members, and white city residents in general. African American church members marched separately, on each side of the procession, reflecting their segregated and separated role in church and in society.[76] Following Furman's death, Baptists throughout the South and throughout the nation paid tribute to Furman's life.[77]

Bereft at the loss of their primary leader, and as an acknowledgment of his pivotal role in the promotion of educational enterprises, Lowcountry Baptists honored Richard Furman by naming their soon-to-be-opened denominational academy in his name. At the time of its opening, leaders envisioned the Furman Academy and Theological Institution as a theological preparatory school, to serve as a stepping stone for pupils who would then attend Washington Seminary. For those who did not have the means, the state seminary would provide the basics of theological education, so that young men could minister ably to their churches. Poor pupils would attend the academy for free; others (both ministerial and lay scholars) would pay for their education.[78] The executive board of the state convention (the Board of Agents) considered several sites for the institution, including Greenville and Pendleton, before settling on the town of Edgefield. The trustees of the Edgefield Village Academy (established in 1822) donated their buildings to the board for use of the school, and wealthy Edgefield Baptist Eldred Simkins Sr. donated land adjacent to the property.[79] The Board of Agents purchased the home of Basil Manly, who was departing for Charleston, as a domicile for the academy's principal.[80] In September 1826 the board unanimously chose Rev. Joseph Warne as principal of the new academy. Warne was "an Englishman from the North" who had hoped to serve as a missionary in foreign lands but whose health issues prevented such a role.[81]

The Furman Academy and Theological Institution welcomed the first class of students on January 15, 1827.[82] As an advertisement in the Charleston *News and Courier* noted in early January, the "Seminary of Instruction . . . is located in the village of Edgefield, of this State, under the patronage of the State Convention of the Baptist Denomination in South Carolina. The immediate supervision of it is committed to the Board of Agents, who have selected the Rev. Mr. Warne its Principal. The object of the Seminary is, to afford instruction to Students, that shall prepare them for the higher classes in the most respectable Colleges of the United States, and also, to impart instruction in Theology to young men designed for the Gospel Ministry."[83]

As they did at the male and female academies in Greenville, Furman students in advanced years studied Latin and Greek as well as English grammar, geography, moral philosophy, criticism, and mathematics.[84] A code of conduct stipulated that "All lying, cursing, swearing, drunkenness, fighting, dueling, dice, card and billiard playing, betting, theft, fornication are forbidden to the students of the seminary."[85] At least three ministerial candidates enrolled in the seminary between January 1827 and December 1828: Issachar J. Roberts, from Tennessee, and South Carolinians Thomas Simons and James Griffith. The institution struggled financially in the first year and a half, and by June 1828, Reverend Warne, suffering from ill health and seeming not "very well suited to the position," resigned and returned to the North. Just six months later, in December 1828, the board and the convention closed Furman Theological Institution, returning land and money to donors.[86] Reverend Jesse Hartwell provided lodging and training for the three ministerial students at his home in High Hills, while Baptist leaders, eager to continue their support of liberal and ministerial education, debated next steps for the academy and seminary.[87]

By 1830, white Lowcountry Baptists remained in the forefront of both southern and national denomination building. They created the first Baptist state convention in the country through which they established a denominational academy to educate and train ministerial students, providing a model for Baptists in other states. White Lowcountry Baptists helped shape the first national Baptist organization and served in crucial leadership roles in the organization throughout the 1810s and 1820s. Many of their efforts were due to the vigorous leadership of Richard Furman, who spearheaded and oversaw educational, missional, and organizational work throughout this long pastorate in Charleston. The Lowcountry denominational vision was not embraced by all Baptists; Upcountry churches opposed the state convention and in some cases fiercely resisted attempts to change their congregational culture and beliefs. Although they fought with one another bitterly over extra-congregational organization, white Baptist ministers found more common ground in their accommodation of slavery and their desire to evangelize to enslaved people as well as to whites. In the first two decades of the nineteenth century, white Baptists under the guidance of Richard Furman shifted from this accommodationist stance toward a more proactive one, proclaiming through the Charleston Association a distinctively proslavery argument and placing Lowcountry South Carolina Baptists in the vanguard of proslavery religious thought in the United States.

CHAPTER FOUR

Defining Sectionalism, 1790–1830

In the early nineteenth century, as they built momentum for a national Baptist organization devoted to missions and a professionalized ministry, white Baptists in the Lowcountry also moved down a distinctively sectional path, taking strategic steps to silence antislavery sentiment in their ranks and to fashion a public and political defense of slavery. Driven largely by vocal minister Richard Furman, their reasons for doing so were to ensure the protection and growth of their churches and their denomination. As early as 1800, well before most religious leaders took such public stances, Furman led an effort to petition the South Carolina legislature for the right of churches to evangelize to enslaved people. Concerned that prominent South Carolinians equated their attempts to evangelize to enslaved people with an antislavery agenda, and adamant that Baptists in South Carolina needed the support, rather than the suspicion, of Charleston's slaveholding elite, Furman and other white Baptist leaders proclaimed publicly that slaveholding, if practiced along Christian lines, was both a biblical right and a gospel duty. Furman, the main force behind this proslavery argument, worked specifically to silence Baptists who disagreed with this view and, by the 1820s, called for the state to promote Christian slavery by passing laws tempering cruel punishments and protecting the religious instruction of enslaved people. Here, in the most slave-conscious part of South Carolina—and the most slave-conscious part of the American South—Charleston Baptists shifted the narrative about slavery in the early 1800s and increased its efficacy by 1830. By actively silencing public doubts about Christian slaveholding within their own ranks, white ministers consciously and deliberately shaped a denominational image intended to reassure the public of their proslavery and pro-order stance. Christian slavery, they argued, if practiced according to biblical mandate, would reinforce social stability and white supremacy, leading to peace and harmony under the aegis of Christian order.

In the early 1800s, Upcountry Baptists did not make official pronouncements about slavery in the same way that their Lowcountry brethren did. However, white Baptists in the Upcountry ordered their churches, racially, in the same hierarchical way as white Baptists in the Lowcountry did: by seating enslaved people in segregated areas during church services, or, in churches with larger numbers of enslaved people, creating entirely separate services for them. Despite this white-enforced hierarchy, enslaved people continued to join Lowcountry and Upcountry churches. Personally convicted of their need for salvation, black Baptists demonstrated the same eagerness to worship as Christians and to share the gospel experience as whites, challenging whites in various ways about their worth as spiritual beings. Although black participation in biracial Christianity provided whites with affirmation that they were following God's commands to evangelize to enslaved people, it also served as a reminder that enslaved people were active shapers of their spiritual fates. Should enslaved people push this humanity too far, social egalitarianism might ensue. Evangelization of enslaved people thus proved a circular argument: white Baptists strove to bring black men and women into the Kingdom of God, but, aware of the egalitarian implications of Christianity, they also constantly reinforced racialized power relations in biracial churches. Through preaching, discipline, and spatial separation and segregation, whites in the Upcountry and the Lowcountry consistently reminded enslaved people of their servility and subordination; indeed, the seeds of postbellum segregation were sown in antebellum churches.[1]

Between 1790 and 1810, a major shift occurred in the way that white South Carolina ministers publicly spoke about slavery. In the 1790s, although white Baptists largely accommodated and reinforced the institution through their religious practices, there remained room for ministers and laypeople to publicly question slavery's permanence. By the early 1800s, prominent white Baptist leaders closed this window of opportunity, shutting down antislavery discussions and creating an institutional narrative that argued for the biblical morality of owning enslaved people and for the right of churches to evangelize to enslaved people. Led by Richard Furman, white Baptists forged a proslavery narrative meant to assure the larger public that the denomination did not pose a threat to the social order. Rather than instigating ideas of freedom and emancipation, whites believed that the Christian model of slavery protected the master-slave relationship and produced loyal, obedient enslaved people. Christian slavery, white Lowcountry Baptists argued, was the only viable way to ensure order and harmony in a slave society.

Although such queries were sporadic, the 1790s witnessed some intra-church questions about slavery in South Carolina. Spartanburg's Cedar Spring Baptist Church in 1799 asked the Bethel Association "whether or not it is agreeable to the gospel to hold Negroes in slavery." The association "evidently suppressed this question in committee," according to one church historian.[2] Along the coast in Georgetown, William Staughton, who came from England to serve the Georgetown church after Richard Furman requested from English minister John Rippon the help of a "young man of promise and character," remained at the church for only seventeen months before departing for northern colonies for health reasons and because of his opposition to slavery. Staughton left South Carolina on friendly terms. Georgetown Baptists had offered to double his salary if he remained, and despite controversy over Staughton's marital relations (his home church in Birmingham, England, refused to recognize him in good standing because he had taken a wife who was still legally married to another man), Richard Furman provided a recommendation letter noting that Staughton had "justified the recommendations given him by his European friends, and procured him the love and respect of his acquaintances in general, who esteem him as a man of piety, and a gospel minister of eminent abilities."[3]

Ironically, the antislavery declaration of a rival evangelical denomination, the Methodist General Conference—the governing body of Methodists in the United States—helped put an end to open and fluid conversations among Baptists about the righteousness of holding enslaved people. In May 1800 the General Conference, meeting in Baltimore, called for an end to the "enormous evil" of slavery, noting that the institution was "repugnant to the inalienable rights of mankind and the very essence of civil liberty" and stating that it violated the "whole spirit of the New Testament." The conference recommended that Methodist ministers, elders, and deacons promote the end of slavery by urging their listeners to sign petitions to state legislatures demanding the gradual emancipation of enslaved people, not stopping until they met their goal.[4] News coursed through South Carolina that Methodist ministers were circulating antislavery pamphlets and petitions in the state, prompting United States senator Jacob Read, a Federalist from Charleston, to write Governor John Drayton calling for the arrest and imprisonment of any Methodist minister who disseminated antislavery materials in the state. Read condemned "all those ignorant vagabonds calling themselves preachers," noting that they were "overrunning our Country imposing on the weak and credulous" and inflicting "infinite mischief on Society."[5]

White anxiety about slave revolt had been on the increase before the Methodist General Conference made its statement against slavery. In the late 1790s, whites throughout the coastal South feared that the slave insurrection in the Caribbean island of Saint-Domingue would lead to revolts among their own enslaved people. In early 1800 the threat of antislavery Methodist agitation in the slaveholding states increased this anxiety. Then, in late summer of 1800, news of Gabriel Prosser's aborted slave rebellion in Richmond, Virginia rippled through the slaveholding states. As news of the insurrection spread, South Carolina governor John Drayton directed slave patrols to search homes and disband gatherings of black men and women when whites were not present, and to exert increased vigilance toward enslaved people traveling without passes. In Georgetown, authorities called out the state militia to prepare for a rumored invasion of black prisoners from Saint-Domingue. Responding to these multiple threats to racial order, South Carolina legislators in December 1800 passed a harsher set of laws to promote the "better governance" of enslaved people. Legislators agreed that "the laws heretofore enacted for the government of slaves, free negroes, mulattoes and mestizos, have been found insufficient for keeping them in due subordination." As a result, they crafted a new law that, among other things, made illegal "all assemblies and congregations" of enslaved people and free persons of color who gathered "for the purpose of mental instruction" in "a confined or secret place of meeting, or with the gates or doors of such place of meeting barred, bolted, or locked." It mattered not if whites were present at such meetings, according to the new law. A second part of the law went even further, banning the gathering of enslaved people or free blacks for any reason at all before dawn or after sunset. Additional laws placed restrictions on the interstate slave trade, gave greater authority to slave patrols, and made it more difficult for enslavers to free their enslaved people.[6] For Baptists as well as other denominations, South Carolina legislators had now severely limited the possibility of church-authorized religious gatherings for enslaved people, which were sometimes held with few if any whites present. As Lacy Ford argues, "If enforced, the new restrictions fell just short of constituting a total ban on the evangelical outreach to slaves and free blacks."[7]

Being no stranger to mixing religion and politics and convinced that properly supervised Christian enslaved people would uphold rather than threaten the social order, Richard Furman quickly organized a religious protest of the new law. In late October 1800, before the legislature met in December, Furman presented in his annual letter to the Charleston Association a portrait of Christian order that sanctified hierarchy and that recognized enslaved people as part of the larger societal family. Members of society, Furman reminded the ministers in the Charleston Association, were not equal in society but rather had "relative duties" toward one another. By following these duties, which were outlined in the Bible, Christians would ensure peace and order among one another; the proper social relations between men and women, as well as between enslavers and enslaved people, would bolster and solidify a social order resting on white supremacy and gendered patriarchy. Furman wrote in 1800, "Let the relative duties be strictly regarded among us, according to the plain doctrines of Christ, and the bright examples of primitive Christianity: That as parents and children, husbands and wives, brethren and sisters, masters and servants, we may walk worthy of the gospel, and adorn the doctrine of God our Saviour, in all things."[8]

In late October 1801, ministers from the thirty churches who belonged to the Charleston Association took stronger political action. During the annual meeting of the association, they drafted a petition to the state legislature seeking to rescind the law prohibiting religious gatherings for enslaved people and free blacks. Another petition with exactly the same wording and signed by numerous residents came from Chester District in 1801, suggesting that Charleston Baptists circulated the document in print to different denominations throughout the state.[9] Claiming that Christian slavery was the best way to enforce societal peace and order, the petitioners argued that the new law infringed on the religious rights of both white and black Baptists in two ways. First, by limiting the "Time and Manner of giving religious instruction to the Persons whose Situation is contemplated in the Act," the legislation severely weakened opportunities for enslaved people and free blacks to partake in religious worship and instruction. Second, the law infringed upon the religious rights of church members by exposing churches "to the

Danger of Interruption and Insult, from the Rudeness of Persons who move in the lowest spheres of Authority, whenever they choose to appear as Enforcers of the Law."[10]

Rather than creating rebellious enslaved people, Charleston ministers argued, the religious instruction of black Carolinians, if applied with white supervision, was the best way to uphold order in society. Ministers argued that "the plain Doctrines and positive Precepts of Christianity" practiced by South Carolinians "have a direct, contrary Tendency" to produce loyalty amongst enslaved people. The petitioners knew this well, for, "as Ministers of the Gospel," many had "long been in the habit of giving religious Instruction to Negros" for two reasons: because it was "a part of their ministerial Duty" and in order to secure "the public peace and Security of the State." As to the latter situation, the petitioners attested that from years of practice they could state that enslaved people who received proper religious instruction remained loyal to their enslavers. Petitioners had "very satisfactory Evidence" that enslaved people had "conscientiously imbibed" Christian values that had "governed their Conduct" and made them loyal to their biblical duties of servitude. This was the case even during the American Revolution, "when Temptations to a contrary Conduct were numerous and powerful."[11]

Stripping enslaved people of their right to practice Christianity, moreover, could actually foment rebellion. The law, with such "aforesaid severe Restrictions," would "have a strong indirect Tendency to produce the Evil it was designed to prevent," the petition warned, by "making that Class, of the religious Negroes, who value religious Privileges, feel unhappy, and consider themselves oppressed." Not only would enslaved people, bereft of religion, no longer serve as role models for the unchurched, they might ultimately be influenced or seduced by *disloyal* enslaved men and women to engage in revolt and rebellion.[12]

The Charleston ministers closed their petition by admitting that the subject of religious instruction for enslaved people was a "delicate" one. They understood the need for laws designed to prevent slave rebellions, but they believed that religious instruction should be provided to enslaved men and women of a Christian character. For these reasons, the petitioners hoped for a revision in the current law to "relieve the virtuous Citizens from the Embarrassment complained of, and have their religious Liberties unimpaired."[13] Although powerful in their arguments, the petitions of Charleston and Chester residents did not persuade South Carolina legislators to amend the 1800 law when they met in December 1801. Furman and other Baptist ministers maintained their political pressure, sending a second petition to the legislature in 1802 reiterating their pleas.[14] Furman undoubtedly collaborated with his close friend Charles Cotesworth Pinckney, as well as with Federalists Thomas Pinckney and Henry William DeSaussure, to enact legal changes.[15] The campaign worked: in 1803 the legislature enacted a modified law permitting enslaved people and free blacks to assemble before 9:00 p.m., so long as a majority of white persons attended. Patrols were prohibited from disrupting such meetings with white-majority attendance. If there were more enslaved people present than whites, regardless of when the meeting occurred, patrols or others could break up the gathering and punish the offenders with lashes.[16] The vote was far from unanimous: the House passed the revisions 50–45, the Senate 21–8.[17] The new law still posed impediments for Baptists in the Lowcountry, where gatherings of enslaved people tended to be larger, making it difficult for a majority of whites to be present. However, the law was not heavily enforced in most years.[18]

Successful in tailoring a political compromise allowing the religious instruction of enslaved people to continue, Richard Furman and Lowcountry Baptist ministers now worked to ensure that the white Baptist image remained firmly aligned with the protection, rather than the disruption, of slavery. In his personal memoirs, William Bullein Johnson remembered that antislavery sentiment amongst Baptists reached its height in the first decade of the nineteenth century. Dissension occurred within the Charleston Baptist Association around 1807, when a white minister belonging to the Charleston Association, having read antislavery tracts penned by "an eminent Baptist Minister of the State of Georgia," preached a sermon and introduced a resolution supporting abolition. The minister, identified only as "W. M.," challenged slavery by asking what would happen if English minister John Rippon, editor of the influential *Baptist Annual Register*, owned the wife and children of a fellow minister. Upon finding out the situation, could that minister fellowship Dr. Rippon "at the Lord's Table"?[19]

The minister's words created a stir, but Richard Furman answered clearly and decisively, according to Johnson. The Charleston minister, "in his mild and respectful manner," responded by unequivocally affirming the biblical legitimacy of slavery. Using scripture, Furman made two central arguments: that racial slavery existed in the Old Testament as a permanent system, as evidenced by the curse of Ham, and that the New Testament sanctioned the practice, as shown by the actions of Jesus and his apostles.[20] Furman concluded his testimony by circling back to W. M.'s scenario about John Rippon and presenting a strong argument for the Christian model of slavery based upon the racialized and gendered notion of patriarchal benevolence. "Suppose," Furman challenged, "that in Great Britain the institution of slavery existed by the laws of the Realm & in agreement with the teachings of the word of God." Suppose also that Furman, paying a visit to Rev. Rippon, found that "by the chances of war, Dr. Rippon had become the owner of my wife & children and that he treated them with all kindness." Wouldn't this benevolent ownership, this care of those who couldn't legally care for themselves, be reason to fellowship with his brother in Christ?[21]

Furman's argument, Johnson narrated, ended the conversation: "The reply of the Doctor was overwhelming." W. M., according to Johnson, did not reply, nor did others, reflecting to Johnson "full proof of entire satisfaction with the argument of the Moderator." After this incident, Johnson wrote, "the subject of Slavery has not, from that time, disturbed the churches of South Carolina."[22]

But the "subject of slavery" did not immediately go away. Sometime after the association meeting, W. M. sent Richard Furman a letter restating his concerns about slavery and asking that ministers in the Charleston Association take steps toward ending the institution. Although W. M.'s letter is not extant, Furman's twenty-one-page reply to him, written in July 1807, has been preserved. In the letter, Furman responded to numerous concerns posed by W. M. about various aspects of slavery, including the African slave trade. Furman's arguments converged around six main points, all elements of a more developed and robust model of Christian slavery: that slavery was morally lawful; that only the actions of slaveholders, if inhumane, made slavery morally wrong; that Christians could alleviate the inhumane nature of the foreign slave trade by purchasing enslaved people so as to treat them well; that moral enslavers, providing religious education to their enslaved people, created loyal and industrious workers, leading to social stability and economic gain; that emancipation would have the opposite effect, creating civil unrest and possibly violence; and that any discussion of emancipation among Baptists would have damaging political implications, as it would hamper their influence as an association.

Furman began his response to W. M. by disputing that slavery was a moral evil and by defending the model of Christian slavery as a system that benefited both enslaved and enslaver. As defined by biblical law—Furman spent almost the entire second half of his letter justifying slavery through scripture—slavery was neither "a sin" nor a "Moral Evil." Only humans could make slavery sinful, by not pursuing their reciprocal duties owed to one another in the enslaver-enslaved relationship. Enslavers were to be humane, just, and benevolent, and enslaved people were to be industrious and respectful. Furman did not shy away from explaining the benefits that both parties would experience in such a Christian relationship. Christian enslavers, serving as "the Guardians and Benefactors of the Slaves," would provide enslaved people great moral and psychological uplift, enabling enslaved people to "enjoy as much satisfaction as if they were free; and in many instances, more." Enslaved people, in turn, "by their virtue and reasonable labour" would "contribute to the general welfare of the nation as well as to themselves and their immediate owners." As he had explained before and would do so again, Furman maintained that Christian slavery would provide a powerful antidote to the instability that would result from emancipation; indeed, it was the solution to emancipation, designed "to promote . . . peace and security" rather than "convulsing our country with domestic commotion."[23]

Just as slavery—through reciprocal relationships—could be scripturally and morally practiced, the foreign slave trade also could be interpreted through a Christian lens. In response to W. M.'s question about what duty Christians held "in respect of the Slave Trade," Furman acknowledged the painful ramifications of the venture. Had the slave trade never existed but been proposed "de novo," Furman would "oppose its being engaged in," due to "the disagreeable nature of the business," and "the opportunity it affords to the exercise of cruelty"—*unless* the slave trade was the only means "of preserving the lives of the poor heathen," and the only way to provide them access to Christian teachings. But the trade was in existence only until the end of the current year. If "all serious Christians should abstain from purchasing the enslaved people that are brought here," Furman noted, the enslaved people "must of course go into other hands, where it is not probable they would fare as well." Instead of boycotting, Baptists should purchase "as many as they can of these poor people with an honest intention to render them as happy as circumstances will admit." This form of benevolent capitalism embraced unapologetically the mutual benefits of slavery. White Christian masters would enrich their economic holdings while simultaneously protecting the "rights" of enslaved people. Here was a way to bring humanity to an inhumane practice, with benefits to enslaver and enslaved person alike.[24]

Again, Furman reinforced the importance of Christian ownership and Christian benevolence toward enslaved people as the best antidote to the problems emancipation would cause. "Our concern is to conduct ourselves aright toward the Slaves in our country," he wrote, not to call for their liberation. The best way to exercise "benevolence" was to buy Africans "as slaves when brought here . . . with an honest intention (and correspondent conduct) to use them well & instruct them in Christianity." Freedom would have the wrong effect. If freed, old and ill enslaved people, as well as young children, "would be left to starve," and, as they had in the North, others would fall into "idleness & vice" that at best would be "a nuisance to Society" and at worst could lead to revolt.[25] "We know the Scenes of desolation & blood," he reminded W. M., pointing to the "tragedy which has lately been exhibited in St. Domingo." Christian slave ownership, rather than "Liberty & Equality," would maintain the social order; Federalist hierarchy, rather than Democratic-Republican individualism, should be put into place.[26]

W. M. posed additional questions to Furman, including whether Christians had a duty to keep enslaved families intact. Although recognizing the humanitarian benefits of not separating enslaved families, Furman's answer ultimately privileged the rights of owners over family unity: enslaved families should remain united if at all possible, Furman answered, particularly for husbands and wives, as well as mothers with very young children.[27] But W. M.'s letter was more than a rhetorical exercise: it was a call for action. W. M. proposed that the Charleston Association should discuss the "subject of Slavery, and what relates to the treatment of Slaves"—the very issues he had previously posed to Richard Furman. Taking his message further, W. M. asked if Lowcountry Baptists could "reasonably hope that such a measure would lead to a necessary reformation and so prepare the way for the latter day of glory?" Was not freedom the moral and political answer to the enslavement of Africans, and the needed reform to hasten Chirst's return?[28]

Furman responded decisively. The association had a duty "to take every subject into consideration in which the glory of God and our duty to him are concerned." Baptists as a group might be able to encourage Christian slaveholding in a "wise, prudent, and becoming matter." But the type of outcome that W. M. hoped for, that slavery be labeled a sin and that steps be taken toward emancipation, would be utterly perilous for two reasons. First, not only could "civil commotion and insurrection" ensue but the newly freed would lose the material care and religious guidance provided by Christian enslavers. Emancipating enslaved people "would lead no otherwise to reformation, and the latter day of Glory, than the Crusades did in former times, and the French Revolution in the present day—by leading us thro previous scenes of Enthusiasm, and martyr's blood." Second, and just as dangerous for white Baptists, any hint of discussion about abolition within associational circles "would destroy the influence of the Association in the community at large," as well as "expose it to just censure." Questioning the morality of slavery endangered the legitimacy of white Baptists in the South and, at its most extreme, could lead to violence and bloodshed. There was no place for such conversation in South Carolina Baptist congregations.[29]

Rather than endorsing formal congregational discussions about how to care for enslaved people—discussions that could open opportunities for slavery to be questioned—Furman suggested a quiet, underground approach to W. M.'s concern about the welfare of enslaved people. "Perhaps the best method an individual, a church, or an Association could take in this respect would be for them with as little noise as possible, to apply themselves (each for himself) to the serious performance of those duties, which they would recommend to others in respect of slaves, and thus furnish examples to all around them of the benign influence of Humanity, Justice, and Religion, in such a state of things." Through *practice and example,* rather than collective conversation or action, Baptists could model the mutual responsibilities of Christian slaveholding, with the aim being to "ameliorate the condition of Slaves, to enlighten them with the knowledge of God & the Redeemer, to inspire them with a just sense of their duty; as well as their Masters of theirs." Order and authority would be upheld, "& subordination produced; as well as kindness and justice exercised."[30] Slaveholder benevolence would benefit enslaver and enslaved alike, providing religious instruction and moral uplift to enslaved people and, just as significantly, preserving white-controlled authority and order.

Furman sent a specific message to W. M. to cease his critique of slavery or risk endangering the great causes of the Baptist denomination. "I hope I shall not be called again to write on this subject," Furman wrote, noting the complications of writing late into the night, the only time available for such an exercise.[31] Furman's remonstrance did not work, for there is a strong chance that W. M. continued to share his antislavery views with those who would hear. In 1808 the association warned of a "certain William McCarty, who calls himself a Baptist Minister, and a Physician; but has proved himself to be a very immoral and base man."[32] While William McCarty may have been an entirely different person than the W. M. who appears in Furman's letter, the two may also have been one and the same.

The Charleston Association's debate shows that, in the early 1800s, divergent beliefs about slavery still permeated white Baptist thought in the Deep South. Egalitarian and antislavery strands of evangelical and Revolutionary thought continued to influence some white Baptists, leading them to challenge slavery and to advocate for its end. Simultaneously, powerful religious and secular leaders, with Charleston Baptist Richard Furman in the vanguard, shaped a second line of thinking, one that applied a well-defined concept of Christian benevolence to the practice of slavery. Drawing from biblical authority, whites believed that this Christian model of slavery benefited both enslaved people and enslavers, providing the former crucial religious and moral guidance, and the latter assurance of slave loyalty and social stability. For the second line of thinking about slavery to triumph, antislavery thought had to be silenced: Baptists had to create a Christian vision of slavery along a united front, in order for their arguments, and their influence, to be taken seriously. Richard Furman set out to achieve that end, actively relegating white support for emancipation to an underground movement at best and unapologetically proclaiming both the biblical righteousness and the social benefits of slave evangelization. In a Lowcountry society where white citizens worried constantly about racial unrest and disorder, Furman and the Charleston Baptist Association stood out for their pronounced and early defense of Christian slavery as the best way to maintain order, harmony, and white supremacy.

As Richard Furman was silencing antislavery sentiment within the Charleston Association, his close friend Edmund Botsford was doing his part to sell the benefits of the Christian model of slavery to a wider public audience. Botsford, who in 1796 had moved to Georgetown to become pastor of the fledgling Baptist church in that town, preached almost wholly to enslaved people; his first two white converts came seven years into his ministry at the church.[33] In 1811 the sixty-six-year-old Botsford wrote to Richard Furman, a man ten years his junior, that "my labor seems in vain, except to the poor blacks," who responded well to the minister's messages.[34] Botsford remained positive about his outreach to enslaved people, noting that "If I was a young man, and possessed of only as much zeal as I once possessed, I should be very fond to go preaching and talking from one plantation to another, and be wholly a preacher to negroes." He recognized his talent for preaching to enslaved people, whom he felt comprised a different audience from whites. Botsford could "suit my talk to them, and enter into their views of things, and doubt not, with the blessing of God, I should be of considerable service."[35] Botsford's efforts at Georgetown led to continued black conversions. As he had at Welsh Neck, he appointed several "leading characters in the church" held in "good esteem by their owners & the world at large" to assist with the spiritual needs of the large black congregation.[36]

Believing fully that a model of Christian slavery benefited both enslaved people and whites in general, in 1808 Botsford published *Sambo and Toney: A Dialogue in Three Parts*. The pamphlet told the story of the successful efforts of Sambo, an enslaved Christian, to convert the enslaved Toney, as well as Toney's wife Fanny, to Christianity. Botsford emphasized two main concepts in his chronicle: that God's message of salvation applied to enslaved people as well as to whites; and that Christianity produced loyal enslaved people by civilizing and reforming their primitive and uncouth behavior. In the narrative, Toney complained to Sambo that the "minister never preach to we black people," but Sambo reminded Toney that the Bible "speaks to every body alike," both black and white, poor and rich, young and old. All enslaved people had the potential to be children of God should they act on it. By doing so, a second concept would be realized: that enslaved people would be morally upright and faithful to their enslavers. This would benefit the enslaver and the enslaved, and indeed all of society, by ensuring social stability. Enslaved people should learn about salvation, and they should also be loyal to their God-given station.[37] Writing to Richard Furman, Botsford reiterated his genuine hope that enslaved people receive the good news of the gospel: he hoped the story would be shared in the slave community and that the message would help "that class of our poor deprived fellow creatures who are too little attended. . . by all of us."[38] Botsford also hoped, however, that whites would realize the benefits of Christian slavery.[39]

Edmund Botsford's enthusiasm for and promotion of a Christian version of slavery had developed over time. Much like George Whitefield in the 1740s, who first criticized but later took part in the ownership of enslaved men and women, Botsford initially questioned slavery but later became an advocate of the Christian model of slavery. When he first arrived in Charleston in the 1760s, Botsford told Rhode Island Baptist David Benedict, who traveled through the country collecting information for his comprehensive *History of the Baptists in the United States*, that he "had never heard much respecting the negroes" and had only seen "four or five" black men or women. Botsford claimed to be no fan of slavery—even in 1813, he confessed, he was "no advocate for it." But through providence, Botsford reported that he had settled in a land where slavery already existed, noting that "as I cannot do as I would, I do as I can." He preferred to hire servants but could not find them to hire, so he purchased enslaved people and offered them paternalistic care: "I feed them, clothe them, instruct them, etc."[40] In contrast to Furman, who saw slavery as a more permanent institution, Botsford often portrayed slavery as a temporary arrangement that, through Christian practice, would not only lead to moral uplift for enslaved men and women but might ultimately result in their freedom. In his essay titled "On Slavery," most likely written in 1812, Botsford claimed that "I do not mean in this Essay to vindicate Slavery." Instead, his goal was to "give a just description of the treatment of slaves in this State." Botsford's account of African slavery vacillated from critical to optimistically cautious. "Upon the whole," he wrote, "slavery is attended with many evils & I do not wish to defend it." The management of enslaved people in South Carolina depended upon both "the temper of the Master & the conduct of the slave," with some punishments being "severe." Yet, "Bad as their situation is," conduct toward enslaved people "is often represented much worse than it really is" and had improved significantly from "forty or fifty years ago," in the years before the American Revolution. The Christianization of enslaved people had begun to change the institution: "Of late years a great number of the slaves have become serious & are united with religious Societies; & many of them are to all appearance truly pious, these are a restraint on some of a bad character." A great gulf existed between enslaved men and women who were religious and those who were not. Religious enslaved men and women helped to foil adverse behavior of enslaved people and in turn encouraged benevolence amongst enslavers, so that enslaved people were treated more humanely, indeed better than many others in the world, including the working class in England. While the slavery practiced in South Carolina by harsh and severe enslavers "is in its best state . . . a very great evil," Botsford concluded, "[i]t is to be hoped that their condition will continue to meliorate, till some way & means shall be fallen on for their emancipation, which however as matters are circumstanced must be a work of time."[41]

Although Botsford admitted that enslaved people, like whites, were capable of salvation, he illustrated a characteristically Eurocentric view of the African race. "It is true, the slaves have no hope of freedom, and it is also true, they have no proper idea of the nature of freedom. Many in their own country were slaves, and many who were not, were miserable. Several with whom I have conversed, have really preferred their present state in this country to their own country, though in that they were free," Botsford told David Benedict. For the time being, Christian slavery was the best answer for the problem of slaveholding in general, for the African race was not ready for freedom. It provided both a more humane treatment of enslaved people and a better way to maintain social control, with black enslaved people providing proper guidance to other black enslaved people.[42]

In the early 1800s, white Baptists such as Edmund Botsford and Richard Furman articulated to the public a Christian model of slavery to assure white southerners that they, like other elite Carolinians, promoted and protected slavery, seeing it as a means to uphold stability and to defend the social order. They differed in the ways they judged the morality of the institution: Furman seemed decidedly supportive of the institution, Botsford less so. Nevertheless, their shared commitment to exemplify the benefits of the Christian *practice* of slavery, with the dual impact of helping enslaved people and reinforcing white supremacy, was striking. While Furman and Botsford conveyed to both enslaved people and enslavers the social benefits of Christian slavery, enslaved peoples' desires for spiritual recognition and relevancy threatened to contradict white desires to enforce social and racial hierarchy. Enslaved people and free blacks repeatedly claimed the right to participate in worship and to partake in religious sacraments. One of the most significant rights they pursued was the opportunity to minister to others. Such requests occurred consistently in the 1700s and 1800s. At Bush River Church (Newberry District) in the 1793, Moses Gift, identified by the church clerk as a "man of colour," sought permission to preach and exhort. White members decided that "he had no call to the work of preaching or exhortation" (one wonders if it is because he advanced an antislavery message) and that "it was best for him to be silent." Moses, who did not heed the mandate, was excluded from the church.[43] In the late 1790s members of Cedar Spring Baptist Church (Spartanburg District) met at the home of a white female member "to hear Brother Titus exercise his gift." Whites then granted Titus permission "to sing, pray, and exhort in public, and appoint meetings in the vicinity of the church," so long as Titus understood that his independence was limited and that his actions were "to be in Subordination to his master, and that his master council him in particular cases as his prudence may dictate." Titus, like Moses, may have preached an antislavery message: in November 1804, white members of Cedar Spring suspended him for violating the church's orders.[44] So too may have "Black Bro Bill," who was allowed to preach within the bounds of Friendship Baptist Church but was charged with disobeying church orders and, in the words of historian Leah Townsend, "giving offense in public talk."[45]

At times, black men assumed significant authority over other enslaved and free black members. At Lower Fairforest Church, "Brother Negro Tom" was granted permission to "exercise his gift" within the bounds of the church and, later, throughout Union District.[46] In addition to preaching, Tom served as a de facto deacon, on at least one occasion citing two enslaved people to church to deal with a disciplinary dispute. In 1811, white leaders compensated him three dollars for taking "Sister Negro Judith," described as a "church charge," into his household. Judith may have been deeded to the church, or the church may have been responsible for her until a court determined her legal ownership status.[47] The church twice withdrew Tom's permission to preach, once in 1812 for no specified reason and a second time in 1820 for failing to attend church and for "retailing spirits." Following each occasion, Tom was restored and allowed to preach again. In 1822 Tom requested formal ordination in the church, a request that white members debated the following year. A disruption in the church minutes obscures what happened; by 1829, when the minutes resumed, Tom's name appeared no more. Here was an enslaved man who had a great deal of autonomy, it seems, both inside and outside of the church.[48]

Black men and women also found opportunities to take their masters to task for not supporting the Christian model of slavery. At Big Creek Church in Anderson District, a slave named Judy spoke of her own version of slavery. In May 1823 Brother Johnson charged "his Black woman Judy" with disobedience."[49] In July the church, "after long debate," decided to forgive both Judy and Brother Johnson for a public feud that was developing in the church between Johnson, his wife, and Judy. In September, at a call meeting of the church, Brother Johnson and his wife brought new charges against their servant. "Brother Johnson first lays in a charge against Judy which is disobedience & telling falcityes [*sic*] he also says that she has she has backers in the church to do the Evil that she has done." Sister Johnson followed, charging Judy with disobedience and "telling of falcityes] also heard her say that she had backers in the church & also heard her say that she was Sorry that she had taken their advice, or done as she had done."[50]

Judy responded that "she did give ill Language to her Master & Mistress because she had not enough to Eat." The aggrieved slave declared, however, that "she never told Bro. Stone's wife the tales that has been stated, she also says that the reason why she did not humble herself to her Master & Mistress, was, because she was afraid of giving a worse hurt, & that they wold tung lash her." Judy had tried at two different times to reconcile with her owners, she claimed. Brother Johnson also stated that "if he has hurt aney of his Brethrens feelings by whipping his servant" or by other actions, "he is sorry for it." Sister Johnson also apologized to the church "for saying that they would sell Judy, & that it should not be to her satesfaction." Judy, by contrast, still would not "confess her faults."[51] By the next regular business meeting, whites voted to exclude Judy from church membership, although in 1833 new problems would arise between Judy and Sister Johnson.[52]

By publicly challenging her enslavers to treat her humanely, Judy asserted agency and standing as a human being before a collective audience of white and black Christians. Disciplinary cases also show how African Americans claimed equal treatment in everyday tasks, and how whites resisted such actions. In July 1830 Salem Church in Edgefield District placed a slave named Harry under censure. Harry and a white man, Albert McCarty, agreed to work for another church member, Daniel Wheeler, for three days in exchange for a shirt for each man. Daniel Wheeler's daughters made both shirts, marking the better-made shirt for Albert McCarty. Harry, however, had switched the shirts, so that McCarty received the lesser-made shirt originally intended for Harry. The church asked: "Harry did you knowingly take Albert McCarty's shirt in place of your own." Harry replied that he did, as he gave "the same price for my shirt that Mr. McCarty gave for his." The church suspended Harry, placing him "under the watch care of the church" for six months.[53] Whites disciplined Harry for taking a shirt that was not designated for him. In doing so, they reminded him of the inequity of race and status. Enslaved people were not free, and their work was not equal to that of a white man. But the fact that Harry exercised his own free will, choosing the better shirt, served as a reminder that whites needed to be constantly vigilant of the enforcement of racial order. Clearly, Harry's version of Christian order differed from that of whites in the church.

In contrast to Harry and to Big Creek's Judy, Lydia Frierson, a member of the Baptist church in Charleston and a woman repeatedly raped by her enslaver, faulted herself for her sinfulness, rather than blaming her owner or the slave system. In 1829 Frierson confided to Basil Manly, her minister, that her enslaver repeatedly compelled her to have sex with him, therefore causing her to be complicit in the act of adultery. Frierson had not taken communion for years because she felt that she was a sinner. She met with Manly to confess her wrongdoings. As a Baptist minister who articulated a Christian model of slavery, one might hope that Manly could have intervened to protect Lydia from her enslaver's abuses. Instead, since Frierson's master was not a church member (and perhaps even *were* he a member), Manly could only concentrate on Lydia's role in the relationship. He thus advised her to do the impossible: to reform her own ways by rebuffing her enslaver's sexual advances and telling him that "she could not consent to sin." Lydia attempted to follow her minister's advice, but to no avail, as her master "threaten[ed] her most dreadfully" for rejecting his overtures. In this scenario, Frierson's sexual misdeeds were *her* fault, not the fault of a master with undue power. The church could do nothing to forestall the situation; although subjected to the sexual desires of an enslaver who owned her as property, Lydia, as a Christian, needed to reform her adulterous ways so that she would not subject herself to final damnation.

Lydia Frierson's agonizing situation reveals a fundamental flaw in the Baptist denominational narrative of slavery: the model of Christian benevolence and mutual obligations between enslaver and enslaved applied only to willing participants. Churches dared not encroach upon the relations between a slave owner and his (or her) enslaved people if the owner was not a church member. Frierson's calamitous situation had no immediate remedy, although after John Frierson died, Basil Manly purchased Lydia to live in the Manly household, ensuring that she would be protected from further sexual or physical abuse from any other enslaver. Manly acted as the benevolent patriarch, but he could offer physical protection only after John Frierson's demise.[54]

Through cases as different as those of Judy, Harry, and Lydia Frierson, church records show that enslaved people took seriously the moral implications of Christianity, exercising their rights as humans and as members of a Christian community. In various ways, they claimed religious rights in Baptist churches, space that whites sometimes gave them, and sometimes, in a show of authority, that whites removed from them. Black agency was tolerated by whites—indeed, at times it was encouraged—but only within the parameters of white control. When black agency threatened to overturn the Christian model of slavery, when it became too close to stressing social equality for enslaved people, white Baptists reinforced their authority and increased their vigilance over the slave community. The Christian model of slavery contained room for blacks to exercise certain rights as members of the Baptist community, but it also, always, served as a conduit for white Baptists to reinforce racial difference and white superiority.

The Christian model of slavery was severely threatened in the late spring and early summer of 1822, when white authorities in Charleston uncovered a plot for a massive slave revolt headed by a free black carpenter Denmark Vesey. Ostensibly Vesey and his coconspirators crafted an elaborate plan for enslaved people to kill their enslavers and escape to Haiti. Leaks about the planned revolt, set to occur on July 14, 1822 (Bastille Day), began to reach white authorities in late May, resulting in the arrest of Denmark Vesey and suspected collaborators in late June. By July 2, 1822, following a hearing by the Magistrates and Freeholders Court, Denmark Vesey and five other accused leaders were hanged for their role in the conspiracy.[55] Authorities ultimately arrested over 130 enslaved people and free blacks. Thirty were released without a court trial, while over 100 were tried before magistrates, resulting in the hanging of 35 alleged conspirators (including Vesey) and the deportation of another 37 black men and women (including Vesey's daughter Sandy). Although historians debate how formalized or widespread the rebellion was, the effect of the alleged conspiracy on both white and black Charlestonians had major implications.[56]

Born into slavery in St. Thomas, Denmark Vesey bought his freedom from his enslaver, a sea captain, in 1799 after winning a street lottery in Charleston. Vesey's name was listed on the rolls of Charleston's Second Presbyterian Church as late as 1817, but by 1818 he was attending and serving as lay preacher of the city's largest black church, the African Methodist Episcopal Church, known simply as the "African Church."[57] Started in Philadelphia in 1816 by Richard Allen, the church spread mainly in the North. In Charleston, black Methodists, frustrated about lack of burial rights in the white-controlled Methodist congregations in the area, created a separate AME congregation. Under the leadership of Charleston free black Morris Brown, the church housed between three and four thousand enslaved people and free blacks. Concerned that the church proved a conduit for abolitionist sentiment, city leaders closed the church in 1818 and again in late 1820 and early 1821.[58] The existence of the AME church illustrates that white political leaders largely disregarded the 1800 and 1803 laws prohibiting large gathering of enslaved people and free blacks for religious gatherings.[59]

More so than previous insurrection plots, the Denmark Vesey insurrection showed to white South Carolinians the dangers of allowing enslaved people and free blacks too much religious autonomy.[60] White and black testimony revealed that Vesey drew deep antislavery inspiration from the biblical teachings, which he passed on to his followers. The official court report noted that Vesey felt that God was behind the revolt and that the success of the participants was "predicted in the Scriptures."[61] One defendant, Rolla Bennett, an enslaved woman owned by Governor Thomas Bennett, explained that Vesey "read to us from the Bible, how the Children of Israel were delivered out of Egypt from bondage." Vesey also recited biblical passages about God's command to the Israelites "that all should be cut off, both men, women, and children," telling his coconspirators that "it was no sin for us to do so, for the Lord had commanded us to do it."[62]

The Denmark Vesey slave insurrection, thwarted before it got off the ground, served as a powerful reminder to many whites in South Carolina that free blacks and enslaved people could use religion not to affirm slavery but to challenge it through armed rebellion. Terrified at the extent of the insurrection plot, white Charlestonians took immediate efforts to bolster security and to restrict and regulate the actions of free and enslaved men and women. City officials demolished the African Methodist Church and exiled its minister, Morris Brown, from South Carolina. The state legislature in December 1822 passed the Seaman's Act, which called for free black sailors on incoming ships to be locked in a city jail until their ships departed the city.[63] White authorities also voiced great concern over the liberties that Christian paternalism seemed to bestow upon enslaved men and women.

City intendant James Hamilton, writing about the Vesey plot in August 1822, decried the excesses of slaveholder paternalism, suggesting the need to restrict religious and educational instruction for both free and enslaved black men and women. "Many slave owners among us," he wrote, "not satisfied with ministering to the wants of their domesticks, by all the comforts of abundant food, and excellent clothing, with a misguided benevolence, have not only permitted their instruction, but lent to such efforts their approbation and applause."[64]

Standing in direct opposition to Denmark Vesey's Christian vision of freedom from bondage, as well as James Hamilton's suggestions to place further restrictions on the actions of enslaved people, was Charleston minister Richard Furman's belief that Christian slavery provided the best model for promoting and protecting the white-controlled social order. Furman's own Charleston church included a large number of enslaved people, who operated in a quasi-independent way but also with crucial white oversight.[65] The church in 1819 had granted black deacons the right "to examine bondspeople in all except 'weighty matters . . . so as to prevent much uneasiness and trouble to the church.'"[66] Like other leading ministers in Charleston, Furman believed that Denmark Vesey and his coconspirators were part of a small group of enslaved people and free blacks who had subverted Christianity for their own gains because they had practiced religion without white oversight. With correct moral guidance and religious instruction from whites, Furman avowed, enslaved people would be loyal and God-fearing subjects.[67] Moreover, should politicians realize this formula for social order, and should the state lend assistance to religious instruction of enslaved people, the likelihood of societal harmony would be greatly strengthened, rather than being threatened by rebellion. Simply put, Christian slavery would help to forestall rather than to promote slave insurrection.

Believing that moral action was required by the state in this time of turmoil, Furman collaborated with his close friend Charles C. Pinckney, Congregationalist minister Benjamin Morgan Palmer, and other members of the Charleston Bible Society—which encouraged biblical literacy for enslaved as well as free South Carolinians—to petition the state's governor, Thomas Bennett, to declare a day of fasting to express appreciation to God that the state had been spared from the violence that might have occurred had the Vesey plot not been thwarted. The Charleston Bible Society also requested that Bennett oppose legislation that would limit the religious instruction of enslaved men and women. Bennett in early October replied to the request, refusing to declare a day of fasting (noting that it would draw greater attention to the plot) but indicating general support for efforts to provide religious instruction to enslaved people.[68] Undeterred by Gov. Bennett's refusal to declare a fast day, Furman—who almost certainly penned the letter from the Bible Society—now worked within his own denominational structure to make the same request. At its annual meeting in late November, the newly formed Baptist State Convention, at the request of the Charleston Association "and in conformity to a plan for acting in concert with the Presbytery and Synod of the Presbyterian Church, lately assembled at Columbia," lobbied successfully for the state's newly-chosen governor, John Lyde Wilson, to appoint a "Day of Humiliation, Prayer, and Thanksgiving" expressing thanks to God for his hand in restraining "two important events," one "the late attempt to raise a murderous Insurrection in this State," which had been "frustrated" by "a kind interposition of Divine Providence," and the second the recent hurricane, which "soon succeeded the other, and ravaged a great part of the State, spreading far and wide desolation and death; but which, evidently, was held under merciful restraints."[69]

The Baptist State Convention attached with its request for a fast day a full statement of its views, authored by Richard Furman, "concerning the lawfulness of holding slaves, and of the right policy to be observed with respect to them, as have been agreed upon in our deliberations on the subject, and as may appear to be necessary, or expedient to exhibit."[70] Furman read the exposition to delegates at the 1822 meeting of the Baptist State Convention, which voted to publish the essay in the *Southern Intelligencer* and the *Columbian Star*, the latter of which would be read by northerners.[71] The essay, titled "Exposition of the Views of the Baptists, Relative to the Coloured Population of the United States, in a Communication To the Governor of South Carolina," was published in pamphlet form in 1823 in Charleston.[72]

Furman's "Exposition" showed his old-school belief that religion and politics could interact for the moral good. One of the earliest proslavery pamphlets to be circulated widely through the South, the publication unabashedly declared Christian slavery the best model of governance in a slave society. The work replicated arguments that Furman made in 1800 and 1801—that the best way to order society was through Christianity and that evangelizing to enslaved people created loyal, well-cared-for enslaved people who would not rebel against their enslavers. It also ascertained that slavery was fully biblical if practiced through Christian means. "Divine Law," Furman wrote, "never sanctions immoral actions." Furman also took his arguments further than he had in the early 1800s by calling for the state to *protect* Christian slavery through laws forbidding cruelty to enslaved people and ensuring that enslaved people could participate in white-sanctioned religious instruction. For Furman, the best way to achieve societal harmony was to blend church and state through laws promoting benevolence toward enslaved people. While religious leaders, including Baptists, called for greater state involvement in the management and care of enslaved people in the late antebellum and Civil War years, Furman's petitions for state protections came at a much earlier date.[73]

Furman's "Exposition" began with a clear message to the governor and other politicians about why a fast day should be held. Both church and state should address the foiled rebellion with "publicity, rather than secrecy" while simultaneously offering a solution to prevent further insurrections. Furman emphasized a number of points in arguing that the state should not be fearful of massive slave revolts. First, although enslaved people formed a majority of the population in some parts of the South, overall they were vastly outnumbered by whites—they comprised, in Furman's words, "little more than one sixth part of the whole number" of residents of the southern states. Second, the difficulty that enslaved people and free blacks had in gaining access to weapons further weakened their potential to rebel successfully. Third, should rebellion occur, "multitudes of the best informed and truly religious" enslaved men and women would remain loyal to their masters and would actively help to thwart plans for insurrection. Fourth, although antislavery men and women in the North supported emancipation, should they witness enslaved people "wading through blood and carnage" to achieve freedom, they would "do what both their duty and interest would require; unite under the government with their fellow-citizens." Whites would ultimately align with other whites, rather than black men and women, to put down rebellion, and to punish the "prime movers" of any such "nefarious scheme."[74]

The best way to confront slave rebellion head-on, Furman contended, was for the state to embrace the model of Christian slavery. Furman offered four primary arguments justifying Christian slavery as the best way to achieve peace and social order. First, Christian slavery was biblically right. Abolitionists threatened to "disturb the domestic peace of the State, to produce insubordination and rebellion among the slaves, and to infringe on the rights of our citizens; and indirectly, to deprive the slaves of religious privileges" by causing enslavers to fear that enslaved people would find an antislavery message in the Bible, thus making them more likely to revolt. But abolitionists were wrong, for "the right of holding slaves is clearly established in the Holy Scriptures, both by precept and example."[75]

Second, Christian enslavers and Christian enslaved people had mutual duties toward one another. Christian masters cared for their enslaved people and, in return, expected loyalty and subservience from enslaved men and women. Distinguishing Christian paternalistic masters from those men and women who viewed enslaved people only as commodities, Furman acknowledged that, while owning enslaved people was justifiable, many Americans, both those engaged in the slave trade and those who were enslavers, had treated their enslaved people cruelly and were accountable for doing so. But another way of slaveholding was also practiced in the country that followed the gospel order of slavery and that, "when tempered with humanity and justice, is a state of tolerable happiness; equal, if not superior, to that which many poor enjoy in countries reputed to be free." In this Christian version of slavery, the "master has a scriptural right to govern his slaves so as to keep them in subjection; to demand and receive from them a reasonable service; and to correct them for the neglect of duty, for their vices and transgressions." The enslaver did *not*, however, have either the "scriptural nor . . . moral" right "to impose on them unreasonable, rigorous services, or to inflict on them cruel punishment." The Christian enslaver had a divine duty to provide his enslaved people "protection, and such necessaries and conveniences of life as are proper to their condition as servants; so far as he is enabled by their services to afford them these comforts, on just and rational principles." Christian enslaved people, in turn, had a "positive duty" to "reverence their master, to be obedient, industrious, faithful to him, and careful of his interests; and without being so, they can neither be faithful servants of God, nor be held as regular members of the Christian Church."[76]

Third, in addition to protecting and caring for their servants, Christian enslavers also had a duty to provide them religious instruction. The fact that Christian masters—as "heads of families"—were entitled this responsibility was very significant, for it meant that enslavers would oversee the correct type of religious instruction, teachings that reminded enslaved people of their relative duties toward their masters just as masters had duties toward their enslaved people. Enslavers were "bound, on principles of moral and religious duty, to give these servants religious instruction; or at least, to afford them opportunities, under proper regulations to obtain it." Enslavers also had a duty to allow enslaved people to engage in religious pursuits, so long as the enslaved people showed "proper evidence of their sincerity and uprightness." Religious instruction should conform to white standards, and masters should examine slave "connexions" so that loyal enslaved people "will not be in danger of having their minds corrupted by sentiments unfriendly to the domestic and civil peace of the community."[77]

Fourth, and quite revolutionary, South Carolina legislators had a duty to enforce the Christian model of slavery. Furman argued that the state should be proactive as well as reactive, punishing those involved in insurrections but also passing laws that promoted paternalism so that insurrection did *not* occur. Here was the most proactive and bold suggestion, one that blended church and state in an effort to uphold a religious model of slavery. Not only should there be laws to prevent cruelty to enslaved people, but enslaved people should be given the right to religious instruction "as may comport with the peace and safety of the state":

> That, where the life, comfort, safety and religious interest of so large a number of human beings, as this class of persons is among us, are concerned; and, where they must necessarily, as slaves, be so much at the disposal of their masters; it appears to be a just and necessary concern of the Government, not only to provide laws to prevent or punish insurrections, and other violent and villainous conduct among them (which are indeed necessary;) but, on the other hand, laws, also, to prevent their being oppressed and injured by unreasonable, cruel masters, and others; and to afford them, in respect of morality and religion, such privileges as may comport with the peace and safety of the state, and with those relative duties existing between masters and servants, which the word of God enjoins.

Enslaved people who demonstrated "suitable evidence of their own good principles, uprightness and fidelity" should be granted "considerable religious privileges." Such opportunities would make these "good" enslaved people appreciate their enslavers and the state even more, "thus rendering their fidelity firm and constant." By contrast, to restrict religious rights for loyal enslaved people because of the actions of a small group of rebellious enslaved men and women "would be felt as oppressive, tend to sour and alienate their minds from their masters and the public, and to make them vulnerable to temptation." Enslaved people needed religion, both for their own mortal selves and to ensure their loyalty to both enslaver and state. The best way to obtain racial order, Furman maintained, was to allow enslaved men and women access to religious instruction under the proper guidance and instruction, rather than prohibiting religion for enslaved men and women.[78]

Richard Furman's "Exposition" emphasized what the well-known minister had publicly proclaimed for decades: that slavery was scriptural and that the best social model for governing enslaved people was a Christian one. By the early 1820s, responding to the actions of enslaved men and women, Furman took his arguments further, calling on South Carolina legislators to fashion a version of Christian slavery for the entire state. Not only did the church need to preach to enslaved people unencumbered by legal restrictions, but the state needed to work with the church to *extend* religious and benevolent protections to enslaved men and women, passing laws to prevent cruelty to enslaved people. Only by the conjoining of church and state would society reap the benefits of Christian harmony, Furman believed. An old Revolutionary in a changing time, Furman held to the belief that church and state should work together to ensure moral and social order, enforcing a Christian model of slavery that offered enslaved people salvation while reinforcing their servility. In the vanguard of preaching a social vision of Christian slavery that would guarantee both white supremacy and social order, Furman's public arguments proved foundational to the larger, more widely embraced proslavery stances of many white politicians and ministers in the South by the 1830s, 1840s, and 1850s.[79]

Between 1790 and 1830, South Carolina Baptists articulated one of the earliest and most forceful religious defenses of slavery in the American South. Slavery, they argued, was legitimate and moral so long as it was practiced along biblical lines. Although enslaved people who joined Baptist churches challenged, in various ways, the model of servility that whites preached to them, biracial church membership also affirmed to whites that the Christian model of slavery was working. The strong stance that the Charleston Baptist Association took in aligning itself with a proslavery and pro-order position took place for two reasons: because of the large presence of enslaved people in the Lowcountry; and because of the leadership of Richard Furman, who was raised since infancy in South Carolina, around enslaved people, and who had no doubts about the biblical lawfulness of slavery practiced according to the gospel. Furman, who believed fundamentally in the role of pastors as moral statesmen, forged an official and institutional Baptist position on slavery, silenced white Baptists who sought to oppose slavery publicly, and called on the state to help forge an alliance with churches to promote Christian slavery. Furman was a force to be reckoned with, an old-school Federalist who felt that religion and politics should be controlled by the elite, that men and women, fathers and sons, enslavers and enslaved people had relative duties toward one another. Many other white Lowcountry Baptists would reinforce this belief after Furman's death in 1825. No South Carolina Baptist took as forceful an approach in shaping public discourse about slavery as Richard Furman, nor did any South Carolina minister—of any denomination—do so at such an early date. Although in denominational matters Furman and his Lowcountry Baptist cohort envisioned a strong, centralized, national Baptist organization coordinating missions and educational outreach (one that many Upcountry Baptists strongly opposed), in defining the correct way to order southern society, Furman's public sentiments helped craft a sectionalized identity for white South Carolina Baptists throughout the state. During Furman's lifetime, the two tangents of Baptist thought—denominational nationalism and social sectionalism—coexisted with one another, as northern and southern Baptists placed slavery to the side and focused on shared missionary goals. By the 1830s and 1840s, the story would shift dramatically.

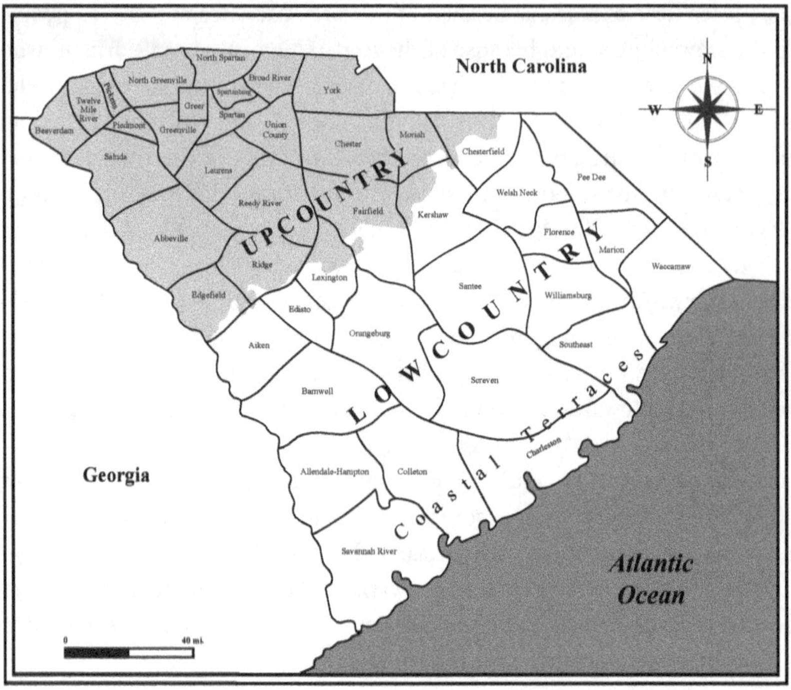

Geographical Divisions and Baptist Associations across South Carolina.

CHAPTER FIVE

Baptist Clashes, 1830–1845

Between 1830 and 1845, South Carolina denominational Baptists expanded their efforts globally, nationally, and on the state level. They remained in significant leadership roles in national Baptist organizations. At home, white Lowcountry Baptists also continued to broaden their base throughout the state, into territory where congregational Baptists held firm ground. They successfully convinced some Upcountry associations to join the Baptist State Convention and to support denominational missionary and educational efforts. They also poured energy and money into the success of Furman Theological Institution, moving it from one location to another in an effort to make it thrive. Despite these efforts, Baptist culture wars continued. Many Baptists in the Upcountry vigorously opposed denominationalism. Instead, they advocated for the autonomy of the local congregation, arguing that the Bible in no place advocated for organized missionary efforts or theological seminaries for ministers. Although a major revival spread through the Upcountry in the early 1830s, aided by ministers-in-training of Furman Theological Institution, Baptists in the region remained strongly divided over denominationalism. Their battles over missions and education reached a crescendo in the mid-1840s, resulting in some churches splintering over efforts to protect their "old school," primitive church ways against "new school" denominational intrusions.

Although they divided with one another over organization, missions, and education, white Baptists united on a second front, in defense of slavery and of their own biblical right to own enslaved people. The rise of immediate abolitionism in the early 1830s put Baptist ministers on a defensive track about their own morality in a way that they had not before envisioned. Faced with allegations by English and northern Baptists that those who tolerated slavery were the worst type of sinners, for the first time white Baptists throughout the state, not just in the Lowcountry, publicly defended their actions as Christian slaveholders. Abolitionists were wrong to criticize them, they argued, for slavery was a gospel institution that, if practiced according to scriptures, was morally right. Abolitionist interference, in the opinion of South Carolina ministers, contradicted and worked against the biblical duties of white enslavers and white-controlled churches to preach to and extend benevolence to enslaved people. Abolitionism also threatened the racial and social order by encouraging enslaved people to revolt from their servile positions. Despite their internal culture wars, Baptist ministers throughout the state assumed a more public, strident, and sectionalized role in defending slavery as a Christian institution. When northern Baptists refused to treat them as equals, white South Carolina Baptists took a leading role in extracting themselves from the northern national movement. They formed a new denomination, the Southern Baptist Convention, that was at once global in outreach and sectional in orientation, allowing them to defend their vision of Christian order on their own terms.

As white Baptists proclaimed their right and duty to hold enslaved people, they also increased their efforts to proselytize to them. For whites, success in this endeavor meant maintaining racial control while simultaneously meeting the religious needs of enslaved people, forging an environment where enslaved men and women could find spiritual fulfillment but where whites could retain proper order and authority. Enslaved people attended biracial churches for reasons that differed from white expectations of social order. Enslaved people sought meaning through the pursuit of Christian citizenship—through opportunities to engage in the life of the church, to take part in its sacraments, and to be part of a sacred community of worship. Through such actions, black Baptists constantly reminded white Baptists of their relevance as children of God. White Baptists and black Baptists operated in a state of tension—a push and a pull—with whites granting enslaved people spiritual recognition but also reminding them, through governance, spatial settings, and discipline, of their secondary status as black men and women, both inside and outside of the church. African American desires for spiritual belonging and meaning, and white desires to both welcome but also differentiate black members, contextualized biracial Baptist church relationships throughout the antebellum period.

In July 1831, a month before Nat Turner began a slave rebellion in Virginia, Upcountry Baptists experienced a tremendous revival. Fueled by students from Furman Theological Institution as well as ministers of churches throughout the region, the revival led to growth that rivaled the awakening of the early 1800s. The revival deepened Baptist influence in the Upcountry and throughout the state, but it did not produce a unified Baptist presence. Divisions between congregational and denominational Baptists reached their highest degree of discord in the late 1830s and early 1840s, as congregational Baptists fought vehemently against the strategic efforts of denominational Baptists to professionalize the ministry and to fund missionary endeavors.

The revival of the early 1830s began in the Edgefield area, which had become an important staging ground for denominational Baptists. Basil Manly had worked to gentrify Baptist congregations in the area in the 1820s, and Baptist leaders had eagerly opened Furman Academy and Theological Institution there in 1827. In late 1830 William Bullein Johnson, president of the Baptist State Convention, moved to Edgefield to take leadership of the local Baptist church. By August 1831, as local ministers met for their quarterly "union" meeting at a church called Sardis, close to the town of Edgefield, revival began. Learning the news of a camp meeting in Virginia the previous year, local Baptists decided to expand the union meeting into a camp meeting. The meeting drew at least five hundred people and sparked great religious interest in the community. Twenty-eight people confessed their sins and asked for salvation; ministers baptized eight people at the meeting.[1]

William Bullein Johnson immediately moved to widen religious interest in the revival. Johnson and other ministers asked the Sardis leaders to visit the Edgefield Church, to spread the revival fervor. "To our surprize [*sic*] and joy," wrote Johnson, "several of them came to see us in the evening of the day on which they left the camping ground." When the revivalists arrived, the church bell was rung, alerting the town residents of a religious meeting. Public services at sunrise, mid-morning, late afternoon, and evening followed for ten days. In between the morning and afternoon public meetings, participants also met at private homes in the village so that "prayer, praise, and exhortations were constantly going on." The church itself, however, was seldom empty. People hurried to find seating in the crowded meeting house during the public services. "Long before the bell would announce the arrival of the hour for preaching," Johnson recounted, "the streets and ways leading to the meeting house would be covered with those who were hastening to obtain seats." Crowds filled the church "from sunrise to ten or eleven o'clock at night."[2] News of the revival—"of these amazing scenes"—spread to nearby regions, motivating crowds of people to "come and see the Lord's doing, so marvelous in our eyes." Edgefield residents hosted guests from surrounding locales. Some businesses closed for parts of the day, and the male and female academies, consisting of a total of one hundred pupils, "were at first partially suspended, and finally dismissed" so that teachers and students could attend the services.[3]

In addition to existing preachers of local congregations, professors and ministerial students at Furman Academy and Theological Institution helped spread the revival—an effect of the Lowcountry denominational vision to train and educate more ministers in the state. Richard Furman's son James C. Furman, a student of Furman Theological Institution during the revival, remembered that "Edgefield District shared largely in [the] gracious awakening." Deluged by "constant and pressing calls for labor," local preachers asked for ministerial help from the school. Professor Jesse Hartwell, principal and teacher, and two unidentified students traveled to Edgefield to assist with services; James C. Furman later participated in at least one revival in Edgefield District, as well as events in other parts of the state. "Everywhere immense congregations gathered, and through the day meetings were held in the open air," the young minister proclaimed.[4] William Bullein Johnson noted that the youthfulness of the ministerial students helped draw young converts to the revival. Though young themselves—"destitute of the advantages of human learning," as Johnson put it, "they spoke well for their Master," displaying both zeal and ability in preaching and exhorting.[5]

Revivalism had a profound impact on the residents of Edgefield District. Between 1831 and 1833, membership increased in some churches by over 200 percent. With a membership of 79 members in 1830, Edgefield Baptist Church baptized 74 people by October 1831, and 130 people the following year. The 25 members of Mt. Moriah witnessed the baptism of 86 people in 1831. And Sardis Church, where the revival began, experienced 50 baptisms, with numbers surging to 115.[6] By 1833 numbers began to wane in most churches—the Edgefield church baptized only 5 people that church year, although Mountain Creek church experienced a late revival, with 150 people baptized between August 1832 and August 1833.[7] Baptisms in the Edgefield Baptist Association escalated from 361 in 1830 to an amazing 1,062 in 1831.[8] Those affected by the revival included enslaved people and whites alike.

Edgefield District witnessed an increase in enslaved people between 1820 and 1830, with 1830 marking the first time that the black population outnumbered the white population.[9] During the revival, black men and women joined churches at a higher rate than whites did. The Edgefield Baptist Association reported 2,854 whites in 1831, as opposed to 776 black members.[10] By 1833 there were 3,843 white members and 1,187 black members belonging to the numerous churches in the association, a 52.96 percent increase for blacks, as compared to a 34.65 percent increase for whites.[11] By 1834 there were 3,997 whites and 1,362 blacks—an increase of 75 percent between 1831 and 1834 for blacks, and of 40 percent for whites between 1831 and 1834.[12] To many participants, both black and white, the awakenings of the 1830s raised millennial hopes, seeming to be, in the words of William Johnson, "indications of the rapid approach of the kingdom."[13]

The Edgefield area was not the only location to witness dramatic Baptist growth. Much further to the north of Edgefield District lay Brushy Creek Baptist Church, in Greenville District. Here, in this more mountainous part of the state, revival began at the annual meeting of the Saluda Baptist Association, hosted that year by Brushy Creek Church. As usual, the association meeting drew a large crowd. Adding to the excitement was the presence of two ministers from Georgia, Jonathan and James Davies, who had overseen magnificent revivals in churches in Georgia in the late 1820s. A heightened sense of the supernatural also contributed to the awakening. Brushy Creek Church's long-term minister, Lewis Rector, had prophesized about a coming revival shortly before dying in 1827. Then, on the day of August 7, 1831, a spot appeared on the sun that resulted in a greenish atmospheric hue. H. P. Griffith, present at the revival, recounted that there occurred "a strange phenomenon in nature" where "the rays of the sun were dimmed by a dark spot on his disk." The eclipse cast a "pale, somber hue" on "the whole face of creation," causing men to be either alarmed or humbled, "as under the finger of God." Preachers, Griffith wrote, "eager to lay hold of every means adapted to the awakening and humbling of sinners, made happy and forcible allusions to the surrounding scene," pointing to the mysterious greenish light of the sun as a sign of the supernatural. With "all things being seemingly ready," the association meeting and accompanying revival began, lasting for four days and bringing large numbers of converts.[14]

The revival had a major impact on Brushy Creek, surging membership almost six-fold. In July 1831, the month before revival hit, roughly 40 members belonged to the church—about the same number of members as the church had in the early 1800s. By 1832 church membership had increased to 190. In 1833 the number declined slightly, to 184.[15] The church clerk wrote of the 1831 associational meeting that people of all ages, from "the old, the middle aged and young yea little boys and girls of ten and Twelve years" joined the church.[16] Enslaved people also attended the meeting and felt the call of the Holy Spirit. But revivalism, like everything in the South, also bore aspects of racial segregation. As they beckoned converts to come forward, the white audience was first given the invitation, followed by the black audience.[17] Enslaved people also needed permission from their enslavers—who were not always in attendance—to join the church. In June 1832, John, who had been expelled from the church in the past, came before the church to express his contrition and ask for forgiveness. His mistress, Sister Horton, was not present at the meeting, so the decision was delayed.[18] Likewise, several enslaved people were not received immediately during the revival because they could not fully or clearly relate their conversion experience. The same month that John sought readmission to membership at Brushy Creek, for instance, a slave named Linia "came forward but not being clear in her experience was not received."[19]

While the revival of the early 1830s lit fires throughout Upcountry, it also affected churches in Lowcountry Beaufort District. The awakening in this area came from two directions: it was assisted by Furman students and no doubt inspired by the Edgefield revivals, but another major force came out of Savannah, Georgia, in the form of Presbyterian Daniel J. Baker. Following a successful interdenominational revival in Savannah, Baker accepted invitations to preach in nearby locations along the coast. In the fall of 1831 he traveled to several towns in Beaufort District, where crowds welcomed his dynamic, energetic preaching. Baker effected about sixty conversions in Gillisonville and made a significant impact in Grahamville, but the town of Beaufort saw the most dramatic results. Unconcerned about denominational affiliation (Presbyterian historian George Howe lamented that of all the converts of the Beaufort revival, "Not one became a Presbyterian"), Baker worked with the local Baptist and Episcopal ministers (these were the only two churches in the town), holding revival services two and three times a day.[20] "A holy atmosphere pervaded the town, and affected the entire population to a degree unparalleled, save in the revival described by President Edwards, at Northampton, in 1735," remembered Baker.[21] Up to three hundred people were converted during the revival, including prominent men and women in the community. Future Baptist minister Richard Fuller, South Carolina radical politician Robert Barnwell Rhett, and future Episcopal bishop Stephen Elliott comprised only some of the well-known converts.[22] Rather than replacing an older Baptist style with a new one, the revival helped solidify an evangelical culture in Beaufort that was already controlled by the elite. In both its origins and its results, the Beaufort awakening differed in important respects from the revivals in the Upcountry.

The revival of the early 1830s led to phenomenal growth in the number of Baptists—white and black, male and female—in the Upcountry and western portion of South Carolina. Baptist ministers, however, disagreed about the degree to which human agency affected the awakening. Congregational Baptists such as those at Brushy Creek placed primary emphasis upon the Pentecostal nature of the revival and prayed for continued "out poor [outpouring]" of the Holy Spirit.[23] By contrast, Lowcountry Baptists recognized the work of the Holy Spirit but also accentuated the importance of organizational evangelicalism. William Bullein Johnson's account of the Edgefield awakening, circulated throughout the South in the Georgia-based *Christian Index*, lauded the role of the Furman Theological Academy in fueling the revival. Without such an institution, the labor needed to expand the revival would have been challenging. "In these scenes of spiritual labor," he wrote, "the advantage of numbers in the ministry was strikingly evident." One minister's sermon "was enforced by the exhortation of another," and then by a third and fourth sermon by yet another revival leader. "And thus in the course of one day, would all the Ministers be engaged in some way or other, helping and sustaining each other," Johnson explained. He applauded the spirit of unity within which the ministers operated: "That too, which tended not a little to the energy and success of their labors, was the spirit of unanimity, which directed the efforts of the whole band to the same grand point, the glory of God in the salvation of souls through our Lord Jesus Christ."[24] Without such properly trained ministers, revival could not have reached the heights that it did. Man's efforts strengthened the workings of the Holy Spirit, creating a marvelous but well-ordered awakening of souls. For William Bullein Johnson, the revival of the early 1830s, a wonderful event in itself, presented yet another sign that ministerial education, a major facet of Baptist denominationalism, enhanced efforts to expand the kingdom of God.

While Baptist ministers celebrated the results of the revival of the early 1830s, their progress was threatened by two issues that caused significant religious conflict and division. One issue, Nullification, was a political conflict that engulfed South Carolinians in the early 1830s. The second was the ongoing division between missionary and anti-missionary Baptists. Between 1832 and 1833, white voters participated in passion-filled debates about Nullification—South Carolina's attempt to nullify two federal tariffs—that took on aspects of a religious crusade. Churches and associations observed fast days to stop the infighting and to plead for political harmony.[25] Politics sometimes overflowed into congregations, and ministers worried that Nullification diverted attention from religious efforts. While he celebrated the recent revival in Edgefield, James C. Furman worried that in Charleston "the great political excitement" occurring over Nullification "exerts an injurious influence on the cause of Christ." Such a passionate and heated political climate exacerbated "those backslidings which characterize too many of our religious professors," Furman wrote, hindering greatly the mission of the church. "'Nearness to God, & the heat of political contest (& who takes of fire into his bosom but is not inflamed?) seem to be utterly incompatible."[26] In the Upcountry, where Unionism was much stronger than in the Lowcountry, politics also spilled into churches, threatening the work of the Lord. Numerous Upcountry Baptist congregations sent queries to their associations about the role ministers should play in the Nullification controversy. The Bethel Baptist Association answered the question of whether "the tenor of the gospel" would "permit the ministers thereof to mix subjects of political controversy in their pulpit discourses." Ministers should abstain from public discourses about politics, the association declared, with the exception of "cases where the liberties of conscience becomes the subject of legislation."[27]

In the divided Upcountry, political tensions between Nullifiers and Unionists were especially strong. Denominational Baptist minister James Chiles, who pastored in many churches in the region, wrote often to his colleague and friend James C. Furman about the religious and political excitement pervading the region. In Edgefield in the summer of 1832, during the highest point of the revival, so at odds were communities over politics that often "the minister's force was divided in conducting *two* meetings of the same kind and at the same time in churches contiguous to the neighborhood."[28] In still another case, on "the Lord's day, at a Baptist Church," a fight broke out between members of the States' Rights and Union parties. Weapons were used: "dirks, knives, and pistols were drawn, and a bloody encounter was then witnessed." The fighting occurred on church grounds and involved church members and nearby residents; serious injuries were reported, although no fatalities. "Each party has indicted the other and we fear the difficulties have not terminated," Chiles wrote. Political battles divided other Upcountry Baptists, as well, worrying Chiles that while "we have enjoyed precious seasons of divine grace for 2 or 3 years," Baptists might have become too sanctimonious and complacent in their gains, allowing the worldly and secular to permeate their bounds. "The day is not far distant, if not it be not now present, when the language of St. Peter will be applicable to some of the Churches; 'The time is come that *judgment* must begin at the house of God.'"[29]

Similar disruptions plagued other Upcountry churches. At Bethel Baptist Church in Spartanburg District in 1833, "a terrible convulsion . . . shook the church to its very centre [*sic*]." After Thomas Ray, a church elder and a wealthy planter, supported the Nullifiers, the church split between Unionists and Nullifiers; not until 1834 did the factions begin to smooth over their differences.[30] By 1833 the Edgefield Baptist Association had connected factional politics to religious declension. "It has been our unhappy lot, in this highly favored land, to have been involved in difficulties, that threatened the extinction of our liberties, or the separation of these States," wrote William Johnson. "In such a state of things, parties will be formed, for all men do not think alike." Because humans were imperfect, they would engage in party politics, "the influence of which is awfully injurious to the vital interests of the christianity in the soul."[31] While the impending storm had passed, Johnson cautioned, "the effects of the threat remain and are felt throughout the country." How? "It is true that, during our difficulties, revivals succeeded revivals in delightful order." The revivals came from "God's immediate and invincible power." When the power "declined, the influence of the political controversy began to be felt," creating a "mighty reaction" that "is operating an unfriendly influence upon the interests of religion."[32] Much more work, it seemed clear, was needed to build the Kingdom of God.

As the immediate controversy over Nullification faded, Baptist division over denominationalism did not. In the Upcountry, opposition to trained ministers and missionary organizations, verging on a full-fledged embrace of antimissionism, continued in the 1830s, reaching a high point by the following decade. The Upcountry Saluda Baptist Association experienced particularly strong resistance to the advancement of missionary ideas. To the dismay of denominational Baptists, the association withdrew from the Baptist State Convention in the early 1820s after joining for only one year. Pro-mission ministers in the association increased their denominational efforts throughout the late 1820s and into the 1830s. In the mid-1830s they formed Anderson District Mission Society, which became an affiliate member of the state convention, allowing pro-mission churches to coordinate missionary efforts with the larger state organization. But antimission sentiment remained strong in some churches. Both Salem and Flat Rock Church, located close the village of Anderson, experienced "serious trouble over the mission question" in 1839. Flat Rock sent two separate sets of delegates to the Saluda Association meeting that year, one representing an antimission faction, the other a missionary faction. Salem Baptist Church did not send any delegates to the 1839 meeting of the association (delegates instead attended the newly formed antimission Fork Shoal Association), prompting the Saluda Association to establish a committee to investigate the conflict. Committee members reported in 1840 that they had attempted "to discharge the duties assigned us" by visiting Salem Church but were "prevented making an effort to reconcile said church" by the church's minister, James H. Hembree, who notified the committee that it "could not be received nor heard, coming in the capacity of a committee from the Association."[33]

Reacting against the missionary tendencies of some in their midst, a small number of churches formally withdrew membership from the Saluda Association and created the antimission Fork Shoal Association.[34] Fork Shoal delegates were clear in their opposition to the Baptist State Convention, asserting their belief "that the Baptist State Convention, with all her train of kindred institutions, are unscriptural, and cannot be supported from the word of the Lord; and therefore have no fellowship for them; and no question relative thereto shall be introduced or discussed in the Association."[35] The association remained in existence until 1844, when it dissolved for lack of membership.

Anderson District's Big Creek Church underwent a particularly tumultuous time in the early to mid-1840s. The congregation divide into two groups and competed, literally, for possession of the meeting house. The anti-missionary faction in 1844 renamed itself the Big Creek Primitive Baptist Church and joined the Fork Shoal Association. Big Creek Primitives carefully delineated their beliefs through the "Articles of our faith at Big Creek as a church of the old School baptists," which resolved that "in obedience with the apostle Paul a chosen vessel of God, we are disposed to Comply with that appossels [*sic*] orders & withdraw from all those that depart from the faith for the love of money." Their command, they felt, came straight from the Bible: "Sd. Orders is on record 1. tim ch. 5 & 6 verse, as also 2nd tim and 3rd Chapter 5, V., and as we take the old and new testament for the onley [*sic*] rule of faith & practice we find that we must withdraw from such or disobey there [*sic*] Com'ds of the apostle above mentioned." Should anyone think that God should want more from His Church that was mentioned in the Bible, Old School adherents warned,

> our answer is its not So for our proof look, duet. 4. Ch. 2nd prob. 30:6 Rev. 22: & 18; 19, and you will find that there is nothing to be added or deminished [*sic*] to his word and he does not require of us anything that he has not told us of and therefore brethern [*sic*] we are disposed to act as we Say & we will not say & then refuse to act as we Say, and if anyone Should Say that they are willing to withdraw from the institution and not from the brethern [*sic*] that patronises them Our answer is that the institution could do no harm if no one wood [*sic*] practice them and therefore Such people as practises [*sic*] them is the eye sore with us & is precisely the people we have no fellowship for, for this reason we think it wood [*sic*] be entirely in consistant [*sic*] Reasoning for any one to Say that he did not fellowship horss [*sic*] Raceing [*sic*] But that he did and wood [*sic*] fellowship the people that done thees [*sic*] things for what harm could hors [*sic*] rasing [*sic*] do if no one wood [*sic*] practice it & what harm could the institution do if no one wood [*sic*] practice it & therefore our resolution is as follows; that we as a church withdraw fellowship from all Benovilant institutions falsly [*sic*] So cald [*sic*] Such as the Baptist State Convention the temperate [*sic*] Society the track society the Sunday School Society, the Baptist furren [*sic*] Mishinn [*sic*] Society the Baptist Home Mishion [*sic*] Society & the abolition Society.[36]

The Primitive faction of the Big Creek congregation, supporting only gospel efforts mentioned specifically in the Bible, seems to have disappeared by 1850, partly because their minister—who had been sentenced to serve jail time for his disruption of the rival faction's church services—left the state for

Georgia. The missionary faction of the church, with a more stable and proactive minister, began to grow. By 1845 the congregation joined the Saluda Baptist Association, which became part of the Baptist State Convention in 1850.[37] Like the Saluda Baptist Association, other associations also joined the Baptist State Convention by the 1850s. The Bethel Association, which had been in existence since 1789, joined in 1852, as well as subsequent Upcountry associations in the late 1850s. By 1860 fifteen associations belonged to the convention.[38] Yet denominational support was not unanimous. Although a majority of Baptists supported missions and education by 1860, an undercurrent of opposition remained in some Upcountry churches. Baptist culture wars had waned but had not completely disappeared.

While their divisions over politics and denomination building were palpable and sometimes even violent, white Baptists drew closer to one another when it came to defending the right to evangelize to enslaved people. Black church membership confirmed to white Baptists that whites were fulfilling their biblical duty to provide the knowledge of salvation to enslaved people. But salvation had deeply significant egalitarian implications. By sharing and practicing the same spiritual tenets as whites, Christian enslaved people could claim a spiritual equality that, if taken to its logical extreme, connoted human equality. Thus, while whites encouraged enslaved people to claim spiritual citizenship, they reinforced racial differences through separation and segregation, through a secondary church citizenship in the temporal world. The Christian model of slavery, designed to provide spiritual and benevolent aid to enslaved people, always carried with it the authority, for whites, to reinforce the racial order.

In the 1830s white Baptist efforts to evangelize enslaved people through a Christian model of slavery drew increasing scrutiny and criticism from two different cross-sections of the country. First, anxiety over the threat of slave insurrection led some white South Carolinians to renew their efforts to restrict religious opportunities for enslaved people. Second, antislavery northern Baptists became more strident in their attacks on slaveholders. White Baptist ministers reacted strategically and defensively to both sets of criticisms, defending the church's right to evangelize to enslaved people and responding vigorously to northern Baptist criticism about the morality of slave ownership. In the process, white Baptists throughout South Carolina strengthened their proslavery orientation and argumentation, underscoring their core beliefs that Christianity benefited enslaved people spiritually and enslavers socially by shoring up the social network. For the first time, they collectively made this public argument to all who would hear it, forging a stronger and more united sectional path within southern Baptist ranks.

Throughout the 1820s and 1830s, Baptists worked aggressively to counter escalating pressure at home to restrict religious opportunities for enslaved people. During these years, in an effort to thwart the dissemination of antislavery and abolitionist literature, numerous southern states passed laws banning slave literacy. In 1829 Georgia legislators made teaching enslaved people or free blacks to read or write a crime subject to fines, whipping, or imprisonment. In 1830 Louisiana legislated jail time for anyone convicted of instructing an enslaved person to read or write. The same year, North Carolina banned literacy for enslaved people and free blacks, stating that literate enslaved people were more likely to "produce insurrection." Virginia law in the early 1830s fined whites who taught blacks to read or write in schools; following the Nat Turner Rebellion, legislators banned preaching by enslaved people and free blacks. Alabama followed with an 1833 law prohibiting the teaching of enslaved people or free blacks to spell, read, or write.[39]

In South Carolina, Whitemarsh Seabrook, state representative, senator, and, by 1834, lieutenant governor, led the charge for more restrictive laws. In 1825 Seabrook proposed banning slave literacy and schools for blacks.[40] Seabrook continued his crusade to stop enslaved people from learning throughout the late 1820s and the early 1830s. Nat Turner's revolt in August 1831 amplified concerns about better ways to control the actions of enslaved men and women. The state's almost total focus on Nullification probably slowed Seabrook's restrictive reforms, but by November 1834 Seabrook's bill to ban enslaved people and free blacks from reading and writing seemed close to passing.[41]

Seabrook's attack on slave literacy came at the same time that white religious leaders advanced a stronger public commitment to evangelizing enslaved people. Methodists in South Carolina and Georgia began to send white missionaries to plantations in Lowcountry South Carolina and Georgia in 1829, and in 1833 South Carolina's Presbyterian Synod passed resolutions signifying the importance of religious instruction of enslaved people. In 1834 Seabrook published a pamphlet harshly criticizing what he perceived to be the liberal religious instruction provided to enslaved people. Although he did not advocate for a full ban on evangelizing enslaved men and women, Seabrook took issue with the religious freedoms he felt that some white evangelicals provided to enslaved people. "Is it advisable," Seabrook wrote, "to make them acquainted with the whole Bible, or to teach them every doctrine of the Bible?" Providing enslaved people and free blacks full religious opportunities was foolish and unwise—those who supported such beliefs belonged "in the Lunatic Asylum."[42]

Acutely aware of attitudes such as Seabrook's, Baptist ministers in Charleston worked strategically to retain the right to preach to enslaved people. Like other ministers in the area, they worried about the recent action of the Charleston city council, which had recently tightened restrictions on religious meetings for enslaved people, in accordance with a more literal interpretation of the 1800 and 1803 laws about slave gatherings. In late November 1834, the city's white ministers—eighteen of them, including Basil Manly—petitioned the state legislature about this turn of events. The memorialists noted that, for the past thirty years, enslaved people had been allowed to worship in the evenings with white oversight but without more than 50 percent whites as the extant laws proscribed. For the enslaved people engaged in domestic work in the city, it was extremely difficult to worship prior to evening, and it was also difficult to amass a large number of whites to attend religious meetings for enslaved people, they noted. Only in times of emergency had such evening meetings been disallowed, and the memorialists could foresee no such emergency in 1834. Additionally, in areas outside of Charleston, no such restriction on religious meetings for enslaved people in the evening had been enforced. The petitioners asked that the city council reconsider its restriction, for, rather than leading to "mischief," religious meetings "are considered to have contributed, more than any cause, to the formation as faithful, valuable, subordinate, and well-affected a body of citizens, as any in the city."[43] At the request of Basil Manly and Christopher Gadsden, rector of St. Philips Church, the city council met with the ministers as a group in late November 1834. The council agreed to support the ministers' memorial "praying for a modification of the Laws in relations to Religious assemblages of Negroes and Persons of Colour" and "Resolved that Council will cheerfully assume the discharge of any of the duties which the Legislature in their wisdom may prescribe in relation to the regulation of religious assemblages of Negroes and Persons of Colour within the limits of the City of Charleston."[44]

Unfortunately for the delegation of Charleston ministers, by December, after repeated attempts, Seabrook's bill to ban enslaved people from reading and writing passed.[45] The law did not include all the restrictions that Seabrook and his allies had proposed. It did not prohibit blacks from preaching or exhorting, nor did it change the measures from the 1800 and 1803 laws about the composition and timing of religious meetings for enslaved people and free blacks. But, in a huge blow to white religious leaders, it banned literacy for the enslaved, making it illegal for anyone to teach an enslaved person to read or write. Free blacks were not included in this ban.[46] White Baptists (like other white evangelicals) were forced to reshape their ministerial efforts to enslaved people. Some quietly continued to teach enslaved people to read. Others, including Presbyterian ministers and other citizens in two Upcountry districts, Abbeville and Chester, petitioned the legislature to revoke the ban on slave literacy.[47]

As concerned as they were about enslaved people not being able to read the Bible, white Baptists were even more affronted by northern abolitionist Baptist condemnations of Christian slavery. On the national and international level, English and northern Baptists in the 1830s began to call for an immediate end to slavery. Baptist ministers in the South felt personally attacked by northern and English Baptist denunciations, for nowhere in the gospel, they claimed, did owning enslaved people make them unchristian. Throughout the state, white Baptists denounced abolitionist intermeddling and proclaimed to northern Baptists that, if practiced along Christian lines, slaveholding was moral and sanctified. Although they evinced differing views on whether emancipation would ultimately occur, all tended to agree that only God would know when enslaved people, through white guidance and amelioration, would be prepared for freedom.[48] In the Triennial Convention, ministers from South Carolina and from other southern states fought specifically to keep slavery out of their national organization's commitment to missionary work at home and abroad. When they could not persuade northern Baptists to concede to their positions, South Carolina Baptists, collaborating closely with ministers in other southern states, withdrew from the national Baptist association to form their own organization. In doing so, they underscored their commitment to missions and education and, even more fundamentally, proclaimed their righteousness as slaveholders, assuring themselves and a larger society that slavery was moral so long as it was practiced within a Christian context. Throughout this period, South Carolina

Baptist ministers took explicit steps to convince their northern and English brothers and sisters, themselves, and the larger South Carolina society that the Christian model of slavery was the only moral way to practice slavery, and that preaching both salvation and servility to enslaved people was the only political way to preserve order in society. In doing so, they preached the gospel and preached race as a way to save black souls and to reinforce white southern supremacy.

White South Carolina Baptists first publicly responded to abolitionism in the mid-1830s. In 1833 Baptist ministers in London sent a letter to American Baptists calling for the immediate abolition of slavery. English Baptists had been active supporters of emancipating enslaved people in the British West Indies, and they celebrated legislation passed by Parliament in 1833 ending slavery in the British Empire by 1838. English Baptists next turned to the United States, sending to the "Pastors and Ministers of the Baptist Denomination throughout the United States of America" a letter calling for American Baptists to support the immediate end of slavery, citing the institution's "awful breach of Divine law."[49] This letter, which they sent to the Acting Board of the General Convention, drew two distinct responses from northern Baptist ministers: some advocated for neutrality within the convention, while others felt that the convention should make abolitionism a primary goal. Moderate voices in the Acting Board prevailed. Citing the constitution of the General Convention, the board proclaimed neutrality, stating that "We have the best evidence that our slaveholding brethren are Christians, sincere followers of the Lord Jesus." Roughly fifty abolitionist Baptist ministers, unhappy with this response, met in Boston on May 26–27, 1835. They composed a letter to British Baptists that condemned slavery, charging that "SLAVEHOLDING is now the most heinous sin with which America is chargeable" and promising to "labor in use of weapons not carnal but mighty through God to the overthrow" of slavery as well as all other "work of wickedness." These American ministers agreed with their British counterparts that slavery was "a sin to be abandoned and not an evil to be mitigated; a high crime against the Majesty of heaven, for the suppression of which every believer in Christ is bound strenuously and prayerfully to labor." They prayed for God's help in their spiritual battle to end slavery, agreeing that "We are verily a guilty nation before God, touching the inalienable rights of many of our fellow-men." Not until all laws legalizing slavery were overturned would this sin be remedied. About 130 Baptists signed the letter.[50]

The censure of abolitionist Baptists against slaveholding church members dovetailed with a larger campaign orchestrated by the American Anti-Slavery Society (the nation's most powerful antislavery organization) to send thousands of antislavery pamphlets to the slaveholding states. When abolitionist mailings came to Charleston from New York via the steamboat *Columbia* in late July 1835, a storm of controversy ensued. Mobs broke into the Charleston post office and burned the abolitionist mailings; the city postmaster, Alfred Huger, then negotiated a solution whereby he separated and confined antislavery materials. In the heat of the moment, officials closed African American schools and stopped all religious meetings of enslaved people, a further blow to Basil Manly and other Charleston ministers who in the previous year had worked with the city council to extend religious protections to enslaved men and women.[51] As a result of both of these measures, almost unilaterally, white Baptists in both the Upcountry and the Lowcountry recalibrated their arguments about slavery. Delegates to the Bethel Baptist Association expressed "deep mortification" over the "fanatical and unchristian doctrines, which have been advanced in certain portions of these States" in regard to slavery. That many abolitionists called themselves Christians proved even more distressing. "If there be true christians among these dangerous agitators, we trust, that God in his mercy, will open their eyes to the guilt and folly of their proceedings," Baptists asserted. The Bible clearly sanctioned slavery, to the point that "no man who is desirous of knowing the will of God, and will read the scriptures . . . can entertain any doubts as to the strict propriety of slaves being held." Like many white southerners, delegates viewed interference with "the relations between the master and the slave" as "mischievous and immoral," and for all these reasons the association recommended that churches "shut their pulpits against any and every Preacher, who advocates the Abolition doctrines, and to abstain from all fellowship and intercourse with him."[52]

Edgefield Baptists went even further in their reaction to abolitionism. In his letter to the 1835 Edgefield Baptist Association, William Bullein Johnson warned that "some of our brethren at the North have indulged themselves in terms of severe reproach upon their brethren at the South, who hold slaves." These northern Baptists had asserted that they would not take communion with slave-owning Baptists, meaning that they viewed the Baptist slave owner as not a true member of Christ's church. Johnson's response was swift and direct. Northern Baptists were following an "unscriptural course" that could well lead to the break-up of the Baptists as a national denomination. They should turn to the Bible for counsel and direction, and should heed Paul's writing to Timothy calling for enslaved people to be loyal to their enslavers, so long as their enslavers were "believing masters." Edgefield Baptists asked those northern Baptists "who speak and write with such asperity against us as slave holders" to reconsider their decision about sharing the communion table with those in the South. Would they not admit the Apostle Paul, who sanctioned slavery? Would they not admit "Jesus Christ himself, who inspired the Apostle" to write the passage? Maybe the real problem was northern Baptists, and maybe it was not northern Baptists who should refuse communion with southern Baptists, but southern Baptists who should exclude from fellowship those following an unscriptural path in the North![53] Not all Baptists in the North were abolitionists, Johnson recognized. A "number of our excellent brethren" had chosen not to interfere with southern slavery. Edgefield Baptists affirmed this group of Baptists "as friends of truth, good order and the Union," and appealed to them to "be firm at their posts, in the maintenance of the word of the Lord, and the concord of the brethren," asking as well that they help maintain unity among northern and southern Baptists "on just and Scriptural grounds."[54]

In the Lowcountry, where whites were the most skittish about slave unrest, the Charleston Baptist Association, in keeping with tradition, sent a petition to the South Carolina legislature relating its concerns about the right to evangelize enslaved people. When they met at their annual conference in November 1835, the association, made up of ministers of Baptist churches spanning Charleston, Georgetown, Williamsburg, Darlington, Sumter, Kershaw, Richland, and Orangeburg Districts, recorded "their sentiments in relation to the question of slavery, now extensively agitated throughout the country." Basil Manly, the moderator of the association, conveyed the views to the legislature in the form of two resolutions, as the ministers felt "it important that the Legislature should be made acquainted with the views and beliefs of their constituents on this subject, (especially of religious bodies) as extensively as possible."[55]

The association's first resolution expressed opposition to abolitionist interference with southern slavery. The association communicated its profound disappointment that "some mistaken philanthropists, and deluded & mischievous fanatics in a portion of our country" thought it necessary "to interfere with the domestic institutions of the Southern and slaveholding states." Such actions would not achieve successful results, for one only had to look to the Bible to see that slavery, if practiced according to scripture, was moral and divinely sanctioned. Moreover, if slavery as a *system* needed reforming—if in its current form in the South change needed to come—the state legislature and the people of each state would make that change "at the most proper period." Outside interference on these issues was not wanted or needed and would not be tolerated by the slaveholding states. White Charleston Baptists viewed intermeddling "not only as officious and unfriendly, but incendiary and murderous in its tendency." Not only did it have an ill effect on enslaved people (by challenging them to leave their beneficial master-slave relationships), it was also "fatal to the feelings of a common brotherhood" among Americans and "fatal especially to the permanency of the union of the states." Slaveholding states should take legal or penal measures to stop abolitionist interference, if "milder measures" did not work. Within the denomination, the Charleston Association called on moderate northern Baptists to halt the actions of radical abolitionists, reminding them "of the consequences which must grow out of any continued interference with this question."[56]

The association's second resolution asked the state legislature not to restrict religious instruction of enslaved people. White Baptists were beholden to evangelize to "this class of people," Manly insisted, not in response to abolitionist attacks but because enslaved people "also have a Master in heaven." The Charleston Association advised all congregations "to use every consistent method, in accordance with the laws of the Land," to teach enslaved people about "salvation through Jesus Christ." White Baptists urged legislators not to restrict rights for enslaved people unless "some existing abuse or obvious danger" existed, for not only had God commanded that slave owners treat their enslaved people humanely, but Christian enslaved people were not a threat to the social order—by contrast, they were a "safeguard" to the enslaver-enslaved relationship.[57]

Slavery, the petitioners concluded, was a matter of political economy. In some states operatives bought and sold their labor only and remained free, but in other states employers had the right to "buy the whole time of laborers at once," with the permanent duty to provide "protection and care over them." God had, in the Bible, "distinctly recognized" the right of enslavers to hold enslaved people as property.[58] Since the right to own enslaved people was "a question purely of political economy," and since states, not churches, regulated the protection and transaction of property, the state "should resist to the utmost every invasion of this right, come from what quarter, and under what pretence it may."[59]

In 1835 white Baptists in South Carolina staked their claim, publicly, about the righteousness of Christian slavery, asserting their right to own enslaved people, to treat them in a Christian manner, and to provide them with religious instruction. Within the denomination, they now redirected the conversation back to the business of missions, emphasizing within official convention business a strategy of neutrality and noninterference with slavery. Because leadership of the Triennial Convention remained in moderate hands, when the Baptist convention met in 1838, no official discussion about slavery took place.[60] Responding to what they perceived as a lack of moral will in the convention, abolitionist Baptists created a new missionary convention, the American Baptist Anti-Slavery Convention, which first met on April 28–30, 1840, in New York City. The convention called for nonfellowship with slaveholding Baptists and for slavery's immediate end.[61] While they established a new abolitionist missionary organization, not all abolitionist leaders withdrew from the Triennial Convention. Most notably, New York minister Elon Galusha, who became president of the new abolitionist convention, also remained on the board of the Triennial Convention (the steering committee of the national denomination), causing an immediate outcry from southern delegates.[62]

Concerned that an avowedly abolitionist minister such as Elon Galusha remained part of the Acting Board of the convention, Baptists in the South again considered separation from their northern brethren. Alabama Baptists led by Basil Manly (who had assumed the presidency of the University of Alabama in 1837, moving from South Carolina) felt that there were "insuperable obstacles to further cooperation in the foreign mission department" and endorsed forming southern-only missions options.[63] The Charleston Baptist Association also recommended the establishment of a separate, southern board of foreign missions. The association suggested that all churches and associations in the state consider "the necessity of the formation, at as early a period as practicable, of a Southern Baptist Board of Foreign Missions." Baptists should continue to send money to the Foreign Mission Board in Boston until a southern board was formed unless "circumstances, more unforeseen, warrant a different course."[64] William Bullein Johnson, president-elect of the 1841 convention, shared through the press the dangers that northern Baptist abolitionism posed to missionary endeavors. For over two decades northern and southern Baptists had been engaged "in the grand Missionary enterprise." Abolitionist actions were "appalling, and most sincerely to be deplored." Would the "connexion" between Baptists in the two regions continue? Only God, who "sees the end from the beginning," knew, Johnson wrote.[65]

Although they considered forming a southern board of missions, white Baptists in South Carolina and in other southern states also sought to maintain their presence in the Triennial Convention, working with moderates in the North to keep slavery out of the organization, which met again in May 1841.[66] Galusha was removed from the Executive Board in 1841, replaced by South Carolina minister Richard Fuller, who actively promoted a noninterference clause.[67] Separation and dissension "must not, will not, shall not, cannot be," Fuller asserted: Baptists must work together to continue their program of missions, rather than fighting over slavery.[68] But increasingly, noninterference proved difficult, for abolitionists, passionate about abolition, continued to wage war against southern slaveholders in the religious press. In 1843 some abolitionist Baptists left the Triennial Convention and formed the American Baptist Free Mission Society, which supported both foreign and home missions; other abolitionists remained in the national bodies, where they worked to purge southern slaveholders from membership.[69] By 1844 white southern Baptists felt increasingly threatened. Both the board of the Triennial Convention and that of the Home Mission Society (the latter formed in 1832) agreed that slavery would not be discussed officially in their meetings, but the abolitionist sentiments of many of the board members worried white southerners. Fearful that abolitionists were taking control of both boards, white southern Baptists made the decision to test the neutrality rules of both the Triennial Convention and the Home Mission Society. Georgia Baptists in 1844 proposed to the Home Mission Board the appointment of a slaveholding missionary, James E. Reeve. Georgia Baptists stated specifically that Reeve was a slaveholder. The Home Mission Board declined to consider the appointment—which they deemed a test case—on the basis that, by revealing that Reeve was a slaveholder, Georgia Baptists had disregarded the 1841 neutrality resolutions mandating that no discussion of slavery take place in the Home Mission Society.[70] That same year, Alabama Baptists led by Basil Manly, promoting their right to be an equal part of the denomination, sent what became known as the "Alabama Resolutions" to the General Board of the Triennial Convention. The resolutions stated that slaveholders should have the same right as non-slaveholders to serve as missionaries or agents in the denomination; they also suggested that churches as well as the Triennial Convention held the power to appoint missionaries. The Triennial Convention answered that the convention itself held the authority to appoint missionaries, and, forced to answer either affirmatively or negatively about slavery, stated that "One thing is certain; we can never be a party to any arrangement which would imply approbation of slavery."[71]

The response of the board of the Triennial Convention to the Alabama Resolutions—that, if asked to violate the noninterference clause and decide whether a missionary could be a slaveholder, the answer would be no—led directly to the formation of a sectional Baptist denomination, the Southern Baptist Convention. Immediately following news of the board's ruling, the Virginia Baptist Missionary Society called for a meeting of southern delegates to decide what course of action to take. Close to three hundred white southern Baptists, as well as a small number of northern Baptists from the American Baptist Publication Society, convened in Augusta, Georgia, on May 8, 1845, to decide their role in national Baptist politics. Some delegates proposed to continue their partnership with northern Baptists in the Triennial Convention, but most were ready to depart. South Carolina Baptist William Bullein Johnson, who had helped create the constitution of the 1814 Triennial Convention, introduced a plan for a new southern convention that combined home and foreign missions, as well as other forms of benevolent outreach, under one organization. The plan, which Johnson purportedly pulled from his coat pocket, set in motion a new, separate, and sectional Southern Baptist Convention.[72]

The formation of the Southern Baptist Convention, as explained by William Johnson, who would preside over the organization in its early years, was not the work of all northern Baptists. It occurred because of the actions of one faction of northern Baptists, the abolitionists, who refused to respect the neutrality of the convention. Abolitionists' efforts to exclude southern slaveholders as missionaries were sinful: "THEY WOULD FORBID US TO *speak unto* THE GENTILES." White southern Baptists would not allow one group of Baptists ("like the Autocratical Interdict of the North") to deny their mission work, however. Abolitionists in the convention threatened to "first drive us from our beloved colored people . . . and from the much-wronged Aborigines of the country; and then cut us off from the whitening fields of the heathen harvest-labor; to which by cogent appeals and solemn prayers, they have so often protested that, without us, they were inadequate."[73] Such being the case, white southern Baptists withdrew to form "their own centre of operations" and committed themselves to two goals: "extension of the Messiah's kingdom, and the glory of our God."[74] Responding directly to the wording of the Foreign Missionary Board when it proclaimed that slaveholders should not serve as missionaries, Johnson countered: "'One thing is certain'—We must go every where preaching the word."[75] "We will never interfere with what is Caeser's," Johnson wrote, nor would white Baptists "compromise what is God's."[76]

By 1845 South Carolina Baptists had reached a denominational crossroads in two important ways. Denominational Baptists pushed their presence further into the Upcountry, articulating a preaching style and a commitment to preaching the gospel that extended well beyond the local congregation. The spread of the denominational vision created significant cultural infighting and opposition within Upcountry churches and Upcountry associations, causing a handful of churches to identify as Primitive Baptists and others to lean closely in that direction. But as divided as they were over *how* to preach, white Baptists in South Carolina between 1830 and 1845 became more unified in their commitment to defending slavery as a Christian right. They shared a belief that Christian slavery was moral and biblical, and that it served a dual benefit, providing for the spiritual and moral well-being of enslaved people as well as preserving the social order. When northern Baptists refused to treat them as co-leaders in their national missionary convention, white Baptists withdrew to form their own organization, the Southern Baptist Convention, with a South Carolina minister and slaveholder at the helm. Finally, it seemed, white Baptists in South Carolina—and in the slaveholding South—would be able to preach the gospel, and to preach about race, as God commanded them to do, as Christian slaveholders who sanctioned spiritual benevolence while legitimizing and perpetuating racial hierarchy and control. Now fully independent from their northern brethren, white southern Baptists took more active steps to promote a Christian moral order that sanctified and sacralized slavery in the church and in the larger society.

CHAPTER SIX

Sectionalism Ordained

Between 1845 and 1860, Baptists in South Carolina shifted their involvement in national Baptist politics to a regional Baptist platform. They became an integral and guiding force within the Southern Baptist Convention, with William Bullein Johnson, the leading denominational Baptist in South Carolina, drafting the convention's new constitution and serving as its president from 1845–1851. Under Johnson's watch, the Southern Baptist Convention continued to promote a full agenda of foreign and domestic missions work. Likewise, in South Carolina, the Baptist State Convention focused aggressively on denominational education, expanding Furman Theological Institution into a four-year college, relocating the school to an area of the state where Baptists had traditionally resisted education, and establishing a women's college in 1854. By the late 1850s, Baptists established a regional seminary in Greenville, the Southern Baptist Theological Seminary, so that the town became a major center of Baptist strength and influence. By the eve of the Civil War, all Baptist associations in the state had joined the Baptist State Convention, and most churches sent monies to support missions and education in an effort to spread the Kingdom of God. Yet some Baptists remained torn about denominationalism. Some church members accepted theologically trained ministers and new, formal styles of worship, but others yearned for the old days of emotional preaching. Internal cultural differences remained, even as overt infighting waned. The Lowcountry Baptist model, so powerful in shaping larger southern Baptist patterns, was still not fully accepted in all of South Carolina.

While denominationalism divided some white Baptists, the practice of Christian slavery did not. Once they had formed their own sectional organization, ministers spoke more urgently and directly about slave evangelization, becoming more intentional about building a biracial Christian kingdom on earth. At the heart of their message was the significance of moral uplift that white Christians should provide to enslaved people and the lack of ability of enslaved people themselves to follow moral dictates. But in biracial churches, enslaved people showed whites a different story. Slave conversions outstripped white conversions in some churches, and enslaved people demonstrated a desire to engage in full Christian citizenship, to partake in Christian rituals including marriages and burials and to share fellowship with fellow church members. Whites struggled to find the right mix for this situation, extending to enslaved people Christian rites only within the parameters of the law and of white control, and always making it clear who held ultimate governing authority. Whites turned their attention toward enslaved people, emphasizing the need for the close moral regulation of black men and women, while simultaneously turning away from them, organizing enslaved people into separate congregations and rejecting enslaved people as equal temporal partners in the church. As their actions would show after the war ended, enslaved people were not content with secondary status they were accorded by whites. For Baptist freedmen and women, the only way to resolve the tension was to leave white-controlled churches in the postwar years, finding, ultimately, both spiritual and physical freedom within the walls of God's meeting house.

In the late 1840s and throughout the 1850s, South Carolina experienced a period of economic prosperity, following more than a decade of depressed prices due to the Panic of 1837. In the 1850s a major cotton boom increased the value of both land and slave property. Significant development of railroad transportation led to the growth of towns and urban areas throughout the state. Eleven different railroads existed in South Carolina by 1860, and all districts in the state had rail lines to either Columbia or Charleston. The Upcountry benefited dramatically from these changes. Between 1840 and 1860, over four hundred miles of railroad track were constructed in the region, with two major lines—the Greenville to Columbia and the Columbia to Charlotte—completed by 1853, and with feeder lines to small towns located all through the region.[1] New towns sprang up along rail lines, and existing towns grew in population. Business increased dramatically in many of these towns, as did property values, wealth, and larger, more grandiose town and city buildings, including churches.[2]

Lowcountry Baptists engaged in this entrepreneurial spirit. Both the Baptist State Convention and individual Baptist associations increased their efforts to support male and female education. The Edgefield Association created a Committee on Education in the late 1840s that raised money for the establishment the Fuller and Hodges Institutes, which opened in 1850 in the fledgling town of Greenwood. Edgefield Baptists touted the natural beauty, healthiness, and accessibility of the region, noting that "The location of these Seminaries [was] on the pleasant and healthy ridge" between the Savannah and Saluda Rivers and was easily accessible via the recently completed Columbia to Greenville Railroad. "By this road, they will be of easy access to nearly all parts of the State," they wrote.[3] Baptists also established Limestone Springs Female High School in Spartanburg District (1845) and Johnson Female Seminary, later Johnson University, in Anderson District (1848). The latter school was named for William Johnson as a tribute to his work with female education.[4] By 1858 numerous students were enrolled at Johnson University, learning Latin, Greek, calculus, and other disciplines.[5] The proliferation of female academies allowed the Baptist denomination to extend its influence into the home and society. In 1854 the Edgefield Committee on Education noted "with pleasure, that the training of the female mind is not forgotten, in the efforts made to extend the facilities of education." Religious education would influence a new generation of men and women who would shape and refine society in gendered ways, Baptists believed, affirming that through education "our sons may be as plants grown up in their youth; that our daughters may be as cornerstones polished after the similitude of a palace."[6]

The establishment of new educational institutions for men and women exemplified white Lowcountry Baptists' desires to increase the denominational presence throughout the Upcountry. Their main focus, however, remained the flagship Furman Institution, which had changed locations and educational scope in the 1830s and 1840s. Started in 1826 in Edgefield as the Furman Academy and Theological Institution, the school was moved to High Hills (where it was called the Theological Institution) and then to Winnsboro (where it was called the Furman Institution); with each relocation, slightly different plans were made for recruiting and training students. In the late 1840s, members of the Baptist State Convention agreed to make two significant changes to the institution. First, they expanded the academy into a four-year university that offered classical as well as theological training. Second, they resolved to move the school to an Upcountry location, where Baptist resistance to ministerial education was pronounced. James C.

Furman explained the logic of relocating to the Upcountry. While the Welsh Neck Association, where the Furman Institution had recently been located, had "for many years past exceeded any other in the practical manifestations of interest in ministerial education," Baptists in other areas of the state had shown much less support for ministerial education and in some sections had "shown downright indifference, if not opposition." It was time for a "remedy for this evil," Furman argued. "We want something which shall draw the Baptist influence of the state to a focal point. We want each season of gathering together of the representatives of the denomination to be a high day, etc."[7]

To secure the best location for the new school, Baptist delegates met with town leaders in Anderson, Greenwood, and Greenville before deciding on Greenville.[8] Greenville was still small in 1850, with roughly 1,750 residents in 1852.[9] Convention Baptists praised the new location, noting the salubrious climate, accessibility to other portions of the state, and, most notably, the opportunity to gentrify Baptists in the region. "We have ventured to style the region, where it now exists, the promised land," James Furman proclaimed. "In this lovely region stands the town of Greenville . . . where the gentle undulation of the surface, and the graceful flow of its river, and the blue line of the mountain in the horizon, justify the appropriateness of a name which blends the ideas of the beauty of spring, and of the quietness of a rural retreat." Furman University stood in line to be "the Acropolis of Greenville" and "a school for the prophets," if Baptists could maintain its operations.[10]

Others also viewed the relocation of Furman Institute as a monumental step for the denomination. One leader referenced his joy at leaving the "captivity" of the prior institution in Winnsboro, where the school resembled a "barn," for an opportunity to "build . . . our Jerusalem."[11] Moreover, a Baptist school would help fight the secular temptations that would soon accompany the urban-industrial growth transforming the Upcountry. The people of Greenville were "about to undergo a great moral experiment," predicted Furman. "The path of the iron horse is even now being opened," and soon transportation would change the nature of the community, subjecting "a quiet rural people" to "the influence of modes of thought, and modes of feeling, and modes of action, transported from a distance." Commerce and vice would change the nature of the pastoral region of small farmers. "How important, then, that we anticipate these dangers, and that we give to Sacred Learning the opportunity to provide against them," wrote Furman.

Religious education would work against "the social influences which shall be brought to bear upon our mountain population." A college "founded on the Bible, and a community trained by the Bible," would fight such a battle against immorality.[12]

Denominational Baptist ministers were thrilled at the religious and social implications of the opening of Furman University. In December 1850 the state legislature chartered the university, and students began classes in 1851 as new buildings were being completed.[13] The three existing faculty members from Fairfield (Peter C. Edwards, James C. Furman, and J. S. Mims) continued in their roles at Greenville; in fall 1851 Charles H. Judson became the fourth faculty member. Edwards, raised close to Society Hill, studied at South Carolina College and at both Newton Theological Institution (Massachusetts) and Union Theological Seminary (New York). North Carolina–born Mims attended Columbian College, Furman Institution, and Newton Theological Institution. James C. Furman graduated from the College of Charleston with a plan to study medicine. After his religious conversion at the age of nineteen, Furman changed his career path, studying at the Furman Theological Institution and serving as pastor of Welsh Neck Church before beginning his teaching career at Furman Institution in 1844. In contrast to Edwards, Mims, and Furman, Charles H. Judson was a northerner by birth. Born in Connecticut, Judson studied at Hamilton Literary and Theological Institution (now Colgate University) as well as the University of Virginia before applying for and being offered his position at Furman University.[14] Two of the four inaugural professors of Furman University can be identified as slaveholders. James C. Furman owned fifty-six enslaved people in 1850 and forty-one in 1860.[15] In the early 1850s, the university hired one of P. C. Edwards's enslaved people to live and work on campus, taking care of buildings and grounds. By 1860 records show that Edwards owned eight enslaved men, women, and children.[16]

The relocation and expansion of Furman University to Greenville helped to anchor a stronger Lowcountry Baptist presence in the Upcountry. Throughout the 1850s denominational Baptists devoted tremendous amounts of time and energy in raising an endowment for the college. Fundraising and concerns about the financial stability of the institution dominated their thinking.[17] Energized by their efforts to launch a four-year denominational college for men, Baptist leaders also engaged in conversation about placing women's education under the control of the state convention. The many female high schools and colleges "which have sprung into existence within the last fifteen or twenty years," wrote John G. Landrum, chair of the convention's Committee on Female Education, "is truly astonishing." This increase "seems to have arisen from the sentiment which prevails every where" in the nation "that female education exerts a wider influence upon society, than the education of the males, and that attention to the former is the surest method of securing increased attention to the latter." A college for women, controlled by the Baptist State Convention, would have a profound impact upon the moral improvement of a rising generation of Baptists. "Our Methodist brethren have already acted; and at this very time, whilst the question of action is pending with us, it is understood that our Presbyterian brethren have a committee appointed on the subject of a suitable location for a female college," wrote Landrum. The call for a "Female College of high order," run through the state convention, would include "all those branches of a liberal education that are pursued in our colleges for young men, with such modifications and differences as experience and sound judgement may dictate; and that the standard of attainment in these branches be high."[18]

Some Baptists opposed the education of females, arguing that establishing a female college would take money and energy from the continued growth and success of the male college. Others opposed centralization in general, believing that female schools should be regulated by local associations. Still others were concerned about the competition that a woman's Baptist college would pose to existing female academies, including Limestone Springs Female High School (Gaffney), Johnson Female University (Anderson), and Fuller Institute (Greenwood).[19] Supporters of the school proceeded onward. Civic leaders in both Anderson and Greenville lobbied to house the school. The convention accepted the offer from Greenville, which transferred the land and buildings of the Greenville Female Academy (once headed by William Bullein Johnson) to the Baptist State Convention, as well as raising $20,000 in funds.[20] Trustees of Furman University were appointed to administer the women's college; they assumed control of the new properties and opened the college, called initially the Greenville Baptist Female College, in 1855.[21] In contrast to Furman University, where, among other requirements, prospective male students were examined by professors on their academic skills, prospective female students did not have to meet admission standards. Although both schools promised a liberal education, women did not receive a degree—they simply graduated after three years of study. Furman students, by contrast, could earn either a B.A. or an M.A. degree.[22]

By the early 1850s, white Baptists had established a significant educational footprint in Greenville and surrounding areas of the far Upcountry. In 1859 another distinctive denominational institution was established: a regional seminary to train southern Baptist ministers. The idea of a southern seminary can be traced back to the 1835, when Basil Manly Sr., at the time pastor of the Charleston Baptist church, proposed such a possibility.[23] Intermittent conversations ensued among southern Baptists in the 1840s and 1850s, culminating in a meeting in 1857 that endorsed the formation and location of a southern seminary in Greenville, South Carolina. The South Carolina Baptist Convention agreed to raise $100,000 for the seminary's endowment—of which $30,000 would come from Furman University funds—contingent on the other southern states, combined, offering $100,000. Should the seminary fail or be moved to a different location, Furman University would retrieve its original donation (as well as additional monies collected by the convention) to be used for theological education at Furman.[24]

In 1858, delegates from Washington, DC, Virginia, North and South Carolina, Georgia, and Louisiana met for five days in Greenville to organize the seminary, nominate professors, and petition the South Carolina legislature for a charter. They secured the former meeting house used by Greenville Baptists—a new, more commodious one was being built across the street—and unanimously selected James P. Boyce, John A. Broadus, Basil Manly Jr., and E. T. Winkler to serve as faculty. When E. T. Winkler declined the nomination, William Williams took his place. All four faculty members were slaveholders from various southern states, and all brought significant pastoral and scholarly recognition to their positions.[25] James P. Boyce, born in Charleston in 1827 to wealthy merchant Ker Boyce, attended Brown University and Princeton Theological Seminary. In the early 1850s he served as pastor of Columbia's First Baptist Church before moving to Greenville as a professor of theology at Furman University.[26] Virginian John A. Broadus completed a Master of Arts at the University of Virginia and served as pastor of the First Baptist Church in Charlottesville, where he was also chaplain at the University of Virginia. He initially turned down the invitation to serve as professor at the seminary—his Charlottesville congregation petitioned him to stay—but after further consideration accepted the position.[27] Basil

Manly Jr. had been raised in South Carolina but moved with his family to Tuscaloosa, Alabama, when his father, Basil Manly Sr., became president of the University of Alabama. Basil Jr. graduated at the top of his class from the University of Alabama, attended Newton Theological Institute in Massachusetts, and completed his training at Princeton Theological Seminary. He preached in Alabama and Mississippi in the late 1840s before becoming pastor of Richmond's First Baptist Church in 1850. In 1854 he resigned his position at First Baptist Church to serve as the first president of the Richmond Female Institute, which he headed until moving to his new position in Greenville in 1859.[28] Edwin Theodore Winkler, born in Savannah, Georgia, attended Brown University and Newton Theological Seminary. He served as editor of various Baptist publications, including the *Southern Baptist Journal*, and in 1854 accepted the call of pastor at Charleston's First Baptist Church. Winkler turned down the invitation to teach at Southern Seminary, not wanting to leave his church congregation.[29] As a result, trustees chose William Williams. Williams, born in Georgia, trained for the law at Harvard and Yale before becoming a minister. He was serving as professor of theology at Mercer University when he accepted the invitation to move to Southern Seminary.[30]

With its faculty positions secured, the seminary began its first session in fall 1859. Twenty-six students from six slaveholding states (Virginia, North Carolina, South Carolina, Alabama, Florida, and Missouri) comprised the first class of the seminary. Student enrollment increased to the mid-thirties the following year, but operations ceased during the Civil War, and the first post-war class had only seven students. Following continued financial and enrollment struggles during the Reconstruction period, Baptists agreed to move the seminary to Louisville in 1877.[31]

By 1860 white Lowcountry Baptists had strategically established a stronger denominational presence throughout the state. By relocating and expanding Furman University, by founding a Baptist college for women, by funding and establishing denominational schools along key transportation routes, and by successfully locating Southern Seminary in Greenville, white Lowcountry Baptists established a permanent footing in the Upcountry. Their transformation was not complete; even during the Civil War, a minority of white congregational Baptists opposed the newer preaching and outreach styles associated with Lowcountry Baptists. Yet overall, white denominational Baptists had achieved significant growth and expansion, establishing a major footprint throughout the state by the eve of the Civil War.

As they celebrated their growing educational and religious influence in the state, white Baptist ministers also devoted greater attention to the conversion of enslaved people. Free of northern Baptist interference and responding to the spiritual interests of enslaved men and women, they more systematically worked to send missionaries to preach to and instruct enslaved people both spiritually and morally. Enslaved men and women joined Baptist churches in large numbers in the late antebellum years. Drawn to a religious framework that offered them individual as well as communal belonging, they worshipped a God who offered them eternal salvation and who affirmed the dignity and worth of their humanity. In various ways—through a desire to preach, a desire to marry, and a desire for Christian burial—black Baptists fought for Christian legitimization despite the segregated worship environment in which they were directed. This spiritual negotiation carried aspects of egalitarianism, and whites were careful to limit the religious freedoms they granted to enslaved people. White Baptists welcomed black men and women into the kingdom of God, but they took clear measures to ensure that the earthly kingdom of God was a segregated one in terms of race. White efforts to evangelize to enslaved people showed both a belief in benevolence toward enslaved people and a deep cognizance of racial difference and need for social control, displayed through segregated practices within churches and through sermons and writings that revealed widespread beliefs in white superiority and black inferiority.

That some white Baptists thought deeply about their Christian duty toward their enslaved people is demonstrated by their wills. Edgefield Baptist James G. Wilkinson illustrates most strikingly a benevolent view of enslaved people. Wilkinson stipulated that all of his enslaved people were to be treated with care: "it is my earnest desire that all my slaves be treated humanely by every one into whose hands they may fall remembering that we shall have to give an account to God for our conduct towards them."[32] Newberry Baptist Church minister Thomas Frean, who was born in Ireland and whose executors included Upcountry civic leader B. F. Perry and judge and Baptist minister John Belton O'Neall, prohibited the sale of his enslaved people after his death and mandated that they be well treated and kept in the family in perpetuity. Frean added a codicil pertaining specifically to his enslaved man, John, who "is a faithful servant, has more than paid me the amount advanced for him, is a member of the same Church with my self and besides a Deacon in the Negro Department." Should Frean die before John, he requested that John "pay such wages only as he conveniently can" and that his executors ensure John's care and provide him a decent burial.[33]

Both missionary-minded and antimission-leaning Baptists made specific reference in their wills to the care of their enslaved people. James Hembree, an antimission preacher, gave his "Black woman Peggy & her son Grief Presley" freedom to select their enslavers, stipulating that one of his executors should provide them a five-day pass to choose their new owner. Peggy, he wrote, "is near forty seven years old and not very sound," while Grief was nearly twelve years of age. Hembree estimated the value of the two enslaved people at six hundred dollars. Additional household items owned by Hembree were to be sold to the highest bidder, "and as for Peggy's household and kitchen furniture that Don't belong to my Estate I have no claim to any thing in her house, except the Cotton wheel and cards and old Table."[34] Thomas Ray of Padgett's Creek Baptist Church in Union District specified that his enslaved people should be "appraised in families." Husbands and wives, as well as their children ages twelve and under, should be kept together, as well as mothers and children ages twelve and under, the women "having no husbands here."[35] In the small congregation of Salem Baptist Church in Edgefield District, church member Nancy Wills hoped "for my negroes to be sold to some merciful man who will treat them well if possible." Nancy Wills signed with her mark; Baptist member John Huiet, the church clerk, served as witness.[36] Like other white Baptists, Nancy Wills stressed the kind treatment of enslaved people while maintaining the assurance of racial difference.

As they addressed the Christian model of slavery, white ministers focused specifically upon the religious instruction of enslaved people. Underscoring the importance of biblical literacy, some ministers (and lay members) taught their enslaved people to read the Bible. Most, however, at least publicly proclaimed to abide by the 1834 law banning slave literacy, although ministers frequently took the opportunity to push for its overhaul. In his 1848 publication *The Negro Law of South Carolina*, John Belton O'Neall argued that the 1834 anti-literacy law "grew out of a feverish state of excitement produced by the *impudent* meddling of persons out of the slave States" and that owners of enslaved men and women should now be ready "to act the part of wise, humane and fearless masters" and repeal the law. How could South Carolinians, as Christians, not allow enslaved people to read the Bible? "It is vain to say there is danger" in withholding such a right from enslaved people, for the best enslaved men and women "are those who can and do read the Scriptures." South Carolinians should not be afraid of their enslaved people, O'Neall continued. "Such a feeling is unworthy of a Carolina master."[37]

Baptist minister Richard Fuller also repeatedly spoke in favor of allowing enslaved people to read the Bible. Fuller wrote that "everywhere the gospel requires of a master the moral and intellectual improvement of the slaves."[38] In his debates with northern Baptist minister Francis Wayland in 1844 and 1845, Fuller critiqued the law banning slave literacy. Although he moved to Baltimore, Maryland, in 1847, Fuller kept some plantations in South Carolina, and in 1850 he petitioned the state for the right to teach his enslaved people to read, suggesting that following the law of God took supremacy over the law of the land. Fuller noted "a higher and paramount allegiance to the law of God," which called for him "to instruct his slaves so that they may be able to read the Scriptures." The Baptist divine also asked permission to "privately & on his plantation" teach his enslaved people to read, "so that they may be able to read the word of God."[39] In 1851 Fuller gave a speech to the American Colonization Society in which he extolled the benefits of colonization as a solution to both northern abolitionism and southern proslavery extremism. Among other issues, he criticized southern society for laws restricting slave literacy.[40]

Whether deliberately or subconsciously, white Baptist ministers provided specific instruction about slave evangelization at times close to meetings of the Triennial Convention. As early as 1822, the same year as the Denmark Vesey insurrection, white Charleston ministers encouraged enslavers to "be regular in releasing . . . their servants from labour on days of public fasting and prayer, and of thanksgiving." Suggestions became more consistent in the late 1830s, as northern Baptist criticism of slavery increased. At its 1837 annual meeting, the Charleston Association noted its "deep concern" for "the spiritual condition of the colored portion of our population" but also requested that ministers of the association provide "careful" instruction to enslaved people and free blacks. Ministers and missionaries, the association advised, should "embrace every opportunity" to preach to enslaved people "the gospel of peace"—of social and religious harmony, of enslaved people performing their dutiful roles. For churches without regular preachers, white members should view it as "*their* solemn and imperative duty to give such instruction as they can, to their colored people."[41] To illustrate the significance of preaching to enslaved people, at the association meeting ministers preached sermons to white audiences while "several sermons were preached to the colored people at the stand."[42] In 1841, the Edgefield Baptist Association recommended that churches "take measures for giving oral instruction from the Scriptures" to enslaved people in separate Sunday services. If "conveniences may not be supplied with all convenient dispatch," enslavers should "impart Religious instruction" to their enslaved people "at home, at stated and convenient seasons."[43] For the first time in 1844, the Charleston Association called for a white missionary specifically to work with enslaved people.[44]

Guidance for slave evangelization also came from the newly formed Southern Baptist Convention, which in 1845 created a Committee on the Instruction of the Colored Population as part of its Domestic Mission Board. Noting that slave owners were "as much the moral guardians of their servants as of their children," the committee in 1846 instructed Baptist masters to include servants during family devotions, which should also include "daily familiar instruction." The slave system was a mutual one, comprised of relative duties: in return for the "services" of enslaved people, "it is reasonable" that enslavers should "provide for their spiritual, as for their physical wants."[45] Ministers should also deliver separate sermons to enslaved people, dividing their white and black congregations, as well as holding separate prayer meetings for enslaved people. The committee also recommended Sunday schools for African American converts to receive oral instruction. Since enslaved children normally didn't attend public worship, Sabbath schools were particularly important for this age demographic. In all of these cases, black deacons should be appointed to supervise and watch over the "moral character" of black worshippers.[46] Finally, missionaries should also be sent to evangelize enslaved people. As enslaved people were "a people that are generally easily excitable," the committee recommended that missionaries employ teachings designed "more to inform than to affect them."[47] Everywhere in these instructions, evangelizing to enslaved people was framed by an awareness of racial difference and, in the eyes of white Baptists, racial dependency. Preaching to enslaved people meant sharing with them the means of salvation as well as showing them how to live moral and orderly lives, in the process helping to guarantee social stability and white supremacy.

In response to the recommendations of the Committee on the Instruction of the Colored Population, ministers of the Charleston Baptist Association made greater organizational efforts to evangelize to enslaved people. Charleston native James Tupper, a lawyer, judge, and ordained minister, emerged as the foremost advocate of the evangelization of enslaved men and women. In addition to his support of Sunday schools and temperance, Tupper, who owned eight enslaved people in 1860, advocated specifically for evangelization of the enslaved, criticizing the state for removing the right of enslaved people to read the Bible.[48] As a member of the Charleston Baptist Association's Home Mission Board, Tupper was unapologetic in his demands for greater missionary outreach to enslaved people, particularly those living on the Sea Islands. "One other field of missionary labor which presents perhaps the greatest destitution and which, although heretofore most neglected," he wrote in 1850, was evangelization of enslaved people on the Sea Islands and along the coast. "Not a single missionary has been sent among them," nor had "a single school" been organized for "their oral instruction," leaving them destitute from learning about God's word. In contrast to members of other denominations, who engaged in organized missionary efforts to preach to enslaved people, Baptists "almost alone are standing idle." Tupper estimated the black membership of churches in the association to be "perhaps equal to that of any other denomination," and he emphasized that enslaved people were thirsty for religious instruction. "The advantage of employing missionaries must be obvious to all," he wrote.[49]

Throughout the 1850s Tupper pleaded for more missionaries to enslaved people. His arguments reflected two prominent beliefs held by white Christians: that enslaved people, as humans with souls, deserved to learn the gospel message, and that they also needed white uplift because they were an inherently inferior race. Slave evangelization was a white duty, Tupper exclaimed. "Thousands of this class of our population are living and dying within our borders without a knowledge of salvation," he wrote in 1850. Because of legal prohibitions, enslaved people could not read the words of the Bible: "We permit them not to take into their own hands the lamp of life, and multitudes are passing on in the darkness that surround them, and will soon sink down into everlasting night." This was unconscionable. Since enslaved people had no access to the Bible, "the means of saving them are in our hands," but what had been done? Nothing! "Not a single Missionary has been sent among them." No one had informed them of Jesus Christ's saving grace. "They are our fellow beings, and are hastening to eternity; they are our servants, and we have kept locked up from them the sacred chart which marks the way to heaven," declared Tupper. White Baptists would be judged for ignoring the spiritual needs of their black brethren, he argued: "Neglect them as we have done, and how can we hope with clean hands to meet them at the judgement?" Compared to the progress other denominations had made in preaching to enslaved people, Baptists were "standing idle." Enslaved people needed specific instruction—"peculiar instruction," in Tupper's words—based upon knowledge rather than emotion. "That kind of preaching which consists more in sound than in anything else" did not work well for enslaved people, who "love the excitement of religion so much, as to be in constant danger of substituting it for principle." Whites should take precautions to exercise concerted oversight of enslaved people, who needed "to be taught as little children the rudiments of the Gospel, and then, step by step, led onward in the acquisition of the Holy precepts and principles of our religion." How terrible that in 1850 in the Charleston Association, there was not a single Sunday school that provided oral instruction to enslaved people, nor was there "a single Missionary preaching upon the plantation of the lower country." Just look at what missionaries could do! They could teach "appropriate hymns and verses of scriptures, the nature and value of prayer, and the plan of salvation," providing a vital spiritual opportunity for enslaved men and women who did not or could not attend church.[50]

To aid in the gospel outreach to enslaved people and in competition with other denominations, the Charleston Association requested in 1854 that the Southern Baptist Publication Society develop a catechism for missionary use. By 1857 Charleston minister E. T. Winkler published *Notes and Questions for the Oral Instruction of Colored People*.[51] Winkler, a native Georgian who supplied churches in his home state and in South Carolina before becoming the pastor of the Charleston church in 1854, had experience with the Southern Baptist Publication Society: in 1852 he began serving as corresponding secretary of the organization. He also became editor of the Charleston-based *Southern Baptist*.[52] Each lesson in *Notes and Questions for the Oral Instruction of Colored People* included a biblical text, "an exposition divided into two or three points, a catechism and a hymn." Similar to many catechisms used by white missionaries to enslaved men and women, Winkler emphasized the duty of the white Christian to provide religious instruction to enslaved people—"those whom Providence has made dependent upon us" and reminded enslaved men and women to "honor their masters" just as "wives should honor their husbands" and as "citizens should honor their governors."[53]

By 1856 the Charleston Association's Mission Board suggested four missionaries to minister to enslaved people, rather than one. Finding missionaries, however, remained a challenge. The board noted that, just as most ministers found it difficult to preach clearly to children, "for the same reason few can preach intelligibly and faithfully to our enslaved people," who like children were "excitable" and could often be attracted to the emotion rather than the substance of religion.[54] Yet, as complicated as it was to find ministers to preach to enslaved people, the task should be continued. Every church should take action. Why? Because "*Our enslaved people are our fellow beings.*" Like whites, black men and women "are destined to unspeakable happiness"—heaven—or "insufferable torment"—hell. White Baptists bore the responsibility for sharing the gospel message with enslaved people. If whites failed to do so, they would "stand before God in judgement" for having the blood of enslaved people's souls on their hands.[55] Whites could not ignore their duty and "hope to appear before the judgment seat of Christ with clean hands." Invested in "an enterprise of love, and mercy and justice," white Baptists should pray, contribute funds, and give their "best efforts" to make the mission work."[56]

As usual, the Baptist effort to evangelize enslaved people, which was part of a larger white evangelical movement to do the same, met significant criticism. The religious instruction of enslaved people remained a cause of apprehension and suspicion from some in the larger white South Carolina community. In order to stem opposition to the religious instruction of enslaved people, in 1845 religious leaders throughout the state coordinated and published a report about the societal benefits of preaching to enslaved people. The publication was directed to "the holders of slaves in South-Carolina" in order to allay white concerns and demonstrate that slave evangelization in all parts of the state benefited enslaved people spiritually and led to a more loyal, obedient workforce.[57] Ministers from different denominations reported about orderly religious services for enslaved people and emphasized the Christian behavior of enslaved people in their congregations. Their reports present a fascinating picture into the varied roles that enslaved people played in biracial worship settings.

Across all the denominations, both Methodists and Baptists continued to gain the most traction with enslaved people because of the personal nature of their religious message. In Georgetown District, Methodists allowed enslaved people to serve as class leaders while Baptists "admit preachers of colour," according to a report by R. F. W. Allston, one of the state's wealthiest planters. Allston constructed a chapel on his plantation "open to all denominations of Christians." Both enslaved Methodists and Baptists used the meeting house separately for twice-weekly prayer meetings as well as worship on Sundays, "when they meet, and pray and sing together."[58] On the island of St. Helena, William Fripp Sr. wrote, apart from Sunday services, black Baptists "meet two or three times a week in the prayer-house on their own plantations and unite in singing, praying and reading the work of God—(when any one is present who can read) and in exhortation." Fripp noted that the practice of an elderly literate enslaved man teaching the catechism to young enslaved people had proved particularly effective. Such religious instruction led to many enslaved people "leading honest and upright and Christian lives."[59]

As Fripp's report makes clear, some enslaved people—including those who could read the Bible—led religious services on plantations. In Fairfield District, minister John Davis specified that of the 12,517 enslaved people and 73 free blacks living in the district, 535 belonged to Baptist congregations. Davis estimated that "[t]he average attendance of negroes on the Sabbath at the 12 Baptist churches, in the spring and summer months, is 200, or 24,400 in all." Davis counted roughly eight to ten "negro exhorters connected with the Baptist churches." Black preachers held meetings in accordance with the law, meaning that whites also had to attend, "except when the congregation is limited to the negroes on one plantation,—which is very common."[60] In Sumter District, George S. C. DeSchamps reported, "watchmen of their own colour" existed in the local Baptist church.[61] William Curtis, pastor of the Baptist church in Columbia, noted that there were 372 members of the church. Curtis preached to black members with the assistance of "two licensed coloured preachers *in the town;* and four others at various *plantations.*" The black preachers led meetings with black members at least twice a week. Additionally, black Baptists served in leadership positions as watchmen (three in the town and one per plantation). Curtis oversaw this work, visiting each plantation once every three months and preaching at mission stations on certain weekday nights. Enslaved and free black leaders managed membership and disciplinary regulations, and watchmen sent reports about membership to the Columbia church. Every three months enslaved people from the plantations were required to come to the Columbia church to participate in a biracial celebration of communion.[62]

Enslavers and enslaved people in the Upcountry engaged in biracial religious interaction more regularly than those in the Lowcountry. "You are well aware," wrote Presbyterian minister John Douglas of Chester District, "that the relation and intercourse between whites and blacks in the upcountry are very different from what they are in the low country." In the Upcountry, enslaved people were "neither so numerous, nor kept so entirely separate, but constitute a part of our households, and are daily either with their masters or some member of the white family: from this circumstance they feel themselves more identified with their owners than they can with you."[63]

In the northwestern districts of the Upcountry particularly, whites and blacks attended the same worship services. Methodist minister James Edward Henry reported that, in Spartanburg District, "the whites and blacks of the different congregations worship together." Two black Baptists served as preachers, without "much benefit," in Henry's view.[64] In Greenville District, by contrast, Thomas Brockman reported that "a few" black Baptists and Methodists were licensed preachers, and "[i]t has been thought they do some good." Their meetings occurred infrequently and only with white permission, he qualified. While white ministers "often address negroes in their discourses," enslaved people sometimes also received religious instruction from white mistresses, who "to their credit," devoted "more attention to the instruction of the negroes than *masters*." Religious instruction "produced a marked difference" in the enslaved population, benefiting enslavers by producing "well-ordered" individuals and providing to enslaved people an "incalculable advantage . . . both for time and eternity."[65]

The 1845 compendium of reports from white ministers about the state of slave evangelization reveals that whites cared deeply about evangelizing enslaved people for two different reasons: one, to help enslaved people find the keys to salvation; and two, to maintain a sense of white-dominated social order. However, it also paints a clear picture of the desire of enslaved people to serve in pastoral and leadership roles. In other ways, enslaved people and free blacks claimed their right to be Christians. One display of black agency, and of white resistance to African American claims for spiritual recognition, emerged in the minutes of Poplar Springs Baptist Church in Laurens District in the late 1840s and 1850s. Here, a dispute about burying black members on church grounds resulted in whites first excluding African Americans and then readmitting them but banning them from serving in segregated leadership roles.[66] Beginning in 1853 whites took control of black church discipline and resolved that "no coloured member shall here after act as deacon in this church."[67] Black members must have held their ground about burial rights, for by 1854 white men agreed to "strike out 4 Words in the 4th rule Which [reads?] thus a majority of the male members, Shall determin, and a minority shall submit, the understanding now is that Both male and female shall have a voice in all matters that may come before the Church."[68] Tellingly, white males allied with white females to offset religious pressure from black members in their church, showing that, while both race and gender factored into structures of power at the Poplar Springs church, racial control proved the central factor in establishing and enforcing political relations within the church.[69]

Just as enslaved people at Poplar Springs refused to relinquish their rights to a Christian burial, many enslaved people also strove to have their marriages recognized by the church. As Erskine Clarke writes, "Slave marriages . . . exposed the vulnerability of blacks to the power of whites and revealed the amazing courage of men and women who took the risk of loving those who could be sold away."[70] Desire to be involved in stable marital unions drew stark attention to the white construction of Christian slavery, which prioritized the rights of owners over those of enslaved people. Although some Baptists pledged not to separate enslaved families, churches did not take moral or disciplinary action against enslavers who, according to their legal rights, sold husbands, wives, or children. White Baptists thus bent to the will of the state and of the enslavers over the needs of the enslaved, subordinating one of the religious sacraments that the church placed the greatest emphasis on—marriage—to the law of chattel slavery.[71]

Nevertheless, enslaved people continued to seek church approval for "unconventional" marriages. Could enslaved people marry a new partner when their former partner had moved away? Could they remarry and remain in the church if an enslaver forbade a slave husband to see a slave wife on a different plantation? Could enslaved people who voluntarily left their partners because of abuse remarry? As more enslaved people joined Baptist churches, the question of marriage and remarriage became increasingly common as enslaved church members expressed a desire to have their unions blessed by the church. White Baptists responded by creating more specific guidelines about the regulation of slave relationships, in the process assuring themselves that they were providing proper Christian care for a group of people who, in their view, lacked the capacity to guide themselves morally.[72]

Church minutes and associational records reveal repeated queries about whether enslaved people could take second husbands or wives, and whether doing so constituted adultery. Sometimes enslaved people directly indicted their partners for infidelity or abuse. At Greenville Church, Dick charged his wife Mary, who belonged to a different owner in the village, with adultery. White members heard Dick's statement as well as Mary's defense before agreeing to exclude Mary from church membership.[73] Likewise, at the Sumterville church, a female slave stated that she had "endured the abuse and infidelity of her husband" for more than one year and had been separated from him for an even longer time. Would it now be possible to marry another person, even though "her real husband, with all his unworthiness, still wishes to retain her?" Was the female slave member "at liberty in the premises" to turn down her real husband and enter into a new partnership?" Uncertain of the biblical answer, white church members sent the query to the Charleston Baptist Association. Responding that the wife's story was the only testimony available, and positing that "the nature and extent of the injury done to the aggrieved party" was not completely established, the Charleston Baptist Association declined making a recommendation, returning the query to the original church to answer the question "as directed by the word of God."[74]

More frequently, the decisions of enslavers impacted slave marriages. In 1843 a slave named Harry explained to Greenville Church, of which he was a member, that as his wife had moved away from town, he sought permission to marry another woman who lived closer to his home. After prolonged discussion, whites in the church ultimately "concluded that they under all the circumstances could do nothing in the matter." After quoting "some scriptures rather against such a proceeding," the church allowed Harry "to act as he thought best."[75] The Charleston church excluded a slave named Martha for living with a man in an unmarried state after Martha's mistress forbade Martha from marrying her partner.[76] The Bethlehem church sought the guidance of the Charleston Association in the case of a male slave who took a second wife. The slave's first wife lived on a nearby plantation, but the enslaver of the first wife prohibited the husband from visiting. Since he couldn't visit his original wife, the male slave took another wife but was willing "to leave the present and take the former wife, if he is permitted." Presented this question, the Charleston Association first inquired as to why the enslaved man could not visit his first wife. Had the slave committed a crime, "rendering his presence on the plantation [of his first wife] inexpedient"? If so, he should not have been allowed to remarry in the first place. However, if the slave husband had done nothing wrong—hence being allowed to marry again—he should not break the second marriage by reconciling with his first wife if he had the chance to do so. The male slave member should remain married to his second wife.[77]

By the mid-1840s white Baptists began to prescribe specific responses and to offer guidance to slave owners about measures to take when slave marriages deviated from the white norm. The Upcountry Bethel Baptist Association defined "valid matrimony" amongst enslaved people as "mutual, voluntary co-habitation of a man and a woman, as husband and wife." If enslaved people separated from their husbands or wives, they would lose their status in the church unless they had "no control" over the separation, or if a separation occurred "contrary to their will." The association concurred that "infidelity to the marriage bed" was the only reason God allowed for a marriage to end. Thus, "when the distances at which they are separate are so great, or the circumstances such as to forbid all hope of their ever coming together, the parties may retain their places in the church."[78]

In 1856 the Charleston Association published very detailed information about slave marriages. A committee of Charleston's three main Baptist leaders—Basil Manly Sr., who in 1855 returned to Charleston from Tuscaloosa, Alabama, to serve as pastor of Wentworth Street Baptist Church; James Ryland Kendrick, pastor of Citadel Baptist Church; and E. T. Winkler, minister of First Baptist Church—came together to respond to a question about slave divorces in the case of an abusive partner. The three ministers, pastors of churches that had split from First Baptist Church, formed the main leadership of the Charleston Baptist Association. The committee penned a long narrative written primarily by Winkler (but signed by Manly) intended to become a guide to how the white church should manage and regulate slave marriages.[79] Tellingly, the committee hoped that the association would use the guidelines to help formulate "a distinct statement of principles with regard to marriage and divorce, especially in the case of slaves."[80] Slave marriages were "peculiar," the committee opined. They were not recognized formally by the state, and, since married enslaved people frequently were owned by separate enlsavers, "their union is liable to separation."[81] Because the state did not formally sanction slave marriages, the church should take the role as the institution legitimizing the union. "In Christian lands," the ministers wrote, "slave marriages are committed by the negligence of civil legislation to the legislation of the Churches."[82]

The committee laid out a concerted plan for slave marriages in Baptist churches, one that involved the participation of the enslaver and the church in the marriage process. Enslaved people should freely choose their partners, but they also should obtain the master's consent to marry. The enslaver could assess the "rightness" of the marriage based upon his knowledge of the enslaved person's character, as well the enslaver's likelihood of moving his enslaved person to another location. Should an enslaver advise against marriage and an enslaved person marry anyway, white Baptist leaders recommended that the marriage "be null and void." Marriages of enslaved partners should be recognized with some type of ceremony, "not too brief or too simple," and with public witnesses, to recognize the solemnity of the arrangement.

Although long-lasting unions were preferable, the separation of enslaved couples was a strong likelihood. No other issue "requiring ecclesiastical action" was "more difficult of adjustment" than the complex questions relating to slave marriages, particularly when separations and divorces were requested. In the committee's opinion, three viable reasons existed for ending a marriage between enslaved people: the death of a husband or wife, infidelity, or separation. Either "involuntary separation" or "compulsory separation" gave enslaved people the right to divorce and remarry. "This is a principle, whose justice civil law admits in so many cases of a prolonged absence. It is a principle which, to a certain extent, the word of God confirms," wrote the ministers.[83]

Baptist churches—not just the Christian master—should also play a role in regulating and overseeing marriages of enslaved men and women. When enslaved people joined churches, whites should exercise "great care" in examining their previous marriage relations. If necessary, churches should "prescribe the marital conditions, which, in each case, must be submitted to before the way of membership is open." Enslaved people whose partners had been forcibly separated and who hoped to marry again should not be shunned by the church, but the church might mandate that the slave wait for a preliminary period—six months or longer was suggested—before the remarriage. After the probationary period, assuming "no reasonable hope of the return of the absent party," enslaved people could divorce and enter into a second marriage. If the former partner returned to the same neighborhood, however, "the parties must consider themselves as dead to each other; just as when, from long absence, one of the parties presumes on the death of the other, and marries again." Of course, voluntary separations were not to be tolerated and would result in exclusion from the church. In all situations, churches should have a hand in overseeing and orchestrating moral guidelines for enslaved people.[84]

The Charleston Association's suggestions for the church's regulation of slave marriages reveals a shift in the stance of Baptist churches in the late antebellum years. In the early 1800s, white Baptists were hesitant to promote a collective, uniform set of instructions for white oversight of slave behavior. Instead, individual congregations were to determine how to best regulate slave morality. At its formation, the Southern Baptist Convention legitimized and made part of its denominational mission the Christian model of slavery, incentivizing white Baptists to regulate and to oversee more clearly and more publicly the moral actions of their enslaved people. From the white perspective, greater religious regulation of enslaved people would have the intended effect of producing a harmonious Christian society of loyal enslaved people who were destined for heavenly rewards. The model, as it always had, deemphasized slave religiosity and agency and emphasized instead the lack of moral integrity of enslaved people. The irony was that, in biracial church settings, by their desire to seek salvation and to be loyal followers of Christ, enslaved people demonstrated to whites their capacity to be just as moral and just as Christian as white believers. This led whites to reinforce—indeed, to emphasize—racial order and control through separation, segregation, and disfranchisement within the biracial church setting. This religious tension between whites and enslaved people, this testing and reinforcing of the Christian model of slavery, would be put to its most dramatic test in the 1860s, when civil war and emancipation created a new set of relations between black and white church members.

Between 1845 and 1860, white Lowcountry Baptists made great progress in preaching the gospel through organized missions and educational efforts. They mounted an aggressive, strategic, and largely successful campaign to create new Baptist academies in the Upcountry, a region traditionally hostile to religious education and missionary activity. By 1850 they had relocated Furman University to Greenville; four years later, they established Greenville Baptist Female College in the same town. By the end of the 1850s, South Carolina Baptists could also boast the opening of a southern Baptist seminary in Greenville. The transformation of Upcountry Baptist culture was by no means complete. Upcountry Baptists engaged in battles over missions and an educated ministry even into the 1860s, revealing the persistence of theological and cultural disagreements within the wider Baptist community. Still, significant inroads and changes were made, and a more general sense of Baptist unity prevailed, as denominational Baptists slowly transformed the Upcountry into a centerpiece for their vision of evangelical life.

In the 1840s and 1850s, Lowcountry Baptists, cognizant of to the wishes of black members to partake fully and equally in Christian worship, fellowship, and sacraments, established a stronger blueprint of the Christian model of slavery, one that reinforced white authority by more deliberately managing the moral actions of enslaved people. White Baptists advocated separate services for slave instruction, sent missionaries to Lowcountry plantations, and specified the best way for whites to regulate slave marriages. Their efforts were replicated on a smaller scale in the Upcountry. Inherent in these efforts of moral management—of creating a harmonious, Christian model of slavery—was a message of racial inequality and of racial separatism: the two races, thought spiritually connected, differed from one another intellectually, culturally, and socially. As they built a more systematic model of Christian slavery, as they convinced themselves that they were fulfilling their duty to evangelize and bring benevolence to enslaved people, white Baptists also furthered the ground for postwar segregation. Thus, at the same time that they invited enslaved people into biracial church settings, white Baptists also turned away from them, segregating enslaved people and in countless ways stressing black inferiority and subordination. Convinced that the Bible sanctioned not only slavery but racial difference, white Baptists agreed that their Christian model of slavery was on the verge of perfection.

CONCLUSION

The Reframing of Christian Order

For all of their internal warfare, Baptists achieved consistent growth in South Carolina. Between 1830 and 1860, their numbers had increased from roughly 10 percent to 26 percent of the state's population.[1] Slave membership outdistanced white membership in the Lowcountry, but slave conversions in Upcountry churches also increased steadily over the antebellum years. During the war, many enslaved people remained in biracial churches, claiming membership in a community of believers of Jesus Christ. Poplar Springs Church in Laurens District protracted its meeting in August 1864, resulting in the addition of twenty-one whites and seven enslaved people. In October of that year, an additional five enslaved people joined the church.[2] To whites in biracial churches, the Christian model of slavery continued to exist within the walls of the church, both in theory and often in practice, even as the institution of slavery began to crumble around them.

In 1860 white South Carolina Baptists who had earlier been so active in creating a national Baptist presence, and who later were leaders in establishing a sectional denomination, now helped lead the most radical southern state out of the union. Convinced that they were on the verge of establishing a perfect Christian moral order, Baptist ministers viewed the 1860 election as a referendum about the world they were building. Vindication and protection of Christian slaveholding led ministers to reengage in politics in ways they had not since the American Revolution. In the Upcountry, where many of the state's top Baptist leaders now resided, Baptist ministers divided over whether slavery could best be safeguarded by remaining in the Union, or whether immediate secession was necessary. In Greenville district, seminary professor James P. Boyce and Baptist minister and prominent judge

John Belton O'Neall initially put their names forth as Unionist candidates to the state secession convention; both men withdrew their names before the election. By contrast, James C. Furman ran as a secessionist candidate. Although Greenville voters overwhelmingly elected the secessionist ticket, the appearance of a Unionist party ticket reflected the divided state of the Upcountry, where pockets of Unionism remained strong. Regardless of their stance on secession, leading Baptist ministers articulated a concerted desire to perpetuate the Christian model of slavery that they had worked so clearly to develop. In their messages about Christian slavery and Christian order, they expressed both a duty to provide moral uplift to enslaved people and a strong need to protect white supremacy and the prevailing social order.[3]

The private correspondence of James P. Boyce, who led the movement to create Greenville's Southern Baptist Theological Seminary, sheds light on the benevolent side of Christian slavery. Boyce was just thirty-three years old in 1860. He owned twenty-three enslaved people and held a great deal of personal and real wealth.[4] Although calling himself "an ultra pro-slavery man," Boyce felt that the South should continue to insist on protections for slavery while remaining in the Union. "I do wish to see the North put entirely in wrong, by making them dissolve the Union, if it must be, through refusing to grant what we ask," Boyce wrote to his brother-in-law H. A. Tupper. He had "always been an old fogy enough to love the past, with all its glorious associations."[5] Boyce also worried that southerners' inabilities to extend full benevolence toward enslaved people had displeased God and contributed to the current crisis. "I believe I see in all this the end of slavery," he stated. "I believe we are cutting its throat, curtailing its domain." Southerners had not extended the full spectrum of benevolence to enslaved people, and now God might end slavery because of such sins: "I feel that our sins as to this institution have cursed us," he wrote. Whites had not sufficiently cared for enslaved people "in their marital and religious relations." Boyce worried that God "is going to sweep it [slavery] away, after having left it thus long to show us how great we might be, were we to act as we ought in this matter."[6]

In contrast to James P. Boyce, Furman University president and Baptist minister James C. Furman, an ardent secessionist, warned white South Carolinians of the chaos and devastation that would come should Christian slavery be eradicated. The fifty-year-old Furman, whose forty-one enslaved people in 1860 made him one of the wealthiest slave owners in the Upcountry,[7] ran and was elected a delegate to the secession convention, where he emphasized the racial chaos and destruction that could come if Christian slavery were overturned. In an explicit effort to reach non-slaveholders, Furman addressed Greenville citizens, tailoring some of his comments specifically to the many Baptists he knew would be in the crowd. In "Letter to the Citizens of the Greenville District," printed in the *Southern Enterprise* on November 22, 1860, Furman and three other religious and civic leaders—Thomas S. Arthur, William H. Campbell, and William M. Thomas—broke down "in plain language" the necessity of secession. Furman and his co-signers cited the many reasons that "our Abolition enemies" endangered white freedoms, civic, constitutional, and religious. In addition to the loss of millions of dollars of property, "universal abolitionism" threatened both Christianity and domestic tranquility. Abolitionism branded slavery as a "gross sin" when in fact it was, according to the Bible, "a sacred right" that if practiced morally by "believing masters" was fully in step with the gospel. Secession was thus religiously righteous as well as constitutionally necessary. "When Southern States separate from Northern ones," the letter proclaimed," they will be doing it under the highest sanction that can warrant human action."[8]

Well aware of the numerical power of Baptists in the Upcountry, and tapping into the congregational, anti-denominational beliefs that had narrated much of the Baptist story in that region, Furman addressed his coreligionists specifically:

> Men of Greenville, show yourself men. Many of you are Baptists. They know the relation which the churches and associations sustain to each other. The, churches are the smaller bodies, and the associations the larger; yet the churches make the association, and if at any time an association should interfere with the rights of a church, that moment that church would secede. Just so here; the States have formed the General Government, and the moment that Government invades, directly or indirectly, the rights of a State, that moment such a State owes it to herself to throw off the odious tyranny.

Throughout his speech, Furman and his co-signers also spoke to the importance of white manhood and white supremacy. Greenville citizens should support secession because a Christian model of slavery protected white supremacy, indeed sacralized it. Should slavery end, the racial order would be turned upside down and total moral depravity would occur:

> Then every negro in South Carolina, and in every other Southern State, will be his own master; nay, more than that, will be the equal of every one of you. If you are tame enough to submit, Abolition preachers will be at hand to consummate the marriage of your daughters to black husbands! Nay, nay! we beg pardon of South Carolina women for such a suggestion. If their fathers and their brothers have not the spirit to break loose from a government whose elected Chief Magistrate aims to establish such a state of things, the daughters of South Carolina would die for shame at the dishonor of the men.[9]

In short, emancipation would bring an end to an ordered, patriarchal, and white-controlled society that was bound by Christian principles. "Self-respect, honor, the safety of our wives, our children, and our slaves themselves, whose well being is inseparably connected with the welfare of their masters all conspire to urge you to sustain the State in the high position which, if she is true to herself, she must assume." White men, whether they owned enslaved people or not, should realize that "[t]he negro is not your equal, unless the Bible be untrue, or you prove yourself unworthy of the name of free men." Abolitionists "are not our masters," nor could they exert authority over southerners unless southerners allowed them to. "Men of Greenville," the authors implored, "*will you submit?*"[10]

James C. Furman's biblical arguments for secession—that the Bible condoned both slavery and white superiority—were part of a larger set of arguments used by the minister to convince Greenville citizens to prize their patriarchal independence and to support secession. Significantly, not all white Baptists agreed with all aspects of Furman's rhetoric. In 1863, frustrated by the horrors of war as well as by their experience in worship, members of Brushy Creek Baptist Church, where Furman had been pastor since 1856, called for the well-known minister's resignation.

Although the congregants' letter to Furman asking for his resignation is not extant, Furman's rejoinder remains preserved. The letter, addressed "To the Brushy Creek Baptist Church" and dated October 1863, responded to three main objections: Furman's vocal leadership of secession; his quiet preaching delivery; and his support for ministerial education.[11] Furman first addressed those in the church who "regard me as instrumental in bringing on the country the evils of the war which now rages on our soil." Furman too felt anguish over "the desolation of this war." But he would not apologize, nor did he regret his role in supporting secession: "I believe that the secession of South Carolina saved civil liberty on this continent," he wrote. Just as his father, Richard Furman, had supported the American Revolution to protect civil and religious liberty, Furman felt that South Carolina's secession was needed to preserve the constitutional freedoms of white southerners. "After-generations will thank the men who saved popular liberty from extinction," he wrote.[12]

A second objection centered upon Furman's rhetorical delivery. Congregants felt that he did not speak loudly enough, which posed a problem for some who were hard of hearing and for those who wished for louder, more emotional sermons. "The ones from hardship of hearing feel themselves shut out from the instruction and comfort of the word preached," Furman responded. "With this class I deeply sympathize, and I duly appreciate their desire for change." Furman felt less connection to those who felt that his sermons should be louder and more emotive. "I do not think that the noise which he makes is any measure of a minister's zeal," the minister wrote.[13]

A third objection, Furman felt, "exists in the shape of a prejudice against education." Furman conceded that education could prove a hindrance to religion if used in the wrong way. "If education makes men proud; if it causes a minister to preach so that plain people cannot understand him, then it is a grievous evil-and instead of promoting it, the sooner we get rid of it the better." Yet "if a minister is a truly pious man, the more knowledge he has the humbler he will be." In the time that Furman had served the church, "I certainly have not attempted to make a vain parade of learning, but have endeavored so to speak that I might feed God's people with understanding and knowledge." Furman wished that he had studied even more "in order to impart to you richer and more varied instruction from God's holy word." He had hoped that the brethren "who some year or two ago" complained about Furman's educational background "would see that it was an unworthy prejudice," but since the feelings remained, "I think I ought at least thus publicly to rebuke it."[14]

Furman concluded his letter by stating that he thought that his work at Brushy Creek had been effective ("I do not believe that any labors have been without fruit," he stated). There would have been more "fruit," he felt, had both the church and the minister "prayed more." But praying about the matter by the point he wrote the letter would not resolve the situation, Furman wrote, noting that "with the prejudices existing, I feel there will not be that united, earnest prayer which is essential to a minister's success." The best answer to the situation, he felt, was to resign as the church's pastor.[15]

James Furman resigned from Brushy Creek Church in 1864, working instead to maintain the solvency of Furman University, which had closed its doors during the war. As Brushy Creek's situation revealed, for all of their efforts to extend their influence in the Upcountry, Lowcountry Baptists still had their work cut out to establish a uniform denominational presence throughout the state. In addition to wartime frustrations, cultural hostilities toward an educated ministry remained strong in some areas. Yet, although Brushy Creek members chafed over the war and resisted changes to the style of preaching that had been part of their longtime tradition, no evidence exists that they questioned the moral righteousness of slavery or the importance of evangelizing to enslaved people. Churches in both the Upcountry and the Lowcountry ministered to enslaved people throughout the duration of the Civil War and voiced a desire to retain black membership in the immediate postwar years. Denominationalism continued to divide white Baptists; race did not. Throughout the war, white Baptists in both the Upcountry and the Lowcountry found common ground in preaching the merits of a racially based Christian social order, one that affirmed and legitimized slavery and one that sacralized racial difference. For white Baptists in both regions, owning enslaved people, evangelizing to them, and reminding them of their racial inferiority had become a biblical right that only God could take away.

Postscript

In 1868, responding to the actions of black members who had left their church, white members of Lower Fairforest Baptist Church formally demarcated themselves from their black brothers and sisters. Noting that "whereas that in the providence of God or in the results of this war now closed we are virtually and nationally and spiritually separated from the colored race," the white church "do this day and forever separate ourselves from the Freedmen in a religious point of view and authorize our deacons to grant all cordially members of our body of Freedmen letters of dismission."[16] White Baptists at Lower Fairforest Church captured aptly the racial reaction of many white South Carolinians to the black exodus from their churches. In the years before the Civil War, the presence of enslaved people in biracial churches helped white Baptists believe that Christian slavery was a fulfillment of God's will. After the war ended, black Baptists, not white ones, were in the vanguard of change. Acting on their religious as well as their social and political freedom, black Baptists left biracial churches to form their own congregations where they could commune with one another freely, without worshipping in subordination to whites. White Baptist ministers attempted to reassert the Christian order and governance that they had created before the war, despite the abolition of slavery. They encouraged black Baptists to remain in white-controlled churches and pledged to provide white oversight and guidance to black brethren and sisters, whom they continued to view as socially and racially inferior. Black Baptists for the first time, however, had the ability to create entirely new congregations, congregations without white oversight, congregations that emphasized spiritual salvation without internal racial hierarchy. Many black Baptists chose to form such congregations in the late 1860s, affirming their dignity as human beings and as brothers and sisters in the full light of God's love. They acted on the desire to be masters of their own fate—the very issue that so worried James Furman and other white Baptist paternalists.[17]

In the immediate postwar years, white South Carolina Baptists had much to reformulate. The Christian model of slavery had imploded after Confederate defeat. White Baptists joined other ex-Confederates in articulating a belief that God had punished the South because southerners had failed to follow biblical commands, including not taking care of their enslaved people adequately, not building a sacred society the way God had tasked them.[18] Ironically, the need for the South to reform it sins in the years following defeat did not prompt white Baptists to form enduring partnerships with black Baptists. Rather, freed of their biblical duty to care for their enslaved people, and believing that independent black congregations were "revolting into barbarity" after rebuffing white guidance, white Baptists reframed racial supremacy to emphasize racial exclusivity rather than racial paternalism. Whites turned to other ways to build their Christian empire, including foreign missions, missions to Native Americans in the West, and continued educational efforts launched through the Baptist State Convention and the Southern Baptist Convention. Postwar Baptist development in the South thus proceeded in a racially segregated way, fashioned by blacks who desired racial equality and whites who became more racially separatist and exclusionary. As white Baptist expressions of racial superiority took a different organizational form, and as black Baptist churches grew in both religious and political influence, race continued to play a crucial role in Baptist life in South Carolina, just as Baptist congregations, still primarily segregated by race, continue to be a powerful force in the state to this day.

South Carolina Baptist Church and Membership Statistics

Appendix 1. *Baptist Adherents In South Carolina*

TABLE 1. Adherents of Charleston Church, 1708

Estimate	Total Population South Carolina	White Members	Black Members	Total Members	Adherent Rate	Assumed Attendance with Family	Population (%)
A	9,580	—	—	90	2.9	261	2.7
B	9,580			90	4.9	441	4.6

TABLE 2. Population of White Baptists according to Gov. Nathaniel Johnson, 1708

White Population South Carolina	White Members	White Population (%)
4,180	418	10

Estimate A is based on the supposition that one church member represented 2.9 adherents, as proposed by Henry K. Carroll. Estimate B is based on Leah Townsend's calculation that one church member represented 4–6 adherents. Some estimations are even more liberal: Baptist historian David Benedict believed that one church member represented 7 adherents. Henry K. Carroll, *The Religious Forces of the United States, Enumerated, Classified, and Described on the Basis of the Government Census of 1890* (New York: Christian Literature, 1893), xxxv; Townsend, *South Carolina Baptists*, 273; Benedict, *General History*, vol. 2, 553. For other estimates, see Patricia Bonomi and Peter Eisenstadt, "Church Adherence in the Eighteenth-Century British American Colonies," *William and Mary Quarterly* 3, no. 39 (April 1982): 245–86; Roger Finke and Rodney Stark, "American Religion in 1776," *Sociological Analysis* 49 (1988): 42.

Sources: Baker and Craven, *Adventure in Faith*, 85; Walter J. Fraser Jr., *Charleston! Charleston! The History of a Southern City* (Columbia: Univ. of South Carolina Press, 1989), 28. Anglican Thomas Nairne in his 1710 *Letter from South Carolina* also reported that Baptists comprised 10 percent of the white population of Charleston. Thomas Nairne, *A Letter from South Carolina; Giving an Account of the Soil, Air, Product, Trade, Government, Laws, Religion, People, Military Strength, &c, of that Province; Together with the Manner and Necessary Charges of Settling a Plantation There, and the Annual Profit it Will Produce* (London: A. Baldwin, 1710), 45–46; Little, *Origins of Southern Evangelicalism*, 68; Coclanis, *Shadow of a Dream*, 64; Wood, *Black Majority*, 144.

TABLE 3. Adherents in South Carolina, 1760

Estimate	Total Population South Carolina	White Members	Black Members	Total Members	Adherent Rate	Assumed Attendance with Family	Population (%)
A	89,740	—	—	720	2.9	2,088	2.3
B	89,740			720	4.9	3,528	3.9

Figures are tabulated from a liberal estimate of 60 members per 12 churches in South Carolina in 1760 (Ashley River, Beech Branch, Cashaway, Catfish, Charleston, Coosawhatchie, Euhaw, Lynch's Creek, Stono, Welsh Neck, a Tunker congregation, and a Seventh-Day congregation). In 1760 four congregations in North Carolina also belonged to the Charleston Association: Fishing Creek, Jersey Settlement, Kehukee, and Three Creeks. These church numbers are not calculated into the above membership figures, nor are members from Separate congregations, who began to move into South Carolina in 1759 or 1760. Edwards, "Materials towards a History of the Baptists in the Province of South-Carolina," vol. 5; King, *History of South Carolina Baptists,* 378–84; Coclanis, *The Shadow of a Dream*, 64.

TABLE 4. Adherents in South Carolina, 1790

Estimate	Total Population South Carolina	White Members	Black Members	Total Members	Adherent Rate	Assumed Attendance with Family	Population (%)
A	249,073	2,909	969	3,878	2.9	11,246	4.5
B				3,878	4.9	19,002	7.6

Source: John Asplund, *The Universal Register of the Baptist Denomination in North America, for the Years 1790, 1791, 1792, 1793, and part of 1794* (Boston: John W. Folsom, 1794), 39–42, 89; Townsend, *South Carolina Baptists*, 272–73; Carroll, *Religious Forces*, xxxv; Julian J. Petty, *The Growth and Distribution of Population in South Carolina* (Columbia: State Council for Defense, 1943), 64. Bishop Francis Asbury, after hearing Richard Furman preach at the Charleston Baptist Church, reported only about "seventy hearers" at the church, which was comprised of 240 members. In the backcountry, where the number of enslaved men and women was significantly lower, black members made up a much smaller portion of congregations. For the entire state, I estimate African American membership to be 25 percent of the Baptist population in 1790. While the African American population in the state was much greater, white Baptists had yet to reach out to black men and women en masse. Townsend, *South Carolina Baptists*, 273.

TABLE 5. Adherents in South Carolina, 1800

Estimate	Total Population South Carolina	White Members	Black Members	Total Members	Adherent Rate	Assumed Attendance with Family	Population (%)
A	345,591	3,908	1,675	5,583	2.9	16,191	4.7
B				5,583	4.9	27,357	7.9

African American membership is estimated at 30 percent of the Baptist population. Of 96 Baptist churches in South Carolina in 1800, 29 (1,682 members) belonged to the Charleston Association, while 45 (2,610 members) belonged to the backcountry Bethel Association, formed in 1794; documentation as to associational membership for the other 22 churches is nonexistent. Townsend uses a formula that each church counts for 58 members, allowing for an adherent rate of 4.8, rather than 4.9, for 1800. Townsend, *South Carolina Baptists*, 273; Petty, *Growth and Distribution*, 64.

TABLE 6. Adherents in South Carolina, 1830

Estimate	Total Population South Carolina	White Members	Black Members	Total Members	Adherent Rate	Assumed Attendance with Family	Population (%)
A	581,185	12,190	8,127	20,317	2.9	58,919	10.1
B				20,317	4.9	99,553	17.1

Source: Minutes of the State Convention of the Baptist Denomination in South Carolina (hereafter Minutes of the State Convention of the Baptist Denomination), 1830, Baptist Historical Collection, Furman University (hereafter BHC, FU) ; *Abstract of the Fifth Census, Showing the Number of Free People, the Number of Slaves, the Federal Representative Number; and the Aggregate of Each County of Each State* (Washington: Duff Green, 1832), 21–22. African American membership is estimated at 40 percent of total Baptist membership. Starting in the 1830s, white Baptists began to differentiate black membership from white, indicating that, while African American membership was on the increase, whites also viewed black members from a racialized perspective.

TABLE 7. Adherents in South Carolina, 1836

Estimate	Total Population South Carolina	White Members	Black Members	Total Members	Adherent Rate	Assumed Attendance with Family	Population (%)
A	589,113	20,092	13,394	33,486	2.9	97,109	16.5
B					4.9	164,081	27.9

Source: John Hayward, *The Religious Creeds and Statistics of Every Christian Denomination in the United States and British Provinces* (Boston: Jonathan Howe, 1836), 119.

TABLE 8. Adherents in South Carolina, 1850

Estimate	Total Population South Carolina	White Members	Black Members	Total Members	Adherent Rate	Assumed Attendance with Family	Population (%)
A	668,507	24,516	20,058	44,574	2.9	129,265	19.3
B					4.9	218,413	32.7

Source: Minutes of the State Convention of the Baptist Denomination, 1850, BHC, FU; *The Seventh Census of the United States: 1850* (Washington: J. D. B. DeBow, 1853), ix. African American membership is estimated at 45 percent of Baptist membership.

TABLE 9. Adherents in South Carolina, 1860

Estimate	Total Population South Carolina	White Members	Black Members	Total Members	Adherent Rate	Assumed Attendance with Family	Population (%)
A	703,708	32,575	30,069	62,644	2.9	181,668	25.8
B				62,644	4.9	306,956	43.6

Source: Minutes of the State Convention of the Baptist Denomination, 1861, BHC, FU; *Population of the United States in 1860; Compiled from the Original Returns of the Eighth Census* (Washington, DC: Government Printing Office, 1864), 452. African American membership is estimated at 48 percent of total Baptist membership.

TABLE 10. Adherents in South Carolina, 1890

Estimate	Total Population South Carolina	White Members	Black Members	Total Members	Adherent Rate	Assumed Attendance with Family	Population (%)
A	1,151,149	76,126	125,572	201,698	2.9	584,924	50.8
B					4.9	988,320	85.6

By 1890, African Americans comprised 62 percent of all Baptists in South Carolina. Source: Bureau of the Census, *Statistics for South Carolina, Containing Population, Agriculture, Manufacture, and Mining for the State, Counties, Cities, and Other Divisions* (Washington, DC: Government Printing Office, 1913), 568; Carroll, *Religious Forces*, xliii, 26, 29. Carroll found that in 1890 South Carolina had the highest percentage of church members belonging to all religious denominations (44.17 percent).

Appendix 2. *Church Growth in South Carolina*

TABLE 11. Upcountry and Lowcountry Church Growth in South Carolina, 1830

Region	No. of Churches	Total Members	Average No. of Members per Church	Total Adherents
Lowcountry	84	10,951	130	31,758
Upcountry	160	9,366	59	27,161

TABLE 12. Upcountry and Lowcountry Church Growth in South Carolina, 1834

Region	No. of Churches	Total Members	Average No. of Members per Church	Total Adherents
Lowcountry	100	15,324	153	44,440
Upcountry	206	18,782	91	54,468

TABLE 13. Upcountry and Lowcountry Church Growth in South Carolina, 1850

Region	No. of Churches	Total Members	Average No. of Members per Church	Total Adherents
Lowcountry	152	21,894	144	63,493
Upcountry	265	22,680	86	65,722

TABLE 14. Upcountry and Lowcountry Church Growth in South Carolina, 1860

Region	No. of Churches	Total Members	Average No. of Members per Church	Total Adherents
Lowcountry	190	32,140	169	93,206
Upcountry	278	30,504	110	88,462

Source: Minutes of the State Convention of the Baptist Denomination, 1830, 1834, 1850, 1860, BHC, FU.

Appendix 3. Numbers of Churches and Membership

TABLE 15. Number of Baptist Churches in South Carolina, 1750–1860

1750	1760	1780	1790	1800	1830	1850	1860
5	12	30	67	96	244	333	468

Source: Asplund, *Universal Register,* 39–42; Edwin Scott Gaustad, *New Historical Atlas of Religion in America* (New York: Oxford Univ. Press, 2001), 20–21; King, *History of South Carolina Baptists,* 378–84; Townsend, *South Carolina Baptists,* 273; Minutes of the State Convention of the Baptist Denomination, 1830, 1850, 1861, BHC, FU. As with membership figures, numbers of churches are conservative. Missing from this count are churches from the following Baptist associations: Moriah, Salem, Broad River, West Union, Tugaloo, and Peedee.

TABLE 16. Baptist and Methodist Membership

Denomination	White Members	Black Members	Total Members
Baptists, 1860	32,575	30,069	62,644
Methodists, 1858	37,095	46,740	83,835

Source for Methodist figures: David Duncan Wallace, *South Carolina: A Short History, 1520–1948* (Chapel Hill: Univ. of North Carolina Press, 1951), 441. African American Methodists comprised 55.8 percent of all Methodists in the state in 1860.

Appendix 4.
Membership by Association

TABLE 17. White and African American Membership, Lowcountry Associations, 1860

Association	Whites	African Americans	Total
Barnwell	1340	689	2,103
Charleston	2912	7489	10,401
Columbia	578	222	800
Edisto	1767	601	2,419
Savannah River	2386	7555	9,941
Welsh Neck	3319	3157	6,476
TOTAL	12,302	19,713	32,140
Percentage total	38.3	61.3	—

Tabulations and estimates are taken from the Minutes of the State Convention of the Baptist Denomination, 1861, BHC, FU, which lists membership figures for the previous year (1860). Membership numbers for whites and African Americans were imprecise; the sums did not always equate to the "Total" category listed for each association.

TABLE 18. White and African American Membership, Upcountry Associations, 1860

Association	Whites	African Americans	Total
Bethel	637	504	1,141
Edgefield	4055	3343	7,421
Moriah	1673	504	2,342
Reedy River	2870	1241	4,111
Salem	1005	1027	2,032
Saluda	2183	846	3,345
Tyger River	4024	829	4,853
TOTAL	16,447	8,294	24,741
Total Percentage	66.5	33.5	—

Tabulations and estimates are taken from the Minutes of the State Convention of the Baptist Denomination, 1861, which lists membership figures for the previous year (1860). Three of ten Upcountry associations are unaccounted for because they did not keep regular tallies of white versus African American members. Those associations are: Broad River (2786 members), Greenville (1198 members), and Twelve Mile (1275 members).

Appendix 5. Membership Statistics, Charleston's First Baptist Church

TABLE 19. Membership, First Baptist Church, Charleston, 1795–1840

Year	Black members	White members	Total
1795	170	70	240
1827	697	165	862
1828	707	191	898
1829	753	195	944
1830	814	235	1,049
1831	840	245	1,085
1832	851	253	1,104
1833	1,020	258	1,278
1834	1,044	259	1,303
1835	1,068	307	1,375
1836	1,091	296	1,387
1837	1,117	280	1,397
1838	1,107	278	1,385
1839	1,124	272	1,396
1840	1,143	288	1,431

Baker and Craven, *Adventure in Faith,* 251, 265; Minutes of the Charleston Baptist Church, 1827–1840, BHC, FU. African American and white statistical breakdowns in membership tabulations cease after 1840.

NOTES

Introduction

1. The British referred to Charleston as Charles Town from 1670 to 1783, when the name changed to its modern-day usage.
2. For the unique and radical nature of South Carolina, see: Peter Wood, *Black Majority: Negroes in Colonial South Carolina from 1670 through the Stono Rebellion* (New York: Knopf, 1974), 3–166, esp. 142–50; Walter Edgar, *South Carolina: A History* (Columbia: Univ. of South Carolina Press, 1998), 63–81, 245–353; Manisha Sinha, *The Counterrevolution of Slavery: Politics and Ideology in Antebellum South Carolina* (Chapel Hill: Univ. of North Carolina Press, 2000); Ryan A. Quintana, *Making a Slave State: Political Development in Early South Carolina* (Chapel Hill: Univ. of North Carolina Press, 2018); Lacy K. Ford Jr., *Origins of Southern Radicalism: The South Carolina Upcountry, 1800–1860* (New York: Oxford Univ. Press, 1988); Stephanie McCurry, *Masters of Small Worlds: Yeoman Households, Gender Relations, and the Political Culture of the Antebellum South Carolina Lowcountry* (New York: Oxford Univ. Press, 1997). The terminology of different regions of South Carolina changed over the decades, as did the territorial designations. I use the term "Lowcountry" to refer to the coastal plain and the area up to the state's fall line, which runs on an east-west diagonal, "backcountry" to mean the areas outside of the settled parishes along the coast in the 1700s, and "Upcountry" to refer to the region to the north and west of the fall line. For more detailed information about the ways the terms changed, see McCurry, *Masters of Small Worlds*, 23, 30–31; Rachel N. Klein, *Unification of a Slave State: The Rise of the Planter Class in the South Carolina Backcountry, 1760–1808* (Chapel Hill: Univ. of North Carolina Press, 1990), 7; and Ford, *Origins of Southern Radicalism*, viii–ix.
3. For studies that argue that Baptists began as "outsiders" and matured into a middle-class, elite denomination over time, see Rhys Isaacs, *The Transformation of Virginia, 1740–1790* (Chapel Hill: Univ. of North Carolina Press, 1982); Donald G. Mathews, *Religion in the Old South* (Chicago: Univ. of Chicago Press, 1977); John B. Boles, "Evangelical Protestantism in the Old South: From Religious Dissent to Cultural Dominance," in *Religion in the South*, ed. Charles Reagan Wilson (Jackson: Univ. Press of Mississippi, 1985), 25–26; Christine Leigh Heyrman, *Southern Cross: The Beginnings of the Bible Belt* (New York: Alfred A. Knopf, 1998); and Robert M. Calhoon, *Evangelicals and Conservatives in the Early South, 1740–1861* (Columbia: Univ. of South Carolina Press, 1988).

By contrast, Thomas J. Little locates a vibrant and diverse evangelical presence in colonial South Carolina. Thomas J. Little, *The Origins of Southern Evangelicalism: Religious Revivalism in the South Carolina Lowcountry, 1670–1760* (Columbia: Univ. of South Carolina Press, 2013). Walter B. Shurden identifies four distinct Baptist traditions—including the "Charleston tradition" distinguished by liturgical and social order—that distinctively influenced southern evangelicalism. Walter B. Shurden, *Not an Easy Journey: Some Transitions in Baptist Life* (Macon: Mercer Univ. Press, 2005), 202–4. For the role of the elite in shaping denominational efforts, see Jon Butler, *Power, Authority, and the Origins of American Denominational Order: The English Churches in the Delaware Valley, 1680–1730* (Tuscaloosa: Univ. of Alabama Press, 2009). Also see Jewel L. Spangler, *Virginians Reborn: Anglican Monopoly, Evangelical Dissent, and the Rise of the Baptists in the Late Eighteenth Century* (Charlottesville: Univ. of Virginia Press, 2008); Keith Harper, *A Mere Kentucky of a Place: The Elkhorn Association and the Commonwealth's First Baptists* (Knoxville: Univ. of Tennessee Press, 2021).

4. Although historians differ in nuance in their definitions of paternalism, the phrase generally describes a white ideology that recognized enslaved people as humans of an inferior station who needed the master's care and guidance to perform their God-given social and economic duties. Under the paternalistic system of slave management, enslaved people were viewed as household dependents, similar to white women and children. In return for the care and benevolence of the household head, paternalists believed, slaves would work productively and bestow loyalty to their masters. For treatments of paternalism as an eighteenth-century development, see Charles F. Irons, *The Origins of Proslavery Christianity: White and Black Evangelicals in Colonial and Antebellum Virginia* (Chapel Hill: Univ. of North Carolina Press, 2008) 13–14, 23–168; and Alan Gallay, *The Formation of the Planter Elite: Jonathan Bryan and the Southern Colonial Frontier* (Athens: Univ. of Georgia Press, 1989). Gallay locates the origins of slaveholder paternalism in the First Great Awakening, giving credit to the reforms made by George Whitefield and the evangelical network formed during his tours of the British colonial South. While Irons identifies examples of Christian benevolence in the early 1700s, he attributes the revival of the 1780s and 1790s, when large numbers of enslaved people joined evangelical churches, as a formative period for the development of white paternalism. For the role of late Enlightenment theorists (especially Common Sense realism thinkers) on modernizing understandings of "humanity" and "humane" relations, see Joyce E. Chaplin, "Slavery and the Principle of Humanity: A Modern Idea in the Early Lower South," *Journal of Social History* 24 (December 1990): 299–315. Also see Mitchell Snay, *Gospel of Disunion: Religion and Separatism in the Antebellum South* (Chapel Hill: Univ. of North Carolina Press, 1993), 83–87.
5. Lacy K. Ford, *Deliver Us From Evil: The Slavery Question in the Old South* (New York: Oxford Univ. Press, 2009), esp. 143–72; Jeffrey Robert Young,

Domesticating Slavery: The Master Class in Georgia and South Carolina, 1670–1837 (Chapel Hill: Univ. of North Carolina Press, 1999) 123–59; Willie Lee Rose, "The Domestication of Slavery," in *Slavery and Freedom*, ed. William W. Freehling (New York: Oxford Univ. Press, 1982), 18–36; William W. Freehling, *The Road to Disunion: Secessionists in Bay, 1776–1854* (New York: Oxford Univ. Press, 1990), 59–97; Eugene Genovese, *Roll, Jordan, Roll: The World the Slaves Made* (New York: Pantheon Books, 1974), 3–10, 658–85; George M. Frederickson, *The Black Image in the White Mind: The Debate on Afro-American Character and Destiny, 1817–1914* (New York: Oxford Univ. Press, 1971), 51–64; David Brion Davis, *The Problem of Slavery in the Age of Revolution, 1770–1823* (Ithaca: Cornell Univ. Press, 1975), 523–64.

6. White Lowcountry Baptists were not the first to espouse a Christian proslavery argument, but through Richard Furman they shaped a powerful and public justification of the institution. Virginia planters in 1785 contested the antislavery petition of Methodist bishops Francis Asbury and Thomas Coke, for instance, noting the scriptural justification of slavery. Calhoon, *Evangelicals and Conservatives*, 126; Edward R. Crowther, *Southern Evangelicals and the Coming of the Civil War* (Lewiston: Edward Mellen Press, 2000), 34-35; Fredrika Teute Schmidt and Barbara Ripel Wilhelm, "Early Proslavery Petitions in Virginia," *William and Mary Quarterly* 30, no. 1 (January 1973): 133-146. Also see Brandon Michael Inabinet, "When Pastors Go Public: Richard Furman's Public Letter on Slavery," *Southern Communication Journal* 76, no. 3 (July-August 2011): 169-190.
7. While this study focuses primarily upon enslaved people of color, free persons of color also belonged to Baptist churches; some held roles as exhorters or lay preachers. Free persons of color accounted for less than 1 percent of the total South Carolina population in 1790 (9,914 of 249,073) and 1.4 percent of the total state population in 1860 (9,914 of 703,708). Edgar, *South Carolina*, 308; Marina Wikramanayake, *A World in Shadow: The Free Black in Antebellum South Carolina* (Columbia: Univ. of South Carolina Press, 1973); Orville Vernon Burton, *In My Father's House Are Many Mansions: Family and Community in Edgefield, South Carolina* (Chapel Hill: Univ. of North Carolina Press, 1985), 203–24.
8. Larry M. James, "Biracial Fellowship in Antebellum Baptist Churches," in *Masters and Slaves in the House of the Lord: Race and Religion in the American South, 1740–1870*, ed. John B. Boles (Lexington: Univ. of Kentucky Press, 1988), 38; Janet Duitsman Cornelius, *Slave Missions and the Black Church in the Antebellum South* (Columbia: Univ. of South Carolina Press, 1999), 20.
9. Stephanie McCurry has shown that white men in antebellum South Carolina, regardless of wealth or social standing, shared a common social and political claim to gendered and racial mastery by the legal control they exercised over white and black household dependents. By underscoring the importance of household and family, she contends, evangelical churches reinforced white male mastery. Although Baptist churches enforced patriarchy in varying degrees through teaching

and discipline, this study argues that smaller congregations in the Upcountry sometimes afforded women more flexible governing roles. McCurry, *Masters of Small Worlds*, 121–97. Also see Monica Najar, *Evangelizing the South: A Social History of Church and State in Early America* (New York: Oxford Univ. Press, 2008), 36–64; Jean Friedman, *The Enclosed Garden: Women and Community in the Evangelical South, 1830–1900* (Chapel Hill: Univ. of North Carolina Press, 1985), 3–20, 39–66; Mathews, *Religion in the Old South*, 109–10. See especially Gregory Wills, *Democratic Religion: Freedom, Authority, and Church Discipline in the Baptist South, 1795–1900* (New York: Oxford Univ. Press, 1997), 51–53; and Elizabeth Fox-Genovese, *Within the Plantation Household: Black and White Women of the Old South* (Chapel Hill: Univ. of North Carolina Press, 1988), 43–46.

10. For treatments of African American religion, see Albert Raboteau, *Slave Religion: The 'Invisible Institution' in the Antebellum South* (New York: Oxford Univ. Press, 1978); Genovese, *Roll, Jordan, Roll*; Sylvia R. Frey and Betty Wood, *Come Shouting to Zion: African American Protestantism in the American South and British Caribbean to 1830* (Chapel Hill: Univ. of North Carolina Press, 1998); Mechal Sobel, *Trabelin' On: The Slave Journey to An Afro-Baptist Faith* (Westport, CT: Greenwood Press, 1979); Mechal Sobel, *The World They Made Together: Black and White Values in Eighteenth-Century Virginia* (Princeton: Princeton Univ. Press, 1987); Cornelius, *Slave Missions*; Michael Mullin, *Africa in America: Slave Acculturation and Resistance in the American South and British Caribbean* (Urbana: Univ. of Illinois Press, 1992); Irons, *The Origins of Proslavery Christianity*; Charles Joyner, *Down by the Riverside: A South Carolina Slave Community* (Chicago: Univ. of Chicago Press, 1984); John B. Boles, *The Irony of Southern Religion* (New York: Peter Lang, 1994), 37–71; Randy J. Sparks, *On Jordan's Stormy Banks: Evangelicalism in Mississippi, 1773–1876* (Athens: Univ. of Georgia Press, 1994), 132–45; John B. Boles, "Introduction," in *Masters and Slaves in the House of the Lord*, 6.
11. See Appendices A–F.
12. See Appendices A–F. Daniel Fountain argues that Christianity did not attract or influence as many enslaved people in the antebellum South as most scholars contend. In postwar years, by contrast, much larger numbers of African Americans converted to Christianity. Daniel Fountain, *Slavery, Civil War, and Salvation: African American Slaves and Christianity, 1830–1870* (Baton Rouge: Louisiana State Univ. Press, 2010).
13. For studies of African American religious actions and experiences after the Civil War, see Paul Harvey, *Redeeming the South: Religious Cultures and Racial Identities Among Southern Baptists, 1865–1920* (Chapel Hill: Univ. of North Carolina Press, 1997); Katharine L. Dvorak, *An African-American Exodus: The Segregation of Southern Churches* (Brooklyn: Carlson Publishing, 1991); Daniel Stowell, *Rebuilding Zion: The Religious Reconstruction of the South, 1863–1877* (New

York: Oxford Univ. Press, 1998); Elizabeth Jemison, *Christian Citizens: Reading the Bible in Black and White in the Postemancipation South* (Chapel Hill: Univ. of North Carolina Press, 2020); Edward J. Blum, *Reforging the White Republic: Race, Religion, and American Nationalism, 1865–1898* (Baton Rouge: Louisiana State Univ. Press, 2005); Paul Harvey, *Freedom's Coming: Religious Culture and the Shaping of the South from the Civil War through the Civil Rights Era* (Chapel Hill: Univ. of North Carolina Press, 2015); Sparks, *On Jordan's Stormy Banks*; and Edward R. Crowther and Keith Harper, eds., *Between Fetters and Freedom: African American Baptists since Emancipation* (Macon: Mercer Univ. Press, 2015).

14. The full name of the Baptist Triennial Convention, which met nationally every three years, was the "General Missionary Convention of the Baptist Denomination in the United States of America for Foreign Missions."

Chapter One

1. Little, *Origins of Southern Evangelicalism*, 9, 27–28, 32, 38–39; Robert A. Baker and Paul J. Craven Jr., *Adventure in Faith: The First 300 Years of First Baptist Church, Charleston, South Carolina* (Nashville: Broadman Press, 1982), 62–70.
2. See Appendix A.
3. Fraser, *Charleston, Charleston!*, 1–81; Wood, *Black Majority*, 218–38; 271–326; Edgar, *South Carolina*, 63–154.
4. Free white settlers utilized European indentured servants, enslaved Native Americans, and enslaved Africans as their early labor force. In 1708, enslaved Native Americans accounted for 14 percent of the total population of South Carolina (1,400 of 9,580). European indentured servants comprised only 1.2 percent of the total population that same year. Enslaved Africans made up 42.79 percent of the total population (4,100 of 9,580). At 4,100, the African population exceeded the white population of 4,080. The number of enslaved Native Americans decreased rapidly as the number of enslaved Africans escalated. By 1738, enslaved Native Americans comprised only about 2.5 percent of the slave population. Wood, *Black Majority*, 144, 155.
5. In 1720 the population of St. James Goose Creek was 79 percent African and that of St. James Santee was 74 percent African, similar to the population of Barbados. Wood, *Black Majority*, 3–166, esp. 142–50; Edgar, *South Carolina*, 69; Walter J. Fraser Jr., *Charleston! Charleston! The History of a Southern City* (Columbia: Univ. of South Carolina Press, 1989), 1–97; Coclanis, *Shadow of a Dream*, 64; Edgar, *South Carolina*, 63–81, 245–353; Sinha, *Counterrevolution of Slavery;* Ford, *Origins of Southern Radicalism*. By 1840 Mississippi had also achieved a slave majority. See Shearer Davis Bowman, *America at the Precipice: Americans North and South during the Secession Crisis* (Chapel Hill: Univ. of North Carolina Press, 2010), 38.
6. Baker and Craven, *Adventure in Faith*, 38.

7. Baker and Craven, *Adventure in* Faith, 43.
8. Baker and Craven, *Adventure in Faith*, 45–46; *The New England Historical and Genealogical Register*, vol. 44 (Boston: New England Historical and Genealogical Society, 1890), 112–13; Wendy Warren, *New England Bound: Slavery and Colonization in Early America* (New York: Liveright Publishing Corporation, 2016), 126.
9. Baker and Craven, *Adventure in Faith*, 45–46; Little, *Origins of Southern Evangelicalism*, 38–39.
10. Baker and Craven surmise that the Screvens became official church members after the birth of their first child, so that their children would avoid infant baptism. Colonial officials targeted the dissenting congregation at various times, closing the newly built meeting house and arresting several leaders in 1679. The following year, the house was reopened for Baptist use. Baker and Craven, *Adventure in Faith*, 47–49.
11. Baker and Craven, *Adventure in Faith*, 47.
12. Baker and Craven, *Adventure in Faith*, 50–61.
13. Baker and Craven, *Adventure in Faith*, 52–62; Nathan E. Wood, *The History of the First Baptist Church of Boston, 1665–1899* (Philadelphia: American Baptist Publication Society, 1899), 179–84.
14. Henry S. Burrage, *History of the Baptists in Maine* (Portland: Marks Printing House, 1906), 24–25.
15. Baker and Craven argue convincingly that the minister remained in Maine until 1696. In 1682 Screven pledged to the Massachusetts General Assembly to leave the colony in a short time; the following year, the Court of Sessions at Wells summoned him "for not departing the Province." Baker and Craven, *Adventure in Faith*, 58–70. For information about early settlement in South Carolina, see Robert M. Weir, *Colonial South Carolina: A History* (Millwood: KTO Press, 1983); and Walter N. Edgar, *South Carolina: A History* (Columbia: Univ. of South Carolina Press, 1998), 47–81.
16. Charles H. Lippy, "Chastized by Scorpions: Christianity and Culture in Colonial South Carolina, 1669–1740," *Church History* 79, no. 2 (June 2010): 253–70; Little, *Origins of Southern Evangelicalism*, 1–115.
17. Baker and Craven, *Adventure in Faith*, 82.
18. Leah Townsend, *South Carolina Baptists, 1670–1805* (Florence: Florence Printing Company, 1935), 10.
19. Will of Lady Elizabeth Blake, September 30, 1725, South Carolina Wills and Probate Records, 1670–1980," vols. 1–2, Ancestry.com, https://www.ancestry.com/search/collections/9080/. Blake's mother, Lady Rebecca Axtell, provided a chandelier for the church. Basil Manly, *Mercy and Judgment: A Discourse Containing Some Fragments of the History of the Baptist Church in Charleston S.C.*

(n.p.: Press of Knowles, Vose and Co., 1837), 12; Baker and Craven, *Adventure in Faith*, 26, 81; Townsend, *South Carolina Baptists*, 13.

20. Roy Talbert Jr. and Meggan A. Farish, *The Antipedo Baptists of Georgetown County, South Carolina, 1710–2010* (Columbia: Univ. of South Carolina Press, 2014), 15; Little, *Origins of Southern Evangelicalism*, 1–47. Also see David Duncan Wallace, *The Historical Background of Religion in South Carolina* (Florence: Order of the Societies, 1917), 4.
21. Baker and Craven, *Adventure in Faith*, 75–78.
22. Baker and Craven, *Adventure in Faith*, 83.
23. Baker and Craven, *Adventure in Faith*, 73–122
24. Little, *Origins of Southern Evangelicalism*, 111; Talbert and Farish, *Antipedo Baptists*, 15; Townsend, *South Carolina Baptists*, 11–18.
25. S. Charles Bolton, *Southern Anglicanism: The Church of England in Colonial South Carolina* (Westport: Greenwood Press, 1982), 16–36; Baker and Craven, *Adventure in Faith*, 85–86; Little, *Origins of Southern Evangelicalism*, 48–83.
26. William Screven to the Church of Christ in Boston, June 2, 1707, in Baker and Craven, *Adventure in Faith*, 86–87.
27. William Screven to Ellis Callender, August 6, 1708, in Baker and Craven, *Adventure in Faith*, 89–90.
28. William Screven to Ellis Callender, August 6, 1708, in Baker and Craven, *Adventure in Faith*, 89–90.
29. Talbert and Farish, *Antipedo Baptists*, 19–20.
30. Talbert and Farish, *Antipedo Baptists*, 22–23.
31. Talbert and Farish, *Antipedo Baptists*, 25–26.
32. Talbert and Farish, *Antipedo Baptists*, 34–35. Talbert and Farish see Screven as a capitalist who bought and sold his Kittery and Somerton lands before moving to Winyah.
33. Baker and Craven, *Adventure in Faith*, 101–3.
34. Baker and Craven, *Adventure in Faith*, 103. For information about Baptists in Pennsylvania, see Jonathan J. Davis, *History of the Welsh Baptists, From the Year Sixty Three to the Year One Thousand Seven Hundred and Seventy* (Pittsburgh: D. M. Hogan, 1835).
35. Thomas Kidd, *George Whitefield: America's First Founding Spiritual Father* (New Haven: Yale Univ. Press, 2014), 102–3; Baker and Craven, *Adventure in Faith*, 112–14; Little, *Origins of Southern Evangelicalism*, 111–22.
36. Baker and Craven, *Adventure in Faith*, 118–19; 217.
37. Baker and Craven, *Adventure in Faith*, 108–11.
38. Baker and Craven, *Adventure in Faith*, 105–6.
39. Baker and Craven, *Adventure in Faith*, 119–20; Townsend, *South Carolina Baptists*, 37–38; Morgan Edwards, "Materials towards a History of the Baptists in the

Provinces of Maryland, Virginia, North Carolina, South Carolina, Georgia," vol. 5, p. 4, Furman University Digital Collections, https://cdm16821.contentdm.oclc.org/digital/collection/jbt/id/241.

40. The group was granted a letter of dismission to join the Charleston church or another Baptist church in South Carolina, or to constitute their own church. John Barrington, ed., *Baptists in Early North America*, vol. 5, *Welsh Neck, South Carolina* (Macon: Mercer Univ. Press, 2019), ii–xxiii.
41. Barrington, *Welsh Neck*, xiii–xvi.
42. Edwards, "Materials," vol. 5, pp. 4–5.
43. David Benedict, *A General History of the Baptist Denomination in America, and Other Parts of the World* vol. 2 (London: Lincoln and Edmands, 1813), p. 324; Eric C. Smith, *Oliver Hart and the Rise of Baptist America* (New York: Oxford Univ. Press, 2020), 74–77.
44. Baker and Craven, *Adventure in Faith*, 124; Eric C. Smith, *Order and Ardor: The Revival Spirituality of Oliver Hart and the Regular Baptists in Eighteenth-Century South Carolina* (Columbia: Univ. of South Carolina Press, 2018), 11–28.
45. Manly, *Mercy and Judgment*, 31; Smith, *Order and Ardor*, 11–28; Baker and Craven, *Adventure in Faith*, 123–75; Edwards, "Materials," vol. 5, pp. 12–13; Benedict, *General History*, vol. 2, p. 324; H. A. Tupper, ed., *Two Centuries of the First Baptist Church of Charleston, 1683–1883* (Baltimore: R. H. Woodward and Co., 1889), 101.
46. Baker and Craven, *Adventure in Faith*, 128–29; Smith, *Order and Ardor*, 11–28. Soon after Hart's arrival, a "great and terrible hurricane" on September 15, 1752, ruined Hart's home, destroyed portions of the newly built meeting house, and destroyed church records. A second, smaller but still damaging storm hit the city on September 30. Conditions were so catastrophic that the assembly banned the exportation of food products in order to have supplies for the colony's inhabitants. St. Philips Anglican church helped the poor, dipping into church reserves. Baker and Craven, *Adventure in Faith*, 128; Fraser, *Charleston! Charleston!*, 83–85.
47. Oliver Hart, *Dancing Exploded: A Sermon, Shewing the Unlawfulness, Sinfulness, and Bad Consequences of Balls, Assemblies, and Dances in General* (Charleston: David Bruce, 1778); Smith, *Order and Ardor*, 34–35.
48. Townsend, *South Carolina Baptists*, 21; Smith, *Order and Ardor*, 52–70.
49. Oliver Hart diary, October 10, 1754, quoted in Townsend, *South Carolina Baptists*, 22.
50. Oliver Hart diary, October 10, 1754, quoted in Townsend, *South Carolina Baptists*, 22.
51. Baker and Craven, *Adventure in Faith*, 151–52; Townsend, *South Carolina Baptists*, 111.
52. Townsend, *South Carolina Baptists*, 111.
53. Townsend, *South Carolina Baptists*, 111; Baker and Craven, *Adventure in Faith*,

152, Wood Furman, *A History of the Charleston Association of Baptist Churches in the State of South-Carolina* (Charleston: J. Hoff, 1811), 8–9.

54. Baker and Craven, *Adventure in Faith*, 156–57; Thomas S. Kidd, *The Great Awakening: The Roots of Evangelical Christianity in Colonial America* (New Haven: Yale Univ. Press, 2007), 258–59; A. D. Gillette, ed., *Minutes of the Philadelphia Baptist Association, 1707 to 1807* (Philadelphia: American Baptist Publication Society, 1851), 72; Terry Wolever, *The Life and Ministry of John Gano, 1727–1804: Pastor-Evangelist of the Philadelphia Association* (Springfield: Particular Baptist Press, 1998), 60–61, 71–73, 78–89; William B. Sprague, ed., *Annals of the American Pulpit*, vol. 6 (New York: Robert Carter and Brothers, 1860), 62–65.
55. Joe M. King, *History of South Carolina Baptists* (Columbia: R. L. Bryan Company, 1964), 156; Kidd and Hankins, *Baptists in America*, 42.
56. *Baptist Memorial and Monthly Chronicle*, vol. 3, no. 11, November, 1844.
57. *Baptist Memorial and Monthly Chronicle*, vol. 3, no. 11, November, 1844.
58. *Baptist Memorial and Monthly Chronicle*, vol. 3, no. 11, November, 1844.
59. Baker and Craven, *Adventure in Faith*, 159–60.
60. Baker and Craven, *Adventure in Faith*, 161–62.
61. See Appendix 1.
62. For examples of other religious groups who modeled paternalism in the 1700s, see Cornelius, *When I Can Read My Title Clear*, 14–15, 21–22; Bolton, *Southern Anglicanism*, 115–18; Alan Gallay, "Planters and Slaves in the Great Awakening," in Boles, *Masters and Slaves in the House of the Lord*, 19–36.
63. Sobel, *Trabelin' On*, 34–39; Frey and Wood, *Come Shouting to Zion*, 45–47; Morgan, *Slave Counterpoint*, 58–101; Raboteau, *Slave Religion*, 126–28; Betty Wood, *Slavery in Colonial America, 1619–1776* (Lanham, MD: Rowman and Littlefield, 2005), 56–58; also see Mullin, *Africa in America*, 243–49.
64. Frey and Wood, *Come Shouting to Zion*, 84–85.
65. Katharine Gerbner, *Christian Slavery: Conversion and Race in the Protestant Atlantic World* (Philadelphia: Univ. of Pennsylvania Press, 2018), esp. 1–12. Also see Irons, *Origins of Proslavery Christianity*, 23–31; Nicolas M. Beasley (who emphasizes the importance of free blacks, particularly, in claiming Christian citizenship), *Christian Ritual and the Creation of British Slave Societies, 1650–1780* (Athens: Univ. of Georgia Press, 2009); Annette Laing, "'Heathens and Infidels'? African Christianization and Anglicanism in the South Carolina Low Country, 1700–1750," *Religion and American Culture* 12, no. 2 (July 2002): 197–228; Herbert S. Klein, "Anglicanism, Catholicism, and the Negro Slave," *Comparative Studies in Society and History* 8, no. 3 (April 1966): 295–327; Michael Anesko, "So Discreet A Zeal: Slavery and the Anglican Church in Virginia, 1680–1730," *Virginia Magazine of History and Biography* 93, no. 3 (July 1985): 247–78. Also see Fred E. Witzig, *Sanctifying Slavery and Politics in South Carolina: The Life*

of Reverend Alexander Garden, 1685–1756 (Columbia: Univ. of South Carolina Press, 2018), 129–57.

66. Thomas Cooper and David J. McCord, eds., *Statutes at Large of South Carolina* (Columbia: A. S. Johnston, 1839), vol. 7, 343.
67. Francis Le Jau to the Secretary of the SPG, October 20, 1709, in Frank J. Klingberg, *The Carolina Chronicle of Dr. Francis Le Jau, 1706-1717* (Berkeley: University of California Press, 1956), 59-60; Bolton, *Southern Anglicanism*, 108–11; Wood, *Black Majority*, 133–36.
68. Cooper and McCord, *Statutes at Large*, , vol. 7, 364–65.
69. Wood, *Black Majority*, 36–37, 61–62, 88–91; Eugene Sirmans, "The Legal Status of the Slave in South Carolina, 1670–1740," *Journal of Southern History* 28, no. 4 (November 1962): 462–66; Thomas J. Little, "The South Carolina Slave Laws Reconsidered, 1670–1700," *South Carolina Historical Magazine* 94, no. 2 (April 1993): 86–101; Daragh Grant, "'Civilizing' the Colonial Subject: The Co-Evolution of State and Slavery in South Carolina, 1670–1739," *Comparative Studies in Society and History* 57, no. 3 (July 2015): 606–36; John Samuel Harpham, "Two Concepts of a Slave in the South Carolina Law of Slavery," *Slavery and Abolition* 39, no. 1 (March 2018): 101–22; Fraser, *Charleston! Charleston!* 15.
70. Cooper and McCord, *Statutes at Large*, , vol. 7. 343, 359–60; Little, "South Carolina Slaves," 97–98, 100; L. H. Roper, "The 1701 'Act for the Better Ordering of Slaves': Reconsidering the History of Slavery in Proprietary South Carolina," *William and Mary Quarterly* 64, no. 2 (April 2007): 410–11; Sirmans, "The Legal Status of the Slave in South Carolina," 465–66; Wood, *Black Majority*, 135–36; Francis Le Jau to the Secretary of the SPG, Feb. 20, 1712, in Klingberg, *Carolina Chronicle*, 108–9. For further information on slavery in colonial South Carolina, see Daniel Littlefield, *Rice and Slaves: Ethnicity and the Slave Trade in Colonial South Carolina* (Baton Rouge: Louisiana State Univ. Press, 1981); Young, *Domesticating Slavery*; S. Max Edelson, *Plantation Enterprise in Colonial South Carolina* (Cambridge: Harvard Univ. Press, 2006).
71. William G. McLoughlin and Winthrop D. Jordan, eds., "Baptists Face the Barbarities of Slavery in 1710," *Journal of Southern History* 29, no. 4 (November 1963): 497.
72. McLoughlin and Jordan, "Barbarities," 497.
73. McLoughlin and Jordan, "Barbarities," 498.
74. McLoughlin and Jordan, "Barbarities," 499.
75. McLoughlin and Jordan, "Barbarities," 497–99.
76. McLoughlin and Jordan, "Barbarities," 499–501.
77. Little, *Origins of Southern Evangelicalism*, 112–15; Sarah E. Kegley and Thomas J. Little, "Records of the Ashley River Baptist Church, 1736–1769," *Journal of the South Carolina Baptist Historical Society* 27 (November 2001), 3–32.

78. *Biographical Memoirs of the Late Rev. John Gano, of Frankfort, Kentucky, Formerly of the City of New York* (New York: Southwick and Hardcastle, 1806), 66–67.
79. *Biographical Memoirs of the Late Rev. John Gano*, 68–69.
80. Townsend, *South Carolina Baptists*, 63–64; Barrington, *Welsh Neck*, xvi–xvii.
81. Will of Martha D'Harriette, May 27, 1758, "South Carolina Wills and Probate Records, 1670–1980," vols. 7–8, Ancestry.com, https://www.ancestry.com/search/collections/9080/; Townsend, *South Carolina Baptists*, 25.
82. Oliver Hart diary, August 26, 1754, in Smith, *Order and Ardor*, 97.
83. Smith, *Order and Ardor*, 97.
84. Pelot inherited land and enslaved people from his two wives. After the death of his first wife, Martha Sealy, Pelot married Catherine Stoll Screven, widow of William Screven (a deacon in the Charleston church and son of Charleston's first Baptist minister, William Screven). Pelot's slave holdings must have been large, although no precise figure exists. Pelot's son Charles Pelot owned seventy-seven enslaved people in 1790. Daniel J. Tortora, "The Life and Ministry of a Forgotten Founder: Rev. Francis Pelot of Euhaw Church, 1720–1774," *Journal of the South Carolina Baptist Historical Society* 30 (2007/2008): 3–14; Townsend, *South Carolina Baptists*, 3–14. For information about the Swiss-founded Purrysburg settlement, see Arlin C. Migliazzo, *To Make This Land Our Own: Community, Identity, and Cultural Adaptation in Purrysburg Township, South Carolina, 1732–1865* (Columbia: Univ. of South Carolina Press, 2007). For information about William Screven, Jr. see Baker and Craven, *Adventure in Faith*, 98-99.
85. In the 1770s Ashley River Church sold the enslaved people and rented the land. Townsend, *South Carolina Baptists*, 34–35. Writing in 1772 about Welsh Neck Church, further in the South Carolina interior, Morgan Edwards noted that "an attempt was made a few years ago to endow it [the church] with a plantation and negroes; the negroes were given, but the purchase of the land failing in their part, the owners took back their negroes." Edward, "Materials," 16–17.
86. Townsend, *South Carolina Baptists*, 64.
87. Townsend, *South Carolina Baptists*, 111; Will of Charles Barker, March 6, 1755, "South Carolina Wills and Probate Records, 1670–1980," vol. 81, Ancestry.com, https://www.ancestry.com/search/collections/9080/; Will of Richard Bedon, December 19, 1756, "South Carolina Wills and Probate Records, 1670–1980," vols. 11–13, Ancestry.com, https://www.ancestry.com/search/collections/9080/; Will of John Mikell, December 13, 1764, "South Carolina Wills and Probate Records, 1670–1980," Ancestry.com, https://www.ancestry.com/search/collections/9080/; Will of James Fowler, Dec. 5, 1752, "South Carolina Wills and Probate Records, 1670–1980," vol. 81, Ancestry.com, https://www.ancestry.com/search/collections/9080/. The grantors often mandated that their support of the church would continue only with selection of a preacher of the Particular

Baptist order. See, for example, Will of Richard Baker, May 20, 1752, "South Carolina Wills and Probate Records, 1670–1980," vols. 7–8, Ancestry.com, https://www.ancestry.com/search/collections/9080/.

88. Will of James Fowler, December 5, 1752, "South Carolina Wills and Probate Records, 1670–1980," vol. 81, Ancestry.com, https://www.ancestry.com/search/collections/9080/.
89. Townsend, *South Carolina Baptists*, 35.
90. Bedgegood's marriage in South Carolina to Mary Murphey caused controversy upon the news that his first wife was still alive in England (the minister claimed to have understood that she died). Although the Charleston Association dismissed Bedgegood from membership, he remained pastor of Welsh Neck Church until his death. Townsend, *South Carolina Baptists*, 69; Barrington, *Welsh Neck*, xxi–xxii. For information about the Bethesda Orphan House, see Kidd, *George Whitefield*, 55–56, 101–2, 192–93.
91. According to Morgan Edwards, Edmund Mathews was a grandson of Thomas Hobbes. Edwards, "Materials," vol. 5, 31; Townsend, *South Carolina Baptists*, 40.
92. Will of Edmund Mathews, May 31, 1784, "South Carolina Wills and Probate Records, 1670–1980," Ancestry.com, https://www.ancestry.com/search/collections/9080/. No will exists for Evan Pugh.
93. Townsend, *South Carolina Baptists*, 68. In 1770 Pugh collaborated with Anglican parish clerk and singing school master Durham Hills to produce *The Cashaway Psalmody,* containing 152 sacred tunes for singing in churches and at home. Pugh and his fiancé, Martha Magee, attended the singing school, and Hills presented the manuscript to the soon-to-be Mrs. Pugh as a wedding present. Marini sees the *Psalmody* as a sign of evangelical ecumenicism. Stephen A. Marini, *The Cashaway Psalmody: Transatlantic Religion and Music in Colonial Carolina* (Urbana: Univ. of Illinois Press, 2020).
94. Will of William Elliott, September 2, 1765, "South Carolina Wills and Probate Records, 1670–1980," vols. 11–13, Ancestry.com, https://www.ancestry.com/search/collections/9080/; Henry A. M. Smith, "The Baronies of South Carolina," *South Carolina Historical and Genealogical Magazine* 15, no. 4 (January 1914): 162; Townsend, *South Carolina Baptists*, 54–56.
95. Smith, *Order and Ardor,* 97. Hart was deeply grieved by Pelot's death, writing "I have lost the best friend and counselor I ever was blest with in the world." Oliver Hart journal fragment, cited in Loulie Latimer Owens, "Oliver Hart, 1723–1795: A Brief Biography," *Baptist History and Heritage* (1966): 31.
96. Will of Francis Pelot, June 13, 1773, "South Carolina Wills and Probate Records, 1670–1980," vols. 14–16, Ancestry.com, https://www.ancestry.com/search/collections/9080/.
97. *South Carolina Gazette and Country Journal*, February 8, 1774, South Carolina Electronic Records Archive, http://e-archives.sc.gov/file/sdb%3AdigitalFile

%7C4a5ea1b3–1784–4aed-9853–03150e7d102e/; Tortora, "Francis Pelot," *Journal of the South Carolina Baptist Historical Society*, 4.

98. *South Carolina Gazette and Country Journal*, April 25, 1774, South Carolina Electronic Records Archive, http://e-archives.sc.gov/file/sdb%3AdigitalFile%7C4a5ea1b3–1784–4aed-9853–03150e7d102e/; Tortora, "Francis Pelot," 4.
99. Will of Isaac Chanler, May 20, 1749, "South Carolina Wills and Probate Records, 1670–1980," vol. 6, Ancestry.com, https://www.ancestry.com/search/collections/9080/.
100. Will of William Tilly, April 1, 1744, "South Carolina Wills and Probate Records, 1670–1980," vols. 72a–72b, Ancestry.com, https://www.ancestry.com/search/collections/9080/. None of the Grimballs spoke in their wills about keeping slave families together. John Jenkins's will is not extant.

Chapter Two

1. Separates also raised the concerns of the Anglican establishment, most descriptively detailed by Anglican missionary Charles Woodmason. Richard J. Hooker, ed., *The Carolina Backcountry on the Eve of the Revolution: The Journal and Other Writings of Charles Woodmason, Anglican Itinerant* (Chapel Hill: Univ. of North Carolina Press, 1953), 45, 103.
2. Philip Morgan estimates that roughly 25 percent of enslaved people in Lowcountry Georgia and South Carolina fled with the British at the end of the revolution. Morgan, *Slave Counterpoint*, 283–85, 492–95, 666; Barrington, *Welsh Neck*, lx.
3. Kidd and Hankins, *Baptists in America*, 30–45.
4. Kidd and Hankins, *Baptists in America*, 36.
5. Benedict, *General History*, vol. 2, pp. 106–8; John Asplund, *The Universal Register of the Baptist Denomination in North America* (Boston: John W. Folsom, 1794), 7; Kidd and Hankins, *Baptists in America*, 33–37. The nine ordinance Separates preached were believer's baptism, the Lord's Supper, love feasts, laying on of hands, washing feet, anointing the sick, the right hand of fellowship, the kiss of charity, and infant devotion. Regular Baptists, by contrast, adhering to the Philadelphia Confession of Faith, accepted only two ordinances, believer's baptism and the Lord's Supper. Kidd and Hankins, *Baptists in America*, 33–37.
6. Kidd and Hankins, *Baptists in America*, 36–38.
7. Benedict, *General History*, vol. 2, pp. 39, 42–43, 49; Kidd and Hankins, *Baptists in America*, 36.
8. Robert Baylor Semple, *A History of the Rise and Progress of the Baptists in Virginia* (Richmond: J. O. Lynch, 1810), 367.
9. Edwards, "Materials," vol. 4, p. 149; Kidd and Hankins, *Baptists in America*, 30–45.
10. Edwards, "Materials," vol. 4, 148-49; G. W. Paschal, "Morgan Edwards'

Materials Towards a History of the Baptists in the Province of North Carolina," *North Carolina Historical Review* 7, no. 3 (July 1930): 386; Elder John Sparks, *The Roots of Appalachian Christianity: The Life and Legacy of Elder Shubal Stearns* (Lexington: Univ. Press of Kentucky, 2001), 29–30.

11. Townsend, *South Carolina Baptists,* 125; Frederick Lewis Weis, *The Colonial Clergy of Virginia, North Carolina and South Carolina* (Boston: copyright by author, 1955), 66; J. D. Bailey, "Rev. Philip Mulkey and the Story of the First Baptist Church Planted in Upper South Carolina," *Review and Expositor* 21, no. 4 (October 1924): 433–45; William L. Lumpkin, *Baptist Foundations in the South: Tracing Through the Separates the Influence of the Great Awakening, 1754–1787* (Nashville: Broadman Press, 1961), 43.
12. Narratives of Baptist ministers Philip James (Welsh Neck) and Edmund Botsford (Welsh Neck and Georgetown, among other churches) also provide examples of God's supernatural intervention. Similarly, members of Lynches Creek Church reported the sounds of a "disembodied voice" near their homes in 1772. Barrington, *Welsh Neck*, xiv–xv. Also see Heyrman, *Southern Cross,* 28–76.
13. Edwards, "Materials," vol. 5, pp. 42–48; Kidd, *Great Awakening*, 263.
14. Baker and Craven, *Adventure in Faith,* 134.
15. Edwards, "Materials," vol. 5, p. 43.
16. Hooker, *Carolina Backcountry*, 112; Klein, *Unification*, 43.
17. Edwards, "Materials," vol. 5, pp. 43–44.
18. Minutes of the Charleston Baptist Association, 1790, BHC FU; Smith, *Order and Ardor,* 92.
19. Townsend, *South Carolina Baptists*, 125.
20. Baker and Craven, *Adventure in Faith*, 134; Thomas Ray, *Daniel and Abraham Marshall: Pioneer Baptist Evangelists to the South* (Springfield, MO: Particular Baptist Press, 2006), 1–28.
21. Benedict, *General History*, vol. 2, p. 39; Semple, *Baptists in Virginia*, 374-75.
22. Townsend, *South Carolina Baptists*, 159; Semple, *Baptists in Virginia,* 375.
23. Townsend, *South Carolina Baptists*, 174–75.
24. Paschal, "Morgan Edwards' Materials," 389–90.
25. Will of Timothy Dargan, March 8, 1761, "South Carolina Wills and Probate Records, 1670–1980," Ancestry.com, https://www.ancestry.com/search/collections/9080/; Edwards, "Materials," vol. 5, pp. 51-52; Townsend, *South Carolina Baptists*, 107–8.
26. Morgan Edwards, *Customs of Primitive Churches; Or a Set of Propositions Relative the Name, Materials, Constitution, Power, Officers, Ordinances, Rites, Business, Worship, Discipline, Government, &c. of a Church; to Which Are Added Their Proofs From Scripture; and Historical Narratives of the Manner in Which Most of Them Have Been Reduced to Practice* (Philadelphia: Andrew Steuart, 1768), 41; Smith, *Oliver Hart*, 61-62; Kidd and Hankins, *Baptists in America*,

37; Catherine A. Brekus, *Strangers and Pilgrims: Female Preaching in America, 1740–1845* (Chapel Hill: Univ. of North Carolina Press, 1998), 63–64.

27. Semple, *Baptists in Virginia*, 374 .
28. Mary Burn McDonald to Richard Furman, October 14, 1797, Richard Furman Collection, Furman University Special Collections, in "Seeking Abraham: A Report on Furman University's Task Force on Slavery and Justice," https://www.elon.edu/u/history-memory/wp-content/uploads/sites/922/2019/11/Seeking-Abraham.pdf; Klein, *Unification of a Slave State*, 44–46, 110–13, 271–72.
29. Brekus, *Strangers and Pilgrims*, 64.
30. Townsend, *South Carolina Baptists*, 174.
31. Semple, *Baptists in Virginia*, 4–5; Townsend, *South Carolina Baptists*, 125.
32. Townsend, *South Carolina Baptists*, 143–44.
33. Townsend, *South Carolina Baptists*, 143–50; Edwards, "Materials," vol. 5, pp. 51–54.
34. James A. Rogers, *Richard Furman: Life and Legacy* (Macon: Mercer Univ. Press, 1985), 3–4; Townsend, *South Carolina Baptists*, 32.
35. Rogers, *Richard Furman*, 5–10; King, *History of South Carolina Baptists*, 21–22; Will of Wood Furman, July 24, 1782, "South Carolina Wills and Probate Records, 1670–1980," vol. 1, Ancestry.com, https://www.ancestry.com/search/collections/9080/.
36. Townsend, *South Carolina Baptists*, 150–51; Rogers, *Richard Furman*, 18–19.
37. Baker and Craven, *Adventure in Faith*, 190–91.
38. Townsend, *South Carolina Baptists*, 145.
39. Baker and Craven, *Adventure in Faith*, 134; Smith, *Oliver Hart*, 88–92, 197–98, 214–21, 237–39, 294–95.
40. Townsend, *South Carolina Baptists*, 175.
41. Furman, *History of the Charleston Association*, 12–13; "Summary of Church Discipline, Shewing the Qualifications and Duties of the Officers and Members of a Gospel Church, by the Baptist Association in Charleston, South Carolina" (Charleston: David Bruce, 1774), in *Polity: Biblical Arguments on How to Conduct Church Life*, ed. Mark Dever (n.p.: Center for Church Reform, 2001), 36.
42. "Summary of Church Discipline," 116.
43. Gregory Wills, "The Church: Baptists and Their Churches in the Eighteenth and Nineteenth Centuries," in Dever, *Polity*, 19–42.
44. Townsend, *South Carolina Baptists*, 177; Durwood Stokes, "The Baptist and Methodist Clergy in South Carolina and the American Revolution," *South Carolina Historical Magazine* 73, no. 2 (April 1972): 87–96.
45. Baker and Craven, *Adventure in Faith*, 190; Rogers, *Richard Furman*, 30–31; Richard Furman, "An Address to the Residents between the Broad and Saluda Rivers Concerning the American War for Independence, November, 1775," in Rogers, *Richard Furman*, 271.

46. Ray, *Daniel and Abraham Marshall*, 23–25, 63.
47. Townsend, *South Carolina Baptists*, 178-82.
48. King, *History of South Carolina Baptists*, 91-95, 149–50; Ford, *Origins of Southern Radicalism*, 5–6.
49. Jeffrey Robert Young, ed., *Proslavery and Sectional Thought in the Early South, 1740–1829: An Anthology* (Columbia: Univ. of South Carolina Press, 2006), 173; Townsend, *South Carolina Baptists*, 177. In 1773 Botsford married Susanna Nun, born in Cork, Ireland, but living in Augusta. Nun had been baptized by Daniel Marshall. Samuel Boykin, *History of the Baptist Denomination in Georgia*, vol. 1 (Atlanta: James P. Harrison & Co., 1881), 21.
50. Smith, *Order and Ardor*, 22; Smith, *Oliver Hart*, 201–11.
51. Baker and Craven, *Adventure*, 129; Townsend, *South Carolina Baptists*, 25; Smith, *Order and Ardor*, 22; Smith, *Oliver Hart*, 219–20.
52. Smith, *Order and Ardor*, 22; Smith, *Oliver Hart*, 219–20.
53. Townsend, *South Carolina Baptists*, 25; Owens, "Oliver Hart, 1723–1795," 37.
54. Loulie Latimer Owens, "Oliver Hart and the American Revolution," *Journal of the South Carolina Baptist Historical Society* 1 (November 1975): 4; Smith, *Order and Ardor*, 91. See Keith T. Krawczynski, *William Henry Drayton: South Carolina Revolutionary Patriot* (Baton Rouge: Louisiana State Univ. Press, 2001); Newton B. Jones, ed., "Writings of the Reverend William Tennent, 1740–1777," *South Carolina Historical Magazine* 61, no. 3 (July 1960): 129–45; Edgar, *History of South Carolina*, 221–25; Smith, *Oliver Hart*, 229–37.
55. Harvey T. Cook, ed., *A Biography of Richard Furman* (Greenville: Baptist Courier Job Rooms, 1913), 50; Baker and Craven, *Adventure in Faith*, 165.
56. J. Glenwood Clayton and Louise Latimer Owens, eds., "Oliver Hart's Journey to the Backcountry," *Journal of the South Carolina Baptist Historical Society* 1 (November 1975): 18–30; Smith, *Order and Ardor*, 90–92; Walter Edgar, *Partisans and Redcoats: The Southern Conflict That Turned the Tide of the American Revolution* (New York: Perennial, 2001), 30–32.
57. Baker and Craven, *Adventure*, 129, 165–67; Smith, *Order and Ardor*, 91.
58. "Petition for Disestablishment," in Edward McCrady, *The History of South Carolina in the Revolution, 1775–1780* (London: MacMillan Company, 1901), 212–13; Cook, *Biography of Richard Furman*, 54–55; Baker and Craven, *Adventure in Faith*, 168; Fletcher M. Green, *Constitutional Development in the South Atlantic States, 1776-1860* (Chapel Hill: Univ. of North Carolina Press, 1930), 109.
59. Baker and Craven, *Adventure in Faith*, 167–68; Green, *Constitutional Development*, 110.
60. "Petition for Disestablishment," in McCrady, *South Carolina in the Revolution*, 212–13.
61. Baker and Craven, *Adventure in Faith*, 169–70.
62. Baker and Craven, *Adventure in Faith*, 170–71.

63. Furman, *Biography of Richard Furman*, 12.
64. James Foster Broome Jr., "Edmund Botsford: A Model of Regular Baptist Ministry in South Carolina" (master's thesis, Southern Baptist Theological Seminary, 1985), 31–32.
65. Smith, *Oliver Hart*, 252–58; Loulie Latimer Owens, "Oliver Hart, 1723–1795: A Brief Biography," *Baptist History and Heritage* (1966): 33–35.
66. Charles O. Walker, "Georgia's Religion in the Colonial Era, 1733–1790," *Viewpoints: Georgia Baptist Historical Society* 5 (1976): 17–44; Noel Lee Erskine, *Plantation Church: How African American Religion Was Born in Caribbean Slavery* (New York: Oxford Univ. Press, 2014), 84.
67. "Letters Showing the Rise and Progress of the Early Negro Churches of Georgia and the West Indies," *Journal of Negro History* 1, no. 1 (January 1916): 70.
68. "Letters," 70–71.
69. "Letters," 70–71.
70. John Rippon, "An Account of the Life of Mr. David George," in *Baptist Annual Register for 1790, 1791, 1792, and Part of 1793*, vol. 1 (London: Dilly, Button, and Thomas, 1793), 473–76; "Letters," 69–71; Erskine, *Plantation Church*, 85; John W. Davis, "George Liele and Andrew Bryan, Pioneer Negro Baptist Preachers," *Journal of Negro History* 3, no. 2 (April 1918): 119–27; Walter H. Brooks, "The Priority of the Silver Bluff Church and Its Promoters," *Journal of Negro History* 7, no. 2 (April 1922): 172–96; Walter H. Brooks, *The Sliver Bluff Church: A History of Negro Baptists Churches in America* (Washington: R. I. Pendleton, 1910).
71. Kidd, *Great Awakening*, 265; Rippon, "An Account of the Life of Mr. David George," 473–76.
72. Ray, *Daniel and Abraham Marshall*, 63; Alfred L. Pugh, "The Great Awakening and Baptist Beginnings in Colonial Georgia, the Bahama Islands, and Jamaica, 1739–1833," *American Baptist Quarterly* 26, no. 4 (Winter 2007): 371; Erskine, *Plantation Church*, 86.
73. In 1840 over two thousand members belonged to First African Baptist Church; over thirteen hundred to Second African; and over two hundred to Third African. Leslie M. Harris and Daina Ramey Berry, "Slave Life in Savannah: Geographies of Autonomy and Control," in *Slavery and Freedom in Savannah*, ed. Leslie M. Harris and Daina Ramey Berry (Athens: Univ. of Georgia Press), 99–102; Whittington B. Johnson, *Black Savannah, 1788–1864* (Fayetteville: Univ. of Arkansas Press, 1996), 7–15, 22. Also see David Benedict, *Fifty Years Among the Baptists* (New York: Sheldon and Company, 1860), 53–54; Ray, *Daniel and Abraham Marshall*, 59–62; Kidd, *Great Awakening*, 265; John Rippon, *The Baptist Annual Register* (London: n.p., 1793), 332–33; Frey and Wood, *Come Shouting to Zion*, 115–17, 131; Gallay, *Formation of a Planter Elite*, 52–53.
74. Elhanan Winchester, *The Reigning Abominations, Especially the Slave Trade, Considered as Causes of Lamentation: Being the Substance of a Discourse Delivered*

in Fairfax County, Virginia, December 30, 1774 (London: H. Trapp, 1778); Nathan A. Finn, "The Making of a Baptist Universalist: The Curious Case of Elhanan Winchester," *Baptist History and Heritage* 7, no. 3 (Fall 2012): 9; Hywel M. Davies, *Transatlantic Brethren: Rev. Samuel Jones (1735–1814) and His Friends: Baptists in Wales, Pennsylvania, and Beyond* (Bethlehem: Lehigh Univ. Press, 1995), 161.

75. Barrington, *Welsh Neck*, xlvii–lxx; Finn, "The Making of a Baptist Universalist," 6–18; Frey and Wood, *Come Shouting to Zion*, 102–4; Joseph Sweeny, "Elhanan Winchester and the Universalist Baptists" (PhD diss., Univ. of Pennsylvania, 1969), 34; Townsend, *South Carolina Baptists*, 69, 256, 296. Also see Edwin Martin Stone, *Biography of Rev. Elhanan Winchester* (Boston: H. B. Brewster, 1836).
76. Elhanan Winchester, *The Universal Restoration, Exhibited in Four Dialogues Between a Minister and His Friend* (Boston: Benjamin B. Mussey, 1831), ix–x; Barrington, *Welsh Neck*, l.
77. Janet Moore Lindman, *Bodies of Belief: Baptist Community in Early America* (Philadelphia: Univ. of Pennsylvania Press, 2008), 142; Finn, "The Making of a Baptist Universalist," 9; Sweeny, "Elhanan Winchester and the Universalist Baptists"; Stone, *Biography of Rev. Elhanan Winchester.*
78. Minutes of Welsh Neck Baptist Church, in Townsend, *South Carolina Baptists*, 69–70.
79. Edmund Botsford to Oliver Hart, March 30, 1785, in Mallary, *Botsford*, 63–64; also see Townsend, *South Carolina Baptists*, 27. Botsford and Furman both preached in Charleston in 1786, resulting in thirty conversions and "a considerable Effusion of the Holy Spirit" in this period of revival. Townsend, *South Carolina Baptists*, 28.
80. Minutes of Welsh Neck Baptist Church, in Barrington, *Welsh Neck*, xciii.
81. Minutes of Welsh Neck Baptist Church, in Townsend, *South Carolina Baptists*, 75.
82. Talbert and Farish, *Antipedo Baptists*, 52; Townsend, *South Carolina Baptists*, 256.
83. Townsend, *South Carolina Baptists*, 256.
84. Smith, *Order and Ardor*, 98; Lindman, *Baptist Bodies*, 141–42.
85. William Rogers, *A Sermon Occasioned by the Death of the Rev. Oliver Hart, A.M.: Who Departed This Life, Dec. 31, 1795, in the 73d Year of His Age* (Philadelphia: Lang and Ustick, 1796).
86. Rogers, *Sermon*, 24. Between 1783 and 1804, Connecticut, New Jersey, New York, Pennsylvania, and Rhode Island passed gradual emancipation laws. New Jersey's law, passed in 1804, stipulated that children born to slave parents after July 4, 1804, would be free upon turning twenty-one (women) or twenty-five (men). James J. Gigantino II, *The Ragged Road to Abolition: Slavery and Freedom in New Jersey, 1775–1865* (Philadelphia: Univ. of Pennsylvania Press, 2015), 1–17.

87. Richard Furman, *Rewards of Grace Conferred On Christ's Faithful People: A Sermon, Occasioned by the Decease of the Rev. Oliver Hart, A.M. Pastor of the Baptist Church at Hopewell, in the State of New-Jersey: Who Departed this Life, December 31, 1795, in the Seventy-Third Year of his Age* (Charleston: J. M'Iver, 1796), 2.

Chapter Three

1. Minutes of the State Convention of the Baptist Denomination, 1822, BHC, FU.
2. Baker and Craven, *Adventure in Faith*, 184.
3. Rogers, *Richard Furman*, 54–55, 59; Hugh Charles Haynsworth, *Haynsworth-Furman and Allied Families (Including Ancestry and Descendants of Sarah Morse Haynsworth)* (Sumter: Osteen Publishing Company, 1942), 122–23. The 1790 census lists Furman as holding six enslaved people. 1790 United States Federal Census, South Carolina, https://www.ancestryheritagequest.com/discoveryui-content/view/376856:5058?_phsrc=fyt1233&_phstart=successSource&gsfn=richard&gsln=furman&ml_rpos=1&queryId=2a96771adc941a1febc1d99cf7dca80a.
4. Carolyn L. Harrell, *Kith and Kin: A Portrait of a Southern Family (1630–1984)* (Macon: Mercer Univ. Press, 1984), 28, 298; Rogers, *Richard Furman*, 67, 184; Baker and Craven, *Adventure in Faith*, 209.
5. Rogers, *Richard Furman*, 84–85.
6. Richard Furman to Sarah Haynsworth, October 29, 1788, cited in Rogers, *Richard Furman*, 84–85.
7. Minutes of the Charleston Baptist Association, October 29, 1788, BHC, FU; Rogers, *Richard Furman*, 85.
8. Baker and Craven, *Adventure in Faith*, 206; *Journal of the Constitutional Convention of South Carolina, May 10, 1790-June 3, 1790* (Columbia: State Commercial Printing Co., 1946), 3, 5, 6, 11; Rogers, *Richard Furman*, 70; James Lowell Underwood, *The Constitution of South Carolina*, vol. 3, *Church and State, Morality and Free Expression* (Columbia: Univ. of South Carolina Press, 1992), 39–40. Others ministers who took part in the 1790 convention included Baptists Nathaniel Walker, Richard Shackelford, and Evan Pugh as well as Episcopal minister Dr. Henry Purcell, who had served as chaplain to Patriot forces during the American Revolution. Rogers, *Richard Furman*, 70.
9. Talbert and Farish, *Antipedo Baptists*, 34.
10. Rogers, *Richard Furman*, 213; Townsend, *South Carolina Baptists*, 31.
11. Rogers, *Richard Furman*, 210–13.
12. "America's Deliverance and Duty: A Sermon Preached at the Baptist Church of Charleston, South Carolina, on the Fourth of July, 1802, before the State Society of the Cincinnati and the American Revolution Society; and the Congregation which usually attends Divine Service in the Said Church, by Richard Furman, D.D.," as cited in Rogers, *Richard Furman*, 212.

13. Rogers, *Richard Furman*, 89–90, 210–11; Cook, *Biography of Richard Furman*, 135–55.
14. Rogers, *Richard Furman*, 210–211; Minutes of the Charleston Baptist Association, 1804, BHC, FU; Aaron Menikoff, *Politics and Piety: Baptist Social Reform in America, 1770–1860* (Eugene: Pickwick Publications, 2014), 51–52.
15. Rogers, *Richard Furman*, 71.
16. *Reports of the British and Foreign Bible Society, with Extracts of Correspondence, &c., Volume the Second, for 1811, 1812, and 1813* (London: J. Tilling, Grosvenor-Row, Chelsea, 1813), 69–73; John Fea, *The Bible Cause: A History of the American Bible Society* (New York: Oxford Univ. Press, 2016), 21; Charleston *Courier*, May 21, July 30, 1817, in Marvin R. Zahniser, *Charles Cotesworth Pinckney: Founding Father* (Chapel Hill: Univ. of North Carolina Press, 1967), 272–75; Rogers, *Richard Furman*, 210.
17. Minutes of the Charleston Baptist Association, 1786, in Cook, *Biography of Richard Furman*, 42; Rogers, *Richard Furman*, 118; Wood Furman, *A History of the Charleston Association of Baptist Churches in the State of South-Carolina: With An Appendix Containing the Principal Circular Letters to the Churches* (Charleston: J. Hoff, 1811), 19.
18. Rogers, *Richard Furman*, 123. British Baptist ministers and missionaries in England had formed the Particular Baptist Society for the Propagation of the Gospel Amongst the Heathen in 1792.
19. Rogers, *Richard Furman*, 117–25; Baker and Craven, *Adventure in Faith*, 223–25. As Hart did, Furman attempted to have churches send money earmarked for education through the association. Furman hoped to incorporate the Charleston Association so that it could "hold and administer funds and property for educational purposes," but many ministers, including Edmund Botsford, disagreed, resulting in Furman suggesting a separate corporation (the Education Fund) that worked in alliance with the association. Rogers, *Richard Furman*, 118.
20. Rogers, *Richard Furman*, 124–25. Brown University began as Rhode Island College. It began in 1764 in Warren, Rhode Island, moving to Providence in 1770. The Philadelphia Baptist Association founded the school as a seminary for Baptists. South Carolina and Georgia Baptists helped raise funds for the college, as did Baptists in England and Ireland as well as in the northern colonies. Rueben A. Guild, *History of Brown University, with Illustrative Documents* (Providence: privately printed, 1867), 113, cited in Rogers, *Richard Furman*, 124.
21. Rogers, *Richard Furman*, 125–27; King, *History of South Carolina Baptists*, 163–65. Furman also supported the founding of South Carolina College in 1801, proposing Baptist minister and president of Rhode Island College Jonathan Maxcy as president; the proposal was accepted. At its inaugural commencement in 1807, the college, which opened to students in 1805, bestowed unto Furman a Doctor of Divinity degree. Daniel Walker Hollis, *University of South Carolina:*

South Carolina College (Columbia: Univ. of South Carolina Press, 1951), 34; Rogers, *Richard Furman*, 131–33.

22. Minutes of the Charleston Baptist Association, 1800, BHC, FU; Baker and Craven, *Adventure in Faith*, 226.
23. Baker and Craven, *Adventure in Faith*, 226–27; Rogers, *Richard Furman*, 138–40.
24. Minutes of the Bethel Baptist Association, 1800, BHC, FU; Townsend, *South Carolina Baptists*, 300. The best treatment of the Great Revival remains John Boles, *The Great Revival: Beginnings of the Bible Belt* (Lexington: Univ. Press of Kentucky, 1972). Also see Dickson J. Bruce Jr., *And They All Sang Hallelujah: Plain-Folk Camp-Meeting Religion, 1800–1845* (Knoxville: Univ. of Tennessee Press, 1981); Ellen Eslinger, *Citizens of Zion: The Social Origins of Camp Meeting Revivalism* (Knoxville: Univ. of Tennessee Press, 1999).
25. Townsend, *South Carolina Baptists*, 297. Also see Peter N. Moore, *World of Toil and Strife: Community Transformation in Backcountry South Carolina, 1750–1805* (Columbia: Univ of South Carolina Press, 2007).
26. Townsend, *South Carolina Baptists*, 297–305.
27. Leah Townsend wrote that "Padgett's Creek received many of its thirty-two negroes during the revival years." Townsend, *South Carolina Baptists*, 258.
28. The proliferation of churches resulting from the revival led to the creation of new Upcountry associations. Fourteen churches that had formerly belonged to the Bethel Association created the Broad River Association in 1800. Three years later, eleven churches were dismissed from the Bethel Association to form, along with six new churches, the Saluda Association. Townsend, *South Carolina Baptists*, 301–5.
29. Richard Furman to John Rippon, August 11, 1802, in Rogers, *Richard Furman*, 109.
30. *City Gazette and Daily Advertiser*, December 10, 1803, in McCurry, *Masters of Small Worlds*, 147–48; Howe, *Presbyterian Church in South Carolina*, vol. 2, pp. 64–65, 112.
31. James Hazzard Cuthbert, *Life of Richard Fuller* (New York: Sheldon and Company, 1878), 20. The Beaufort church began as an "arm" of Euhaw Church, off of the "high road leading from Georgia to Charleston, about sixty miles down the coast from Charleston," and was established in 1746. Dr. Henry Holcombe served as pastor of Euhaw church from 1791–1798. Because of sickness, Holcombe moved his family to Beaufort—about twenty-five miles away—in 1795, where he began Beaufort Church originally as an arm of Euhaw. Holcombe moved to Savannah in 1799 to take charge of the church there. His successor, Joseph B. Cook, saw an increase in church membership in both Euhaw and Beaufort, so much so that the Beaufort church became its own church in January 1804. Cook became the pastor of the church, leaving the pastorate at Euhaw. William Johnson's

father, Joseph Johnson, also joined the Beaufort church (leaving Euhaw). Revival occurred in full later that year. Henry Holcombe later became pastor of Philadelphia's First Baptist Church. Hortense Woodson, *Giant in the Land: The Life of William B. Johnson, First President of the Southern Baptist Convention, 1845–1851* (Springfield, MO: Particular Baptist Press, 1950), 7–11, 36; John B. Boles, "Henry Holcombe, A Southern Baptist Reformer in the Age of Jefferson," *Georgia Historical Quarterly* 54, no. 3 (Fall 1970): 381–407.

32. Townsend, *South Carolina Baptists*, 299; Rogers, *Richard Furman*, 107–15.
33. J. Glenwood Clayton, ed., "Reminiscences of William Bullein Johnson, Part 2," *Journal of the South Carolina Baptist Historical Society* 5 (November 1979): 10; G. Winfred Hervey, *The Story of Baptist Missions in Foreign Lands: From the Time of Carey to the Present Date* (St. Louis: Chancy R. Barns, 1882), 172–98.
34. Clayton, "Reminiscences of Johnson, Part 2," 10. Luther Rice credited Johnson with the idea behind the Philadelphia meeting. Rice wrote to Georgia Baptist Jesse Mercer that Rice discussed with Johnson the possibility of "a general combination or concert of action" between the newly formed foreign mission societies in the southern states. Johnson supported a national meeting and proposed Philadelphia as a convenient location. Rogers, *Richard Furman*, 144–45.
35. Clayton, "Reminiscences of Johnson, Part 2," 10–11; *Proceedings of the Baptist Convention for Missionary Purposes; Held in Philadelphia, in May, 1814* (Philadelphia: A. Coles, 1814), 6-7.
36. Rogers, *Richard Furman*, 147–57.
37. Rogers, *Richard Furman*, 157.
38. *Proceedings of the Baptist Convention for Missionary Purposes; Held in Philadelphia, in May, 1814*, 3.
39. *Proceedings of the Baptist Convention for Missionary Purposes; Held in Philadelphia, in May, 1814*, 24.
40. Clayton, "Reminiscences of Johnson, Part 2," 11. Baptists formalized their support for domestic missions into the American Baptist Home Mission Society in 1832. The Home Mission Society had an independent board separate from the General Convention for Foreign Missions. When southern Baptists formed the Southern Baptist Convention in 1845, they placed foreign and domestic missions under centralized control. Robert Baker, *Relations Between Northern and Southern Baptists* (n.p.: n.p., 1948), 28–42, 156–83; Robert Baker, *The Southern Baptist Convention and Its People* (Nashville: Broadman Press, 1974), 113–17.
41. Guild, *History of Brown University*, 3–27; Kidd and Hankins, *Baptists in America*, 42–43.
42. *Proceedings of the Baptist Convention for Missionary Purposes; Held in Philadelphia, in May, 1814*, 42; Woodson, *Giant*, 39; Nathan O. Hatch, *The Democratization of American Christianity* (New Haven: Yale Univ. Press, 1989), 94–95.
43. Minutes of the Triennial Convention, 1817, in King, *History of South Carolina Baptists*, 168.

44. Furman preached in 1817 about "the very serious and religious importance of a well-informed ministry." Woodson, *Giant*, 39. Baptist missionary Luther Rice took the lead in founding Columbian College, which opened in 1821 in Washington, DC. King, *History of South Carolina Baptists*, 168; Baker and Craven, *Adventure in Faith*, 232–37; Rogers, *Richard Furman*, 190–95.
45. Charles Herbert Stockton, "Historical Sketch of George Washington University, Washington, D.C., Formerly Known as Columbian University and Columbian College, Accompanied by a Sketch of the Lives of the Presidents," *Records of the Columbia Historical Society, Washington, DC* 19 (1916): 18–19.
46. Stockton, "George Washington University," 18.
47. For information about Georgia Baptists, see Colyer Meriwether, *History of Higher Education in South Carolina, With A Sketch of the Free School System* (Washington, DC: Government Printing Office, 1889), 60–71; Samuel Boykin, *History of the Baptist Denomination in Georgia*, vol. 1 (Atlanta: James P. Harrison and Co.), 143–60; Spright Dowell, *A History of Mercer University, 1833–1953* (Macon: Mercer Univ. Press, 1958).
48. Fannie Exile Soudder Heck, *In Royal Service: The Mission Work of Southern Baptist Women* (Richmond: Foreign Mission Board, Southern Baptist Convention, 1913), 28, 35; *Baptist Magazine* 7 (December 1815): 520.
49. Hortense Woodson, *History of the Edgefield Baptist Association, 1807–1957*, (Edgefield: Edgefield Advertiser Press), 69–70; Loulie Latimer Owens, *Banners in the Wind* (Columbia: Women's Missionary Union of South Carolina, 1950), 1–10. Hepzibah Townsend must have been a forceful personality within her own household. In 1833 her husband Daniel attached a codicil to his will stating that he had "reason to fear" that his wife might be unhappy with the "the just and ample provision" he had allotted her in his will. Daniel hoped "to do everything in my power" to make Hepzibah "contented and happy," so he made it possible for her to claim a specific tract of land that Daniel had initially willed to one of his sons. Will of Daniel Townsend, March 7, 1833, "South Carolina Wills and Probate Records, 1670–1980," Ancestry.com, https://www.ancestry.com/search/collections/9080/. By the 1830s female mite societies existed in churches in Beaufort as well as Charleston District. McCurry, *Masters of Small Worlds*, 189. The earliest women's missionary society started in 1800 in Boston. By 1814, the date of the first Triennial Convention, almost fifty local societies existed, primarily in the North. Heck, *In Royal Service*, 35–36.
50. Heck, *In Royal Service*, 26–27.
51. King, *History of South Carolina Baptists*, 260; Cornelius, *Slave Missions*, 27–29; W. J. Megginson, *African American Life in South Carolina's Upper Piedmont, 1780-1900* (Columbia: University of South Carolina Press, 2006), 99.
52. Minutes of the Edgefield Baptist Association, 1831, BHC, FU.
53. Rogers, *Richard Furman*, 217–19; Manly, *Mercy and Judgment*, 61–62.
54. Richard Furman, John M. Roberts, and Joseph B. Cook, *To the Different*

Associations of the State Baptist Convention of South Carolina, November 8, 1820, cited in Rogers, *Richard Furman*, 232–33.

55. Furman, Roberts, and Cook, *To the Different Associations*, in Rogers, *Richard Furman*, 232–33.
56. King, *History of South Carolina Baptists*, 169–71.
57. Minutes of the State Convention of the Baptist Denomination, 1821, BHC, FU.
58. Minutes of the State Convention of the Baptist Denomination, 1821, BHC, FU.
59. Minutes of the State Convention of the Baptist Denomination, 1822, BHC, FU; King, *History of South Carolina Baptists*, 173–75.
60. King, *History of South Carolina Baptists*, 341.
61. Minutes of the State Convention of the Baptist Denomination, 1822.
62. Basil Manly to Iveson Brookes, September 24, 1821, in A. James Fuller, *Chaplain to the Confederacy: Basil Manly and Baptist Life in the Old South* (Baton Rouge: Louisiana State Univ. Press, 2000), 43–44.
63. Basil Manly to Iveson Brookes, September 24, 1821, in Fuller, *Chaplain*, 43–44.
64. Fuller, *Chaplain*, 43–56.
65. J. Glenwood Clayton, ed., "Reminiscences of William Bullein Johnson, Part 3," *Journal of the South Carolina Baptist Historical Society* 7 (November 1981): 4; Woodson, *Giant*, 50; Judith T. Bainbridge, *Academy and College: The History of the Woman's College of Furman University* (Macon: Mercer Univ. Press, 2001), 7.
66. Clayton, "Reminiscences of Johnson, Part 3," 5; Archie Vernon Huff Jr., *Greenville: The History of the City and County in the South Carolina Piedmont* (Columbia: Univ. of South Carolina Press, 1995), 89–94.
67. Clayton, "Reminiscences of Johnson, Part 3," 5; Bainbridge, *Academy and College*, 6–7. In a survey of Greenville newspapers, Archie Vernon Huff found that "thirty-four private schools and academies were mentioned" between 1820 and 1860. "Sixteen of these were located in the village and eighteen in rural areas." Huff, *Greenville*, 94–95.
68. As Judith Bainbridge writes, teaching women Greek and Latin "was unusual, perhaps unique at the time." Bainbridge, *Academy and College*, 8. She references ads in the Greenville *Republican*, June 30, 1827.
69. Clayton, "Reminiscences of Johnson, Part 3," 5; Woodson, *Giant*, 51.
70. Clayton, "Reminiscences of Johnson, Part 3," 5. Mary died in 1825 at the age of twenty. Johnson wrote in his reminiscences that Mary died at the age of "20 years, 10 months and 5 days. She was a child universally beloved." Woodson, *Giant*, 51–52.
71. Clayton, "Reminiscences of Johnson, Part 3," 4–6.
72. Clayton, "Reminiscences of Johnson, Part 3," 4.
73. Clayton, "Reminiscences of Johnson, Part 3," 11; Woodson, *Giant*, 52; Minutes of the Greenville Baptist Church, 1831, BHC, FU.

74. Clayton, "Reminiscences of Johnson, Part 3," 5; King, *History of South Carolina Baptists*, 229–30.
75. King, *History of South Carolina Baptists*, 229–30; Garrett, *Saluda Baptist Association*, 30. When the association withdrew from the Baptist State Convention, missionary delegates formed an auxiliary society to collect money to send to the convention. Clayton, "Reminiscences of Johnson, Part 3," 4.
76. "Rev. Dr. Furman," *American Baptist Magazine* 5, no. 10 (October 1825): 317; Rogers, *Richard Furman*, 254–55.
77. Minutes of the Charleston Baptist Association, 1825, BHC, FU; "Memoir of Richard Furman, D.D., Late Pastor of the Baptist Church in Charleston, S.C.," *American Baptist Magazine* 6, no. 3 (March 1826): 69–76.
78. King, *History of South Carolina Baptists*, 181.
79. King, *History of South Carolina Baptists*, 184–85.
80. Board of Agents minutes, March 16–17, 1826, in King, *History of South Carolina Baptists*, 186.
81. Minutes of the State Convention of the Baptist Denomination, 1834, in King, *History of South Carolina Baptists*, 186. Warne left $40,000 to foreign missions upon his death.
82. King, *History of South Carolina Baptists*, 180–88.
83. King, *History of South Carolina Baptists*, 188. January 3 and 5, 1827.
84. Greenville *Mountaineer*, August 8, 1829, cited in Bainbridge, *Academy and College*, 9–10.
85. Minutes of the State Convention of the Baptist Denomination, 1826, BHC, FU; King, *History of South Carolina Baptists*, 188.
86. King, *History of South Carolina Baptists*, 189.
87. King, *History of South Carolina Baptists*, 190–98.

Chapter Four

1. Eighmy, "The Baptists and Slavery," 666–73. Both whites and blacks were subject to church discipline, where church members held one another accountable for acting in godly ways. Church discipline followed a specific racial hierarchy. While enslaved people could at times instigate charges against whites, very seldom were they allowed to testify against them. Discipline provided enslaved people (as well as white women) significant opportunities to claim agency for themselves but also reinforced both a racial and gendered hierarchy within churches. See especially Wills, *Democratic Religion;* Robert Elder, *The Sacred Mirror: Evangelicalism, Honor, and Identity in the Deep South, 1790–1860* (Chapel Hill: Univ. of North Carolina Press, 2016).
2. Townsend, *South Carolina Baptists*, 242.

3. Staughton's church in England refused to grant him a letter of dismission because of the "adulterous" connection the minister had with divorcee Maria Hanson. The two traveled to South Carolina together and were married by Furman, who corresponded closely with English Baptists before performing the sacrament. After leaving South Carolina, the Staughtons traveled first to New York. Staughton later served as pastor of Philadelphia's First Baptist Church as well as Sansom Street Baptist Church (which broke away from the Philadelphia Church). One of the best-known preachers in Philadelphia, Staughton served as the first president of Columbian College, later George Washington University. S. W. Lynd, ed., *Memoir of the Rev. William Staughton, D.D.* (Boston: Lincoln, Edmands, 1834), 27–37; Talbert and Farish, *Antipedo Baptists*, 37–39. Furman felt some concern that some of his Charleston parishioners wished Staughton to serve as assistant or co-pastor of the Charleston church. See Rogers, *Richard Furman*, 78–84; Tupper, *Two Centuries*, 147.
4. Ford, *Deliver Us from Evil*, 87.
5. Ford, *Deliver Us from Evil*, 88.
6. David J. McCord, ed., *The Statutes at Large of South Carolina*, vol. 7 (Columbia: A. S. Johnston, 1840), 440–43; Talbert and Farish, *Antipedo Baptists*, 53; Ford, *Deliver Us From Evil*, 82–92. The law making manumission more difficult stipulated that masters had to present their petition to a local magistrate's court, attesting that they were freeing enslaved people who could provide for themselves and whose behavior would not be a deterrent to society. The manumission law "constituted a dramatic departure from South Carolina's usual policy of refusing to interfere with a master's authority over [enslaved people]. Breaking with tradition, the new law limited the master's control over his property in the interest of white safety." Ford, *Deliver Us from Evil*, 86–90.
7. Ford, *Deliver Us from Evil*, 88.
8. Minutes of the Charleston Baptist Association, 1800, BHC, FU. Furman also referenced the mutual duties of masters and enslaved people at the 1779 meeting of the Charleston Association. Tise, *Proslavery*, 38.
9. "Petition of the Inhabitants of Chester District Asking a Revision in the Law Which Impairs the Giving of Religious Instruction to Slaves and Free Persons of Colour," c. 1801, Petitions to the General Assembly (S165015), South Carolina Department of Archives and History (hereafter SCDAH).
10. "Petition of the Members of the Charleston Baptist Association Asking Revision in the Law Which Impairs Ministers in Giving Religious Instruction to Slaves and Free Persons of Colour," October 31, 1801Petitions to the General Assembly (S165015), SCDAH; "Petition of the Inhabitants of Chester District," 1801, SCDAH.
11. "Petition of the Charleston Baptist Association," 1801.
12. "Petition of the Charleston Baptist Association," 1801.

13. "Petition of the Charleston Baptist Association," 1801.
14. Ford, *Deliver Us from Evil*, 93.
15. Benedict, *General History*, vol. 2, pp. 145–46. For discussion of the hierarchical and racialized religious perspectives of Federalists Henry William DeSaussure and Charles Cotesworth Pinckney, see Jonathan J. Den Hartog, *Patriotism and Piety: Federalist Politics and Religious Struggle in the New American Nation* (Charlottesville: Univ. of Virginia Press, 2015), 141–64. Also see James H. Broussard, *The Southern Federalists, 1800–1816* (Baton Rouge: Louisiana State Univ. Press, 1978); Lisle A. Rose, *Prologue to Democracy: The Federalists in the South, 1789–1800* (Lexington: Univ. Press of Kentucky, 1968).
16. Talbert and Farish, *Antipedo Baptists*, 54; Ford, *Deliver Us from Evil*, 93.
17. Ford, *Deliver Us from Evil*, 93.
18. Courts "were hesitant to allow the interruption of a religious service unless a clear black majority was present. In fact, some courts refused to allow slave patrols to disperse a peaceful congregation even if a black majority was present, or if the racial makeup of the service could not be ascertained." Nicholas May, "Holy Rebellion: Religious Assembly Laws in Antebellum South Carolina and Virginia," *American Journal of Legal History* 49, no. 3 (July 2007): 246–47; Ford, *Deliver Us from Evil*, 93–94.
19. Clayton, "Reminiscences, of Johnson, Part 2," 15–16.
20. Clayton, "Reminiscences, of Johnson, Part 2," 16–17. For the Curse of Ham, see Stephen R. Hayne, *Noah's Curse: The Biblical Justification of American Slavery* (New York: Oxford Univ. Press, 2002); and David M. Goldenberg, *Black and Slave: The Origins of the Curse of Ham* (Berlin: De Gruyter 2017), 146–59.
21. Clayton, "Reminiscences of Johnson, Part 2," 17.
22. Clayton, "Reminiscences of Johnson, Part 2," 17.
23. Richard Furman, "Questions on Slavery," 36–37, Richard Furman D.D. Papers, 1777-1825, BHC, FU.
24. Furman, "Questions on Slavery," 4. Recent histories have viewed southern slavery (and southern proslavery) as modern in orientation, part of a capitalist world, in contrast to earlier assertions that the southern slave system was strongly premodern. See Dale W. Tomich, *Through the Prism of Slavery: Labor, Capital, and World Economy* (Lanham, MD: Rowman and Littlefield, 2004); Adam Rothman, *Slave Country: American Expansion and the Origins of the Deep South* (Cambridge: Harvard Univ. Press, 2005); Edward E. Baptist, *The Half That Has Never Been Told: Slavery and the Making of American Capitalism* (New York: Basic Books, 2014); Sven Rockman, *Empire of Cotton: A Global History* (New York: Knopf, 2014); Anthony Kaye, "The Second Slavery: Modernity in the Nineteenth-Century South and the Atlantic World," *Journal of Southern History* 75, no. 3 (August 2009): 627–50; Luke E. Harlow, "The South, The North, Hope,

and Historical Change," *Journal of Southern Religion* 18 (2017): jsreligion.org /vol18/harlow.

25. Furman, "Questions on Slavery," 22–23.
26. Ibid., 23.
27. Ibid., 5.
28. Ibid., 4–5.
29. Ibid., 6–7. The colonization movement of the late 1810s and 1820s did not gain widespread traction in South Carolina. Baptist Associations in South Carolina made no direct reference to such efforts, although some ministers supported colonization. In 1819, while a student at South Carolina College, Basil Manly Sr., made a speech to the Clariosophic Society in favor of colonization, although it is unclear if his arguments were his own beliefs or whether they were designed specifically for debate. More than a decade later, in the early 1830s, Manly supported the colonization efforts of a group of free blacks in Charleston. Basil Manly Jr. also advocated for colonization. When Richard Fuller made public remarks about colonization in the early 1850s, he faced a backlash in South Carolina. Fuller, *Chaplain to the Confederacy*, 30–35, 122–23; Anne C. Loveland, *Southern Evangelicals and the Social Order, 1800–1860* (Baton Rouge: Louisiana State Univ. Press, 1980), 213–16; James M. Manley, "The Southern Baptist Mind in Transition: A Life of Basil Manly, Jr., 1825–1892" (PhD diss., University of Florida, 1999), 120. For white South Carolina's repudiation of colonization efforts, see Ford, *Deliver Us from Evil*, 304, 311–17.
30. Furman, "Questions on Slavery," 6–8.
31. Ibid., 21.
32. Minutes of the Charleston Baptist Association, 1808, BHC, FU.
33. Talbert and Farish, *Antipedo Baptists*, 50–51.
34. Mallary, *Botsford*, 151–52; Talbert and Farish, *Antipedo Baptists*, 52.
35. Mallary, *Botsford*, 132, 209; Talbert and Farish, *Antipedo Baptists*, 55.
36. Edmund Botsford to Richard Furman, May 26, 1812, cited in Talbert and Farish, *Antipedo Baptists*, 52.
37. Edmund Botsford, *Sambo and Toney: A Dialogue in Three Parts* (Georgetown: Francis M. Baxter, 1808), 4–18.
38. Edmund Botsford to Richard Furman, October 15, 1808, Edmund Botsford Papers, SCHBC, cited in Mallary, *Botsford*, 91; Talbert and Farish, *Antipedo Baptists*, 59, 149–50.
39. Ford, *Deliver Us from Evil*, 157–61.
40. Benedict asked southern ministers their views of slavery, but only a handful responded; "few," wrote Benedict, "seemed inclined to say much about it." Botsford, by contrast, "entered cheerfully and ingenuously upon the subject." David Benedict, *A General History of the Baptist Denomination in America, and Other Parts of the World*, vol. 2 (London: Lincoln and Edmands, 1813), 207–13,

quote on 209. For a study of Whitefield and slavery, see Kidd, *George Whitefield*, 97–100, 108–12, 188–90; Jessica M. Parr, *Inventing George Whitefield: Race, Revivalism, and the Making of a Religious Icon* (Oxford: Univ. Press of Mississippi, 2015), 61–70, 76–80, 103–5, 109–11, 146–53.

41. [Edmund Botsford], "Essay On Slavery," n.d., Botsford Family Papers, 1769–1869, BHC, FU. Also see Andrew Lee Feight, "Edmund Botsford and Richard Furman: Slavery in the Lowcountry, 1766–1825," *Journal of the South Carolina Baptist Historical Society* 19 (November 1993): 2–22; Andrew Lee Feight, "'The Good and the Just': Slavery and the Development of Evangelical Protestantism in the American South, 1700–1830 (PhD diss., University of Kentucky, 2001); Ford, *Deliver Us from Evil*, 157–61, 169–70.
42. Benedict, *General History*, vol. 2, p. 209.
43. Minutes of Bush River Baptist Church, Newberry District, September 1793; October 1794; October 1795; 1802–1805, all cited in Townsend, *South Carolina Baptists*, 258.
44. Minutes of Cedar Spring Baptist Church, Spartanburg District, November 1795–1804, cited in Townsend, *South Carolina Baptists*, 258.
45. Minutes of Tyger River Baptist Church [Friendship], March–June 1802; October 1804, both cited in Townsend, *South Carolina Baptists*, 259.
46. Minutes of Lower Fairforest Baptist Church, Union District, November 1811; March 26, 1812; April 27, 1816; July 27, 1817, all cited in Allan D. Charles, "Black-White Relations in an Antebellum Church in the Carolina Upcountry," *South Carolina Historical Magazine* 89, 4 (October, 1998): 222–23.
47. Minutes of Lower Fairforest Baptist Church, Union District, April 27, 1811, cited in Charles, "Black-White Relations," 222.
48. Minutes of Lower Fairforest Baptist Church, July 27, 1817; August 3, 1817; May 27, 1820; December 1820; October 1822, all cited in Charles, "Black-White Relations," 222–23.
49. Minutes of Big Creek Baptist Church, May 3, 1823, South Caroliniana Library, University of South Carolina (hereafter SCL, USC).
50. Minutes of Big Creek Baptist Church, September 10, 1823, SCL, USC.
51. Minutes of Big Creek Baptist Church, September 10, 1823, SCL, USC.
52. Minutes of Big Creek Baptist Church, September 17, 1823; June 29, 1833; July 28, 1833; November 16, 1833, SCL, USC.
53. Minutes of Salem Baptist Church, Edgefield District, July 1830; October 25, 1830, BHC, FU.
54. Fuller, *Chaplain to the Confederacy*, 72–74.
55. Fraser, *Charleston, Charleston!*, 201; Douglas R. Egerton, *He Shall Go Out Free: The Lives of Denmark Vesey* (Madison: Madison House, 1999), 126–202; Ford, *Deliver Us from Evil*, 205–56.
56. See Edgerton, *He Shall Go Out Free*, 3–288; Douglas R. Egerton and Robert L.

Paquette, *The Denmark Vesey Affair: A Documentary History* (Gainesville: Univ. Press of Florida, 2017). For a compelling story about differing perspectives on slavery in Charleston from 1865 to modern times, see Ethan J. Kytle and Blain Roberts, *Denmark Vesey's Garden: Slavery and Memory in the Cradle of the Confederacy* (New York: New Press, 2018).

57. Ford, *Deliver Us from Evil*, 209–27; Egerton, *He Shall Go Out Free,* 3–125; David Brion Davis, *The Problem of Slavery in the Age of Emancipation* (New York: Knopf, 2014), 78–79, 209–10; May, "Holy Rebellion," 248–50.
58. May, "Holy Rebellion," 249–50; Egerton, *He Shall Go Out Free*, 109–11, 116, 120–23; Ford, *Deliver Us from Evil,* 181–83, 185, 196.
59. May, "Holy Rebellion," 250; Ford, *Deliver Us from Evil,* 181–85.
60. May, "Holy Rebellion," 249.
61. May, "Holy Rebellion," 249.
62. Lionel H. Kennedy and Thomas Parker, *An Official Report of the Trials of Sundry Negroes Charged with an Attempt to Raise an Insurrection in the State of South-Carolina* (Charleston: James R. Schenck, 1822), cited in May, "Holy Rebellion," 249.
63. Edgar, *South Carolina,* 328–29; Fraser, *Charleston, Charleston!,* 202–3
64. James Hamilton, *Negro Plot: An Account of the Late Intended Insurrection among a Portion of the Blacks in the City of Charleston, South Carolina* (Boston: Printed and Published by Joseph W. Ingraham), 31; Ford, *Deliver Us from Evil*, 229-33.
65. The Charleston church minutes did not include separate tallies for black versus white members until 1827. That year, the church clerk recorded 165 white and 697 black members (19 percent white, 81 percent black). Baker and Craven, *Adventure in Faith*, 251. In 1795 Bishop Francis Asbury estimated that only about 70 (29 percent) of the 240 members were white. Townsend, *South Carolina Baptists*, 29.
66. "Rules and Regulations of the Colored Ministers, Elders and Members of the Baptist Church in Charleston, South Carolina, University of South Carolina," (Charleston: First Baptist Church, 1819), cited in Timothy James Lockley, *Line in the Sand: Race and Class in Lowcountry Georgia, 1750–1860* (Athens: Univ. of Georgia Press, 2001), 239.
67. Others, such as Episcopalian minister Frederick Dalcho and Federalist politician William Henry DeSaussure, made similar arguments. Frederick Dalcho, *Practical Considerations Founded on the Scriptures Relative to the Slave Population of South-Carolina* (Charleston: A. E. Miller, 1823); William Henry DeSaussure, *A Series of Numbers Addressed to the Public, on the Subject of the Slaves and Free People of Color* (Columbia: State Gazette Office, 1822).
68. Robert Paquette and Douglas Egerton, "Of Facts and Fables: New Light on the Denmark Vesey Affair," *South Carolina Historical Magazine* vol. 105, no. 1 (January 2004): 11–16; Ford, *Deliver Us from Evil*, 253–57.

69. Minutes of the State Convention of the Baptist Denomination, 1822, BHC, FU.
70. Minutes of the State Convention of the Baptist Denomination, 1822, BHC, FU.
71. Rogers, *Richard Furman*, 224.
72. Richard Furman, *Exposition of the Views of the Baptists, Relative to the Coloured Population of the United States, in a Communication to the Governor of South Carolina* (Charleston: A. E. Miller, 1823).
73. Furman, *Exposition*, 9. Andrew Lee Feight argues that Furman's 1822/23 *Exposition* retained many of the arguments he made in his 1807 letter about Christian slavery but with one significant change—Furman in 1822/23 no longer admitted that slavery could be a natural, political, or moral evil. This "shift in tone" reveals the changing nature of South Carolina society by the 1820s, whereby questioning slavery because of revolutionary beliefs had shifted to a more conservative stance. Feight, "Edmund Botsford and Richard Furman," 14. Also see Anne C. Loveland, "Richard Furman's 'Questions on Slavery,'" *Baptist History and Heritage* 10 (July 1975): 191; Loveland, *Southern Evangelicals and the Social Order*, 217.
74. Abolitionist Thomas Wentworth Higginson noted sardonically in June 1861 that Charleston whites proposed various reasons for the revolt. "The negroes rebelled because they were deluded by Congressional eloquence, or because they were excited by a church squabble, or because they had been spoilt by mistaken indulgences, such as being allowed to learn to read," Higginson wrote. "So the Baptist Convention seems to have thought it was because they [the insurrectionists] were not Baptists, and an Episcopal pamphleteer [Dalcho] because they were not Episcopalians. It never seems to occur to any of these spectators that these people rebelled simply because they were slaves and wished to be free." Thomas Wentworth Higginson, "Denmark Vesey," *Atlantic Monthly* 7 (1861): 728–44, in Doulas R. Egerton and Robert L. Paquette, *The Denmark Vesey Affair: A Documentary History* (Gainesville: Univ. Press of Florida, 2017), 759.
75. Furman, *Exposition*, 7.
76. Furman, *Exposition*, 17.
77. Furman, *Exposition*, 18.
78. Furman, *Exposition*, 19.
79. Also see Dalcho, *Practical Considerations Founded on the Scriptures*; Ford, *Deliver Us from Evil*, 261–67.

Chapter Five

1. Clayton, "Reminiscences of Johnson, Part 3," 12–22; Woodson, *Giant*, 73–77; Minutes of the Edgefield Baptist Association, 1831, BHC, FU.
2. Clayton, "Reminiscences of Johnson, Part 3," 12–22; Woodson, *Giant*, 74–75.
3. Clayton, "Reminiscences of Johnson, Part 3," 12–22; Woodson, *Giant*, 75.
4. Harvey Toliver Cook, *The Life Work of James Clement Furman* (n.p.: Alester G.

Furman, 1926), 15–35, quote on 17. Students from Furman also assisted in the revival efforts at Beaufort District's Black Swamp Church and Beaufort Church. Cook, *James Clement Furman*, 16.

5. Clayton, "Reminiscences of Johnson, Part 3," 12–22; Minutes of the Edgefield Baptist Association, 1831, BHC, FU; Woodson, *Giant*, 76–77.
6. Minutes of the Edgefield Baptist Association, August 1831, August 1832, BHC, FU.
7. Minutes of the Edgefield Baptist Association, August 1833, BHC, FU; Woodson, *Giant*, 77.
8. Minutes of the Edgefield Baptist Association, 1830, 1831, BHC, FU.
9. Burton, *In My Father's House*, 20.
10. Minutes of the Edgefield Baptist Association, 1831, BHC, FU.
11. Minutes of the Edgefield Baptist Association, 1833, BHC, FU.
12. Minutes of the Edgefield Baptist Association, 1834, BHC, FU.
13. Minutes of the Edgefield Baptist Association, 1831–1835, BHC, FU.
14. H. P. Griffith, *The Life and Times of John G. Landrum* (Philadelphia: H. B. Garner, 1885), 66–68.
15. Membership began to wane by 1834, partly because new churches grew out of the Brushy Creek membership, including Mountain Creek, established in 1832; Pleasant Grove, established in 1833; and Rocky Creek, formed in 1834. In October 1834 an updated roll—because there were so many people who had left the church after the revival—showed 114 white members and 30 enslaved people. That number would remain fairly consistent throughout the pre–Civil War years. Minutes of Brushy Creek Baptist Church, 1831–1834, BHC, FU.
16. Minutes of Brushy Creek Baptist Church, August 1832, BHC, FU.
17. Minutes of Brushy Creek Baptist Church, August 1832, BHC, FU.
18. Minutes of Brushy Creek Baptist Church, June 1832, BHC, FU.
19. Minutes of Brushy Creek Baptist Church, June 1832, BHC, FU. White Baptists did not allow enslaved people to join churches if their masters objected. The Charleston Baptist Association answered Mount Carmel Baptist Church that it was not right "where the owners of slaves object to their joining the church, to receive and baptize them." Minutes of the Charleston Baptist Association, 1839, BHC, FU. Sometimes churches refrained from immediately accepting for membership white men or women who failed to relate an adequate conversion experience, but slave memberships tended to be delayed more frequently than white memberships.
20. George Howe, *History of the Presbyterian Church in South Carolina* vol. 1 (Columbia: Duffie and Chapman, 1870), 556–57; McCurry, *Masters of Small Worlds*, 150–53.
21. William M. Baker, *The Life and Labours of the Rev. Daniel Baker, D.D., Pastor and Evangelist* (Philadelphia: William S. and Alfred Martien, 1858), 145–59, quote on 152; Fuller, *Chaplain to the Confederacy*, 110.

22. McCurry, *Masters of Small Worlds*, 150–58.
23. Minutes of Brushy Creek Baptist Church, August, 1832, BHC, FU.
24. W. B. Johnson, "Animating Scenes in Zion," *Christian Index*, September 3, 1831; Clayton, "Reminiscences of William Bullein Johnson, Part 3," 12–22.
25. Minutes of the Bethel Baptist Association, 1827, BHC, FU; Minutes of the Edgefield Baptist Association, 1828, BHC, FU; Minutes of the Saluda Baptist Association, 1830, 1832, BHC, FU. During the early 1830s, in a reflection of the nation's increasing sectional tensions, white South Carolinians fiercely divided over the explosive question of whether the state should nullify the federal tariffs of 1828 and 1832. Politician Robert Barnwell Rhett, a convert of the 1831 Beaufort revival, employed revivalist techniques and language in his arguments for Nullification; other prominent Lowcountry politicians followed suit. In the Upcountry, where Unionist support was stronger, churches argued and sometimes fractured over this heated topic. Although Nullification excitement may have precipitated religious enthusiasm, most Baptist ministers took aggressive measures to keep politics out of the religious arena. For a discussion of what she terms the "Nullification revivals," see McCurry, *Masters of Small Worlds*, 150–58. Also see Orville Vernon Burton and David Herr, "Religious Tolerance and the Growth of the Evangelical Ethos in South Carolina," in *The Dawn of Religious Freedom in South Carolina*, ed. James Lowell Underwood and W. Lewis Burke (Columbia: Univ. of South Carolina Press, 2006), 152–53. For detailed analyses of South Carolina's Nullification controversy, see Ford, *Origins of Southern Radicalism*, 120–44; William W. Freehling, *Prelude to the Civil War: The Nullification Controversy in South Carolina, 1816–1836* (New York: Harper and Row, 1968); and William W. Freehling, *The Road to Disunion: Secessionists in Bay, 1776–1854*, vol. 1 (New York: Oxford Univ. Press, 1990), 253–86.
26. James C. Furman to C. C. P. Crosby, August 18, 1831, James Clement Furman D.D. Papers, BHC, FU; Snay, *Gospel of Disunion*, 42–46.
27. Minutes of the Bethel Baptist Association, 1830, BHC, FU.
28. James M. Chiles to James C. Furman, November 8, 1833; also see James M. Chiles to James C. Furman, December 5, 1832, both in James Clement Furman D.D. Papers, BHC, FU.
29. James M. Chiles to James C. Furman, November 8, 1833, BHC, FU; Snay, *Gospel of Disunion*, 42–44.
30. Minutes of the Spartanburg Baptist Association, 1882, BHC, FU.
31. Minutes of the Edgefield Baptist Association, 1833, BHC, FU.
32. Minutes of the Edgefield Baptist Association, 1833, BHC, FU.
33. Garrett, *Saluda Baptist Association*, 43–54; Minutes of the Saluda Baptist Association, 1839, BHC, FU. For literature about Antimission Baptists in the South, see Kimberly R. Kellison, "A Seceding State of Mind: The Antimission Controversy in Upcountry South Carolina, 1820–1860," *American Baptist Quarterly* 23, no. 1 (March 2004): 35–49; James R. Mathis, *The Making of the Primitive Baptists:*

A Cultural and Intellectual History of the Antimission Movement (New York: Routledge, 2004); Donald Mathews, *Religion in the Old South* (Chicago: Univ. of Chicago Press, 1977), 124–28; Bertram Wyatt-Brown, *The Shaping of Southern Culture: Honor, Grace, and War, 1760s–1880s* (Chapel Hill: Univ. of North Carolina Press, 2001), 106–35; Bertram Wyatt-Brown, "The Antimission Movement in the Jacksonian South: A Study in Regional Folk Culture," *Journal of Southern History* 36 (November 1970): 501–29; Nathan O. Hatch, "The Democratization of Christianity," in *Religion and American Politics: From the Colonial Period to the 1980s*, ed. Mark A. Noll (New York: Oxford Univ. Press, 1990), 92–120. Also see Byron Cecil Lambert, *The Rise of the Anti-Mission Baptists: Sources and Leaders, 1800–1840* (New York: Arno Press, 1980); Henry L. Burkitt, *A Concise History of the Kehukee Baptist Association From Its Original Rise Down to 1803* (Philadelphia: Lippincott, Grambo and Co., 1850); James L. Peacock and Ruel W. Tyson Jr., *Pilgrims of Paradox: Calvinism and Experience among the Primitive Baptists of the Blue Ridge* (Washington: Smithsonian Institution Press, 1989); John G. Crowley, *Primitive Baptists of the Wiregrass South, 1815 to the Present* (Gainesville: Univ. Press of Florida, 1998).

34. Garrett, *Saluda Baptist Association*, 43–54; Minutes of the Saluda Baptist Association, 1837, BHC, FU. Other Upcountry Associations experienced similar difficulties. See Minutes of the Bethel Baptist Association, 1847; Minutes of the Tyger River Baptist Association, 1840, BHC, FU.
35. Minutes of the Third Annual Meeting of the Fork Shoal Association, October 4, 1839, BHC, FU.
36. Minutes of Big Creek Baptist Church, Book 1, February 7, 1844, SCL, USC.
37. Kimberly R. Kellison, "South Carolina Baptists, The Primitive-Missionary Schism, and the Revival of the Early 1830s," *South Carolina Historical Magazine* 110, nos. 3–4 (July-October 2009): 154–79.
38. The Enoree and Twelve Mile Associations joined in 1857, Barnwell in 1858, and Columbia in 1859. King, *History of South Carolina Baptists*, 229–31.
39. Cornelius, *When I Can Read My Title Clear*, 32–33; John G. Aikin, *A Digest of the Laws of the State of Alabama* (Tuscaloosa: D. Woodruff, 1836), 397.
40. Cornelius, *When I Can Read My Title Clear*, 40–41.
41. Ford, *Deliver Us from Evil*, 463–75.
42. Whitemarsh Seabrook, *An Essay on the Management of Slaves, and Especially on Their Religious Instruction, Read Before the Agricultural Society of St. John's Colleton* (Charleston: A. E. Miller, 1834), 13–26; Donald G. Mathews, "The Methodist Mission to Slaves, 1829–1844," *Journal of Southern History* 51, no. 4 (March 1965): 615–31, esp. 628; Ford, *Deliver Us from Evil*, 469–70; Loveland, *Southern Evangelicals and the Social Order*, 219–56; Donald G. Mathews, "Charles Colcock Jones and the Southern Evangelical Crusade to Form a Biracial Community," *Journal of Southern History* 41, no. 3 (August 1975): 299–320; Ernest Trice Thompson, *Presbyterians in the South*, vol. 1 (Richmond: John

Knox Press, 1963), 207, 443; William W. Freehling, "James Henley Thornwell's Mysterious Antislavery Moment," *Journal of Southern History* 57, no. 3 (August 1991): 383–406.

43. Sundry Ministers in St. Philips and St. Michaels Parishes, "Petition and Supporting Papers, Including Minutes of the Meeting of Said Ministers, Asking for the Modification of an Existing law so as to Empower the City Council of Charleston to Allow Religious Meetings of Persons of Color in Charleston," c. 1834, Petitions to the General Assembly (S165015), SCDAH; Ford, *Deliver Us from Evil*, 471–72.

44. William Roach, Clerk of Council, November 25, 1834, in Sundry Ministers, "Petition and Supporting Papers," c. 1834, SCDAH.

45. Ford, *Deliver Us from Evil*, 467–70. The 1834 law also made it illegal to hire enslaved people or free blacks as clerks or salesmen; harsher penalties were also enacted for liquor trafficking and gambling with enslaved people.

46. *Acts and Resolutions of the General Assembly, of the State of South Carolina, Passed in December, 1834* (Columbia: E. F. Branthwaite, 1834), 13–15, https://www.carolana.com/SC/Legislators/Documents/Acts_and_Resolutions_of_the_General_Assembly_of_the_State_of_South_Carolina_1834.pdf; Ford, *Deliver Us from Evil*, 472-73

47. Cornelius, *Slave Missions*, 100.

48. Loveland, *Southern Evangelicals and the Social Order*, 212–14; Ford, *Deliver Us from Evil*, 50. See, for example, William Bullein Johnson, "To the Editor of the *Biblical Recorder* and *Southern Watchman*," reprinted in the Edgefield *Advertiser*, April 8, 1841. For discussions about ameliorative efforts during the 1850s and during the Civil War, see Kimberly R. Kellison, "Toward Humanitarian Ends? Protestants and Slave Reform in South Carolina, 1830–1865," *South Carolina Historical Magazine* 3, no. 103 (July 2002): 210–25; Eugene Genovese, *A Consuming Fire: The Fall of the Confederacy in the Mind of the White Christian South* (Athens: Univ. of Georgia Press, 1998), 32–33; Eugene Genovese, *The Slaveholders' Dilemma: Freedom and Progress in Southern Conservative Thought, 1820–1860* (Columbia: Univ. of South Carolina Press, 1992), 46–72; Clarence Mohr, *On the Threshold of Freedom: Masters and Slaves in Civil War Georgia* (Athens: Univ. of Georgia Press, 1986).

49. Robert A. Baker, *The Southern Baptist Convention and Its People, 1607–1972* (Nashville: Broadman Press, 1974), 156; Robert A. Baker, *A Baptist Source Book, With Particular Reference to Southern Baptists* (Nashville: Broadman Press, 1966), 87–88.

50. Baker, *Southern Baptist Convention and Its People*, 156; Baker, *Source Book*, 90; Kidd and Hankins, *Baptists in America*, 125-26; A. T. Foss and E. Matthews, *Facts for Baptist Churches* (Utica: American Baptist Free Mission Society, 1850), 25, 28–29.

51. Ford, *Deliver Us from Evil*, 481–85; Snay, *Gospel of Disunion*, 19–52; Richard R.

John, *Spreading the News: The American Postal System from Franklin to Morse* (Cambridge: Harvard Univ. Press, 1995), 257–80; Bertram Wyatt-Brown, "The Abolition Postal Campaign of 1835," *Journal of Negro History* 50 (October 1965): 227–38.

52. Minutes of the Bethel Baptist Association, October, 1835, BHC, FU; Snay, *Gospel of Disunion*, 19–49.
53. Minutes of the Edgefield Baptist Association, 1835, BHC, FU.
54. Minutes of the Edgefield Baptist Association, 1835, BHC, FU.
55. Minutes of the Charleston Baptist Association, 1835, BHC, FU; "Charleston Baptist Association, Resolutions in Support of Slavery," November 24, 1835, Miscellaneous Communications to the General Assembly (S165029), SCDAH.
56. Minutes of the Charleston Baptist Association, 1835, BHC, FU; "Resolutions in Support of Slavery," SCDAH.
57. Minutes of the Charleston Baptist Association, 1835, BHC, FU; "Resolutions in Support of Slavery," SCDAH.
58. Minutes of the Charleston Baptist Association, 1835, BHC, FU; "Resolutions in Support of Slavery," SCDAH.
59. Minutes of the Charleston Baptist Association, 1835, BHC, FU; "Resolutions in Support of Slavery," SCDAH. As Charleston Baptists were reinforcing, publicly, the right to practice Christian slavery, some in their midst were rethinking the institution. Beaufort-born William Henry Brisbane, an ordained Baptist minister and slaveholder, began to have doubts about slavery after reading an antislavery pamphlet in November 1833. Soon after, he defended slavery in the *Charleston Mercury*. Brisbane served as the first editor of the *Southern Baptist and General Intelligencer* periodical, which began publication in 1835 and which advocated for the biblical right to own enslaved people. However, Brisbane's doubts about slavery persisted. In July 1835 he read Brown University president Francis Wayland's commentaries about slavery, which had a "powerful effect" on his views. By 1838 Brisbane had resigned his editorship and moved to Cincinnati. There, he freed his enslaved people and preached in churches in Ohio and Wisconsin, as well as making speeches on the antislavery circuit. He also attempted to repurchase and set free enslaved people he had sold in the past. Brisbane returned to South Carolina during the Civil War as a federal tax commissioner, helping to teach enslaved people to read. Baker and Craven, *Adventure in Faith*, 267–68; J. Brent Morris, "'We are Verily Guilty Concerning our Brother': The Abolitionist Transformation of Planter William Henry Brisbane," *South Carolina Historical Magazine* 111, nos. 3–4 (July-October 2010): 118–50; Willie Lee Rose, *Rehearsal for Reconstruction*, 196, 280–81, 287–89; "Obituary," Boston *Daily Advertiser*, April 8, 1878. Massachusetts Independent minister Cyrus Pitt Grosvenor, visiting South Carolina in the 1820s, was baptized by Richard Furman in 1823. Grosvenor was ordained a Baptist minister and served as pastor of the Georgetown church before

returning to Massachusetts, where he became heavily involved in abolitionism by 1833. Baker and Craven, *Adventure in Faith*, 218–19.

60. Kidd and Hankins, *Baptists in America*, 125–26.
61. Woodson, *Giant*, 91–92; Kidd and Hankins, *Baptists in America*, 126; Baker, *Southern Baptist Convention and Its People*, 157; Robert A. Baker, *Relations Between Northern and Southern Baptists* (n.p.: n.p., 1948), 53; Mary Burnham Putnam, *The Baptists and Slavery, 1840–1845* (Ann Arbor: George Wahr, 1913), 21–33.
62. Baker, *Southern Baptist Convention and Its People*, 156–58; Kidd and Hankins, *Baptists in America*, 126–27.
63. Woodson, *Giant*, 92.
64. Minutes of the Charleston Baptist Association, 1840. Both abolitionist and proslavery Baptists used the religious press to argue for their beliefs, intensifying the denominational conflict. Baker, *Southern Baptist Convention and Its People*, 158.
65. Minutes of the Edgefield Baptist Association, 1840, BHC, FU.
66. Baker, *Southern Baptist Convention and Its People*, 157–58.
67. T. Furman Hewitt, "Richard Fuller (1804–1876): Preacher, Pastor, and Prisoner of His Times," *Journal of the South Carolina Baptist Historical Society* 28 (2003/2004): 10; Kidd and Hankins, *Baptists in America*, 127.
68. Hewitt, "Richard Fuller,"10–11.
69. Baker, *Southern Baptist Convention and Its People*, 158–59; Baker, *Source Book*, 94–95.
70. Baker, *Southern Baptist Convention and Its People*, 158–59.
71. Baker, *Southern Baptist Convention and Its People*, 159; Baker, *Source Book*, 106–8; Kidd and Hankins, *Baptists in America*, 128.
72. Kidd and Hankins, *Baptists in America*, 128–29; Baker, *Southern Baptist Convention and Its People*, 161–77.
73. William Bullein Johnson, "Address of the Southern Baptist Convention," in *Proceedings of the Southern Baptist Convention held in Augusta, Georgia* (Richmond: H.K. Ellyson, 1845), 19–20.
74. Johnson, "Address of the Southern Baptist Convention," 19.
75. Johnson, "Address of the Southern Baptist Convention," 19.
76. Johnson, "Address of the Southern Baptist Convention," 19.

Chapter Six

1. Ford, *Origins of Southern Radicalism*, 215–77; Edgar, *South Carolina*, 283–84. Also see Tom Downey, *Planting a Capitalist South: Masters, Merchants, and Manufacturers in the Southern Interior, 1790–1860* (Baton Rouge: Louisiana State Univ. Press, 2006).
2. Ford, *Origins of Southern Radicalism*, 234–38; Huff, *Greenville*, 120–26; Burton, *In My Father's House*, 32–34.

3. Minutes of the Edgefield Baptist Association, 1850, BHC, FU; Bruce W. Eelman, *Entrepreneurs in the Southern Upcountry: Commercial Culture in Spartanburg, South Carolina, 1845–1880* (Athens: Univ. of Georgia Press, 2008); Huff, *Greenville*, 120–26.
4. John Belton O'Neall Landrum, *History of Spartanburg County: Embracing an Account of Many Important Events, and Biographical Sketches of Statesmen, Divines and Other Public Men, and the Names of Many Others Worthy of Record in the History of Their County* (Atlanta: Franklin Printing and Publishing Company, 1900), 73–74. Also see Eelman, *Entrepreneurs in the Southern Upcountry*; and Timothy P. Grady and Melissa Walker, eds., *Recovering the Piedmont Past: Unexplored Moments in Nineteenth-Century Upcountry South Carolina History* (Columbia: Univ. of South Carolina Press, 2013). Union troops destroyed most of the records of Johnson University, as well as of the Baptist church in Anderson, during a raid on May 1, 1865. Woodson, *Giant*, 146.
5. Joyce Wood, *Anderson University* (Charleston: Arcadia Press, 2011), 9–11.
6. Minutes of the Edgefield Baptist Association, 1854, BHC, FU.
7. Robert Norman Daniel, *Furman University: A History* (Greenville: Furman Univ., 1951), 1-77; Cook, *Life of Furman*, 142.
8. King, *South Carolina Baptists*, 220–21; McGlothin, *Baptist Beginnings in Education*, 96–101; Huff, *Greenville*, 124.
9. Greenville's population increased from 1,100 in 1843 to 1,750 in 1852. By 1860 the size of the town had increased only minimally, to 1,815 residents. Numbers in the 1850s were mitigated by migration to western states, a trend that worried town leaders. Huff, *Greenville*, 112–15. For figures on Charleston, see Fraser, *Charleston, Charleston!*, 228.
10. James C. Furman, "An Historical Discourse, Delivered before the Charleston Baptist Association, at its Hundredth Anniversary" (Charleston: A.J. Burke, 1851), 18-19; Minutes of the Charleston Baptist Association, 1851, BHC, FU; Daniel, *Furman University*, 53; Harvey Toliver Cook, *The Life Work of James Clement Furman* (Greenville: Alester G. Furman, 1926), 125; King, *History of South Carolina Baptists*, 222. In 1852 Benjamin Perry, editor of the Greenville *Southern Patriot*, noted the remarkable economic and cultural transformations Greenville had witnessed over the last several decades. "If anyone had predicted thirty years ago, that we should have had a college commencement in Greenville in the summer, and a steam car running her the next spring, from Charleston in fifteen hours, he would have been regarded as a fit subject for the Lunatic Asylum." *Southern Patriot*, August 19, 1852, cited in Huff, *Greenville*, 114.
11. Cook, *James Clement Furman*, 126; King, *History of South Carolina Baptists*, 221; W. J. McGlothlin, *Baptist Beginnings in Education: The History of Furman University* (Nashville: Sunday School Board of the Southern Baptist Convention, 1926), 96–108.

12. Furman, "An Historical Discourse," 18–19; Minutes of the Charleston Baptist Association, 1851, BHC, FU.
13. King, *History of South Carolina Baptists*, 222–23.
14. McGlothin, *Baptist Beginnings in Education*, 107–8.
15. US Census, Manuscript Returns and Slave Census, South Carolina, 1850, 1860.
16. US Census, Manuscript Returns and Slave Census, South Carolina, 1860; "Seeking Abraham," Furman University website, https://www.furman.edu/about/wp-content/uploads/sites/2/2019/11/Seeking-Abraham-Second-Edition.pdf.
17. King, *History of South Carolina Baptists*, 224–25.
18. Minutes of the State Convention of the Baptist Denomination, 1854, BHC, FU; Bainbridge, *Academy and College*, 33–34; King, *History of South Carolina Baptists*, 228. Methodists established Columbia Female College in the state's capitol in 1859. The same year, Associate Reformed Presbyterians opened Due West Female College. Edgar, *South Carolina*, 300; Wallace, *History of South Carolina*, vol. 3 (New York: American Historical Society), 40–47; Mathews, *Religion in the Old South*, 119–20. Also see Beth Barton Schweiger, *The Gospel Working Up: Progress and the Pulpit in Nineteenth-Century Virginia* (New York: Oxford Univ. Press, 2000), 55–76.
19. King, *History of South Carolina Baptists*, 228, Bainbridge, *Academy and College*, 28, 34–35.
20. Bainbridge, *Academy and College*, 29–32, 39.
21. Bainbridge, *Academy and College*, 39–40.
22. Bainbridge, *Academy and College*, 44–45; Christie Anne Farnham argues that antebellum southerners, not northerners, "evidenced the greatest interest in female colleges." Northerners worried that college-educated women would challenge their roles in society, seeking greater professional accomplishments. By contrast, classical education for women in the South—reserved primarily for the upper classes—served as "a marker of gentility." Christie Anne Farnham, *The Education of the Southern Belle: Higher Education and Student Socialization in the Antebellum South* (New York: New York Univ. Press, 1994), 1–8, quote on 2.
23. King, *History of South Carolina Baptists*, 241; Gregory A. Wills, *Southern Baptist Theological Seminary, 1859–2009* (New York: Oxford Univ. Press, 2009), 7–14.
24. King, *History of South Carolina Baptists*, 241–43; Wills, *Southern Baptist Theological Seminary*, 7–25.
25. King, *History of South Carolina Baptists*, 244–45; Wills, *Southern Baptist Theological Seminary*, 42–47. In 1860 John A. Broadus owned two enslaved people, William Williams owned five, Basil Manly, Jr. seven, and James P. Boyce twenty-three. Slave schedules, 1860 Federal Census; Southern Baptist Theological Seminary, "Report on Slavery and Racism in the History of the Southern Baptist Theological Seminary," 9, Southern Baptist Theological Seminary website, https://www.sbts.edu/southern-project.

26. Wills, *Southern Baptist Theological Seminary*, 4.
27. Wills, *Southern Baptist Theological Seminary*, 42–47.
28. Wills, *Southern Baptist Theological Seminary*, 43–46.
29. Baker and Craven, *Adventure in Faith*, 288–301; Wills, *Southern Baptist Theological Seminary*, 42–47.
30. Wills, *Southern Baptist Theological Seminary*, 47.
31. King, *History of South Carolina Baptists*, 245–46. Wills, *Southern Baptist Theological Seminary*, 53–107.
32. Will of J. G. O. Wilkinson of Edgefield, October 11, 1859, "South Carolina Wills and Probate Records, 1670–1980," box 81, Ancestry.com, https://www.ancestry.com/search/collections/9080/. Other evangelicals made similar arrangements for their enslaved people. Associate Reformed Presbyterian and former orphan Alexander Downer, who in his will in 1818 endowed money to create a school for orphans in Edgefield District, made plans for eleven of his thirteen enslaved people to be sold upon his death. Each of these eleven enslaved people "shall have a ticket from one or more of my Executors to make a choice of a Master or Mistriss [*sic*] and such person shall have the liberty to purchase such Negro at a fair and true valuation." The other two enslaved people, Old Charles and Old Rose, were not to be sold but were to be "comfortably provided for in food clothes and house during their natural lives and that the funds necessary for that purpose be taken from any monies that my executors may have, after the first year, but for that year I wish a Sufficiency reserved for them, from what I may leave on the plantation, and before the Sale of the Personal property." Will of Alexander Downer, 1818, "South Carolina Wills and Probate Records, 1670–1980," vols. A–C, Ancestry.com, https://www.ancestry.com/search/collections/9080/. Edgar W. Knight, *A Documentary History of Education in the South Before 1860* (Chapel Hill: University of North Carolina Press, 1949), 333.
33. Will of Thomas Frean, April 23, 1861, "South Carolina Wills and Probate Records, 1670–1980," vol. 4, Ancestry.com, https://www.ancestry.com/search/collections/9080/. John Belton O'Neall, *The Annals of Newberry, Complete in One Volume* (Newberry: Aull and Houseal, 1892), 78–79, 599–602.
34. Will of James Hembree, May 5, 1847, "South Carolina Wills and Probate Records, 1670–1980," vol. 1, Ancestry.com, https://www.ancestry.com/search/collections/9080/.
35. Will of Thomas Ray, June 11, 1860, "South Carolina Wills and Probate Records, 1670–1980," vol. C, Ancestry.com, https://www.ancestry.com/search/collections/9080/.
36. Will of Nancy Wills, October 7, 1844, "South Carolina Wills and Probate Records, 1670–1980," vols. 1–2, Ancestry.com, https://www.ancestry.com/search/collections/9080/.
37. John Belton O'Neall, *The Negro Law of South Carolina* (Columbia: J. G. Bowman, 1848), 23; Presbyterian missionary John B. Adger also vocally contested

the law and noted that it was often ignored. John B. Adger, *My Life and Times, 1810–1899* (Richmond: Presbyterian Committee of Publication, 1899), 54–55; Cornelius, *When I Can Read My Title Clear*, 54.

38. Richard Fuller, *Domestic Slavery Considered as a Scriptural Institution: In a Correspondence Between The Rev. Richard Fuller, of Beaufort, S.C., and The Rev. Francis Wayland, of Providence, R.I.* (New York: Lewis Colby, 1845), 207; Lawrence S. Rowland, Alexander Moore, and George C. Rogers, Jr., *The History of Beaufort County, South Carolina: Volume 1, 1514-1861* (Columbia: Univ. of South Carolina Press, 1996), 408-415; Cornelius, *When I Can Read My Title Clear*, 115; Kellison, "Toward Humanitarian Ends?," 210–25.
39. Richard Fuller, "Petition For Permission to Teach His Slaves To Read the Bible," Petitions to the General Assembly (S165015), December 9, 1850, SCDAH. For information about the Wayland-Fuller letters, see Cuthbert, *Richard Fuller*, 152–59; Richard Fuller and Francis Wayland, *Domestic Slavery Considered as a Scriptural Institution*, eds. Nathan A. Finn and Keith Harper (Macon: Mercer University Press, 2008).
40. Fuller faced backlash amongst South Carolinians for his criticism of proslavery radicalism and for his endorsement of colonization. Cuthbert, *Life of Fuller*, 193–201; Cornelius, *When I Can Read My Title Clear*, 138; Loveland, *Southern Evangelicals and the Social Order*, 214–17, 247.
41. Minutes of the Charleston Baptist Association, 1822, 1837, BHC, FU.
42. Minutes of the Charleston Baptist Association, 1837, BHC, FU.
43. Minutes of the Edgefield Baptist Association, 1841, BHC, FU.
44. Minutes of the Charleston Baptist Association, 1844, BHC, FU.
45. *Proceedings of the First Triennial Meeting of the Southern Baptist Convention, Held in Richmond, Virginia, June 10, 11, 12, 13, and 15, 1846* (Richmond: H. K. Ellyson, 1846), 16, Report of the Home Missionary Board of the Charleston Association, Minutes of the Charleston Baptist Association, 1846, BHC, FU.
46. *Proceedings of the First Triennial Meeting*, 16.
47. *Proceedings of the First Triennial Meeting*, 16. Also see Paul Stripling, *Turning Points in the History of Baptist Associations in America* (Nashville: B&H Publishing Group), 22–23.
48. Tupper was appointed to a judgeship in Charleston in 1850 and served as state auditor of South Carolina during the Civil War. Along with fellow judge and Baptist John Belton O'Neall, Tupper toured the state in support of temperance. "The Death of Mr. James Tupper," Charleston *Daily News*, August 31, 1868.
49. Report of the Home Missionary Board of the Charleston Association, Minutes of the Charleston Baptist Association, 1850, BHC, FU; Susan Markey Fickling, *Slave-Conversion in South Carolina, 1830–1860* (Columbia: University of South Carolina, 1924), 40.
50. Report of the Home Missionary Board of the Charleston Association, Minutes of the Charleston Baptist Association, 1850, BHC, FU.

51. Minutes of the Charleston Baptist Association, 1854, BHC, FU; E. T. Winkler, *Notes and Questions for the Oral Instruction of Colored People: With Appropriate Texts and Hymns* (Charleston: Southern Baptist Publication Society, 1857).
52. Tupper, *Two Centuries of the First Baptist Church*, 254.
53. Winkler, *Notes and Questions for the Oral Instruction of Colored People*, iii, v, 86; Baker and Craven, *Adventures in Faith*, 295-96.
54. Ninth Annual Report of the Charleston Mission Board, Charleston Baptist Association, 1856.
55. Ninth Annual Report of the Charleston Mission Board, Charleston Baptist Association, 1856.
56. Ninth Annual Report of the Charleston Mission Board, Charleston Baptist Association, 1856. Also see Minutes of the State Convention of the Baptist Denomination, 1853, 1857, 1859, BHC, FU.
57. *Proceedings of the Meeting in Charleston, S.C., May 13–15, 1845, On the Religious Instruction of the Negroes, Together with the Report of the Committee, and the Address to the Public* (Charleston: B. Jenkins, 1845), 3.
58. *Proceedings of the Meeting in Charleston, S.C.*, 34.
59. *Proceedings of the Meeting in Charleston, S.C.*, 49; Talbert and Farish, *Antipedo Baptists*, 78–79.
60. *Proceedings of the Meeting in Charleston, S.C.*, 27.
61. *Proceedings of the Meeting in Charleston, S.C.*, 28.
62. *Proceedings of the Meeting in Charleston, S.C.*, 31–32.
63. *Proceedings of the Meeting in Charleston, S.C.*, 24.
64. *Proceedings of the Meeting in Charleston, S.C.*, 21.
65. *Proceedings of the Meeting in Charleston, S.C.*, 21.
66. In the late 1840s and early 1850s a dearth of male members frequently led to church business being suspended "in concequence [*sic*] of there being verry fiew [*sic*] of the male Members present." Minutes of Poplar Springs Baptist Church, Laurens District, May 15, 1846; June 20, 1846, South Caroliniana Library, University of South Carolina (hereafter SCL, USC). Other Upcountry congregations, in both town and country, experienced similar problems with male attendance. In 1844 Greenville Baptist Church postponed the monthly business meeting because only two males were present. Minutes of Greenville Baptist Church, January 7, 1844, BHC, FU. Also see Minutes of Poplar Springs Baptist Church, Laurens District, January 16, 1847; May 18, 1850; January 18, 1851; December 20, 1851, SCL, USC.
67. Minutes of Poplar Springs Baptist Church, Laurens District, June 18, 1853; October 23, 1853, SCL, USC.
68. Minutes of Poplar Springs Baptist Church, Laurens District, April 15, 1854, SCL, USC.
69. Minutes of Poplar Springs Baptist Church, Laurens District, January 16, 1847; May 18, 1850; January 18, 1851; December 20, 1851, SCL, USC. Also see Erskine

Clarke, *Wrestlin' Jacob: A Portrait of Religion in the Old South* (Tuscaloosa: University of Alabama Press, 2000), 135–39.

70. Clarke, *Wrestlin' Jacob*, 81.
71. For scholarship about antebellum slave marriages in South Carolina, see Emily West, *Chains of Love: Slave Couples in Antebellum South Carolina* (Urbana: Univ. of Illinois Press, 2004); Clarke, *Wrestlin' Jacob*, 135–39. For treatment of slave marriages in the colonial period, see Wood, *Slavery in Colonial America*, 51–52; Frey and Wood, *Come Shouting to Zion*, 48–51; Barrington, *Welsh Neck*, lxvii–lxviii.
72. Clarke, *Wrestlin' Jacob*, 79–81, 134–35; Jeff Forret, "Slaves, Sex and Sin: Adultery, Forced Separation and Baptist Church Discipline in Middle Georgia," *Slavery and Abolition: A Journal of Slave and Post-Slave Studies* 33, no. 3 (2012): 337–58; Cornelius, *Slave Missions*, 37–45.
73. Minutes of Greenville Baptist Church, January 11, 1844, BHC, FU. Later that year, the white church excluded Dick for making "proposals of a lewd nature" to the wife of another slave. Dick answered the white church by reporting that he was drunk when he made the comments. Minutes of Greenville Baptist Church, August 4, 1844, BHC, FU.
74. Minutes of the Charleston Baptist Association, 1843, BHC, FU.
75. Minutes of Greenville Baptist Church, January 21, 1843; November 5, 1843, BHC, FU.
76. Minutes of the Board of Deacons, First Baptist Church, Charleston, July 11, 1847; January, 1848, cited in Clarke, *Wrestlin' Jacob*, 135.
77. Minutes of the Charleston Baptist Association, 1856, BHC, FU.
78. Minutes of the Bethel Baptist Association, 1845, BHC, FU.
79. Fuller, *Chaplain to the Confederacy*, 274–75. Wentworth Street Baptist Church was established in 1841, and Citadel Square Baptist Church in 1856. Baker and Craven, *Adventure in Faith*, 264, 286.
80. Minutes of the Charleston Baptist Association, 1856, 10–20, BHC, FU. Also see Cornelius, *Slave Missions*, 43–45.
81. Minutes of the Charleston Baptist Association, 1856, BHC, FU.
82. Minutes of the Charleston Baptist Association, 1856, BHC, FU.
83. Minutes of the Charleston Baptist Association, 1856, BHC, FU.
84. Minutes of the Charleston Baptist Association, 1856, BHC, FU.

Conclusion

1. Minutes of the State Convention of the Baptist Denomination, 1860, BHC, FU; Petty, *Growth and Distribution*, 226.
2. See, for example, Minutes of Rabun's Creek Baptist Church, SCL, USC; Minutes of Poplar Springs Baptist Church, SCL, USC.
3. Huff, *Greenville*, 134–35; Lillian A. Kibler, "Unionist Sentiment in South

Carolina in 1860," *Journal of Southern History* 4, no. 3 (August 1938): 346–66; James W. Gettys, "Mobilization for Secession in Greenville District," *Proceedings and Papers of the Greenville Historical Society, 1975–1979* 6 (1981): 50–66. Mitchell Snay argues that both northern and southern religious leaders, viewing their efforts in terms of God's providence, intervened in politics when they felt a moral—but not party—compulsion to do so. As Snay writes, both northern and southern ministers "denied any interest in politics when it meant issues of party or policy but claimed that a political question became a legitimate topic for pulpit discourse if it possessed any kind of moral dimension." Snay, *Gospel of Disunion*, 182–83. Snay also argues that religious leaders provided a spiritualization of the sectional controversy, uniting whites by sanctifying slavery and affirming an organic social order based upon race and gender, in the process sacralizing the efforts of white southern politicians. Snay, *Gospel of Disunion*, 214–16. Also see John Patrick Daly, *When Slavery Was Called Freedom: Evangelicalism, Proslavery, and the Causes of the Civil War* (Lexington: Univ. Press of Kentucky, 2002); Crowther, *Southern Evangelicals*; C. C. Goen, *Broken Churches, Broken Nation: Denominational Schisms and the Coming of the American Civil War* (Macon: Mercer Univ. Press, 1985); Richard J. Cawardine, *Evangelicals and Politics in Antebellum America* (New Haven: Yale University Press, 1993).

4. 1860 United States Federal Population Census, South Carolina; 1860 United States Federal Slave Census, South Carolina.
5. James P. Boyce to H. A. Tupper, December 18, 1860, in John A. Broadus, *Memoir of James Petigru Boyce, D.D., LL.D.* (New York: A.C. Armstrong and Son, 1893), 184–85.
6. James P. Boyce to H. A. Tupper in Broadus, *Memoir of James Petigru Boyce*, 184–85.
7. Huff, *Greenville*, 134.
8. James C. Furman, Thomas S. Arthur, William H. Campbell, and William M. Thomas, "Letter to the Citizens of the Greenville District," *Southern Enterprise*, November 22, 1860. Furman chaired the committee that wrote the letter, and likely framed much of the arguments. Huff, *Greenville*, 134; Lillian Kibler, *Benjamin F. Perry, South Carolina Unionist* (Durham: Duke University Press, 1946), 341–42.
9. Furman, "Letter," *Southern Enterprise*.
10. Furman, "Letter," *Southern Enterprise*.
11. James C. Furman to Brushy Creek Baptist Church, October 18, 1863, in Susan Frazier Kahl, *The Bicentennial History of Brushy Creek Baptist Church, Taylors, South Carolina, 1784–1994* (n.p.: Brushy Creek Baptist Church, 1994), 72, 217–19; original manuscript is in the James Clement Furman D.D. Papers, BHC, FU. Kahl supposes that Furman did not send this letter, because he preached until the following year.
12. James C. Furman to Brushy Creek, in Kahl, *Bicentennial History*, 217–18.

13. James C. Furman to Brushy Creek, in Kahl, *Bicentennial History*, 218.
14. James C. Furman to Brushy Creek, in Kahl, *Bicentennial History*, 218.
15. James C. Furman to Brushy Creek, in Kahl, *Bicentennial History*, 218–19.
16. Minutes of Lower Fairforest Baptist Church, April 27, 1868; Charles, "Black-White Relations," 225.
17. Harvey, *Redeeming the South*, 17–196; Stowell, *Rebuilding Zion*; Blum, *Reforging the White Republic*; Harvey, *Freedom's Coming.*
18. For literature on the Lost Cause, see Charles Reagan Wilson, *Baptized in Blood: The Religion of the Lost Cause, 1865–1920* (Athens: Univ. of Georgia Press, 1980); W. Scott Poole, *Never Surrender: Confederate Memory and Conservatism in the South Carolina Upcountry* (Athens: Univ. of Georgia Press, 2004); Lee Ann Whites, *The Civil War as a Crisis in Gender* (Athens: Univ. of Georgia Press, 1995); Keith Harper, "What's Wrong with this Picture? James P. Boyce, John A. Broadus, and Reflections on the Lost Cause," *Journal of Southern Religion* 17 (2015): http://jsreligion.org/issues/vol17/harper.html; Edward R. Crowther, ed., *The Enduring Lost Cause: Afterlives of a Redeemer Nation* (Knoxville: Univ. of Tennessee Press, 2020).

INDEX

A Short Treatise Concerning a True and Orderly Gospel Church, 46
Abolitionism, 11, 56, 83–88, 96, 99–100, 105–6, 115, 117
—English and northern U.S. Baptist abolitionists, 119–27, 139, 155–59
Adger, John B., 208–9
African Americans
—African religious beliefs, 25
—Burial rites, 96, 130, 137–38, 146
—Choice of churches, 25
—Conversion experiences, 6–7, 12, 25–26, 51, 89, 110, 130, 137, 153
—European missionaries, 25–27
—Free blacks, 6, 8, 25, 51–52, 66, 80–81, 83, 86–87, 91–92, 95–97, 99, 117–19, 130, 139, 144–46, 171, 177, 193, 196, 203
—Independent black congregations, 9, 12, 51–52, 127, 159
—Involvement in Baptist churches, 6, 24–26, 30, 34, 35, 38, 51–55, 57, 66, 78, 89, 91–92, 95, 97, 106, 109–10, 116, 130, 137, 144–51, 153, 158–60, 193
—Marriage, 12, 130, 146–51, 212
—Religious leadership roles: deacons, 25, 92, 97, 138, 140, 146; preachers, 6, 51–52, 95–96, 144–45, 171; resistance to white-constructed Christian benevolence, 24–25, 92–95, 102, 146–51, 158–60; watchmen, 144–45
Alabama, 117, 124–26, 136, 148
"Alabama Resolutions" (1844), 125–26
Allen, Richard, 95
Allston, R. F. W., 144
American Anti-Slavery Society, 121
American Baptist Anti-Slavery Convention, 123
American Baptist Free Mission Society, 125
American Baptist Home Mission Society, 125, 190
American Baptist Publication Society, 126
American Bible Society, 63
American Colonization Society, 139
American Revolution, 53, 153, 157
—Anglican disestablishment, 37, 49, 63
—Baptist divisions over, 9–12, 45, 47–48, 50, 57
—British occupation of Charleston, 49–50
—Chattel slavery, 9, 37, 57, 82, 90
—Loyalists, 9, 38, 47–48, 51
—South Carolina Council of Safety, 48
—South Carolina Provincial Congress, 48–49
American Revolution Society, 62–63, 74
Anderson, SC, 47, 114, 131–32, 134
Anderson District Mission Society, 114
Anglican Church. *See* Church of England
Antipaedobaptists (Antipedobaptists), 16, 18
Antislavery sentiment, 5, 9–10, 50, 53, 56–57, 77–80, 83–84, 87–88, 91–92, 96, 99–100, 103, 106, 116–17, 121, 171, 204
Arminianism, 20
Arthur, Thomas S., 155
Associate Reformed Presbyterian Church, 207–8
Augusta, Georgia, 41, 47, 52, 74, 126

Backcountry, definition, 1, 3, 10, 37–50, 57, 62, 64

Backus, Isaac, 38
Baker, Daniel, 110
Baldwin, Thomas, 67
Baptist Annual Register, 83
Baptist churches in South Carolina
—Ashley River (Charleston County), 17, 20, 22, 30–31, 33, 179
—Beaufort (Beaufort County), 190
—Bethel (Spartanburg County), 65, 113
—Bethlehem (Florence County), 65, 147
—Bethlehem (Spartanburg County), 65
—Big Creek (Anderson County), 92–93, 114
—Big Creek Primitive (Anderson County), 114
—Big Steven's Creek (Edgefield County), 72
—Black Swamp (Jasper County), 66
—Brushy Creek (Greenville County), 73, 109–11, 156–58
—Bush River (Newberry County), 91
—Cashaway (Darlington County), 22, 32
—Cedar Spring (Spartanburg County), 79, 92
—Charleston First (Charleston County), 16–30, 49–50, 54, 56, 59–60, 69–70, 72, 94, 97, 135, 147–49
—Citadel (Charleston County), 148
—Columbia First (Richland County), 70, 135, 144–45
—Congaree (Richland County), 40, 43
—Edgefield First (Edgefield County), 72, 107–8, 138
—Edisto (Jasper County), 17, 20
—Euhaw (Jasper County), 17, 22, 31
—Fairforest (Union County), 40, 47–48, 65
—Flat Rock (Saluda County), 114
—Friendship (Spartanburg County), 92 (*see also* Tyger River)
—Georgetown First (Georgetown County), 19, 79, 88–89
—Goucher (Cherokee County), 47
—Greenville First (Greenville County), 73, 135, 147, 212
—High Hills of Santee (Sumter County), 40, 43, 45, 49, 61, 64
—James Island (Charleston County), 21, 32
—Lower Fairforest (Union County), 92, 158
—Lynches Creek (Darlington County), 182
—Mountain Creek (Anderson County), 108
—Mountain Creek (Greenville County), 200
—Mt. Carmel (Pickens County), 201
—Mt. Moriah (Greenwood County), 108
—Newberry First (Newberry County), 138
—Padgett's Creek (Union County), 65, 138
—Pleasant Grove (Greenville County), 200
—Poplar Springs (Laurens County), 146, 153
—Rocky Creek (Greenville County), 200
—Salem (Anderson County), 114
—Salem (Edgefield County), 93, 138
—Sardis (Saluda County), 107–8
—Silver Bluff (Aiken County), vii, 51–52
—Stevens Creek (Edgefield County), 41, 47
—Stono (Charleston County), 17, 20
—Sumterville, (Sumter County), 147
—Tyger River (Spartanburg County), 197 (*see also* Friendship)
—Welsh Neck (Darlington County), 20, 22, 30–32, 53–56, 89, 133, 136
—Wentworth Street (Charleston County), 148

—Woodruff First (Spartanburg County), 65
Baptist State Convention of South Carolina (South Carolina Baptist State Convention), 12, 59, 63–64, 70–73, 75, 98, 105, 107, 114, 116, 129–31, 134–35, 159
Baptists in England, 3, 6, 14–19, 20, 24, 27–30, 34, 37, 63, 79, 105, 188–89, 194
Baptists in South Carolina
—African American challenges to white constructions of Christian slavery, 24–25, 92–95, 102, 146–51, 158–60, 194
—African Americans in Baptist churches, 6, 24–26, 30, 34, 35, 38, 51–55, 57, 66, 78, 89, 91–92, 95, 97, 106, 109–10, 116, 130, 137, 144–51, 153, 158–60, 194
—Baptist Associations (*see* individual associations)
—Children, 33, 51, 69–71, 81, 83, 86, 110, 140, 143
—Church adherents, 6–7, 60, 65, 108–9, 153, 161–68
—Church discipline, 6, 46, 55, 93–94, 146, 171–72, 193
—Churches (*see* Baptist churches in South Carolina)
—General Baptists, 17–20
—German Baptists, 20
—Ministerial training, 13, 23–24, 34, 37, 59–60, 63, 66, 69–70, 111, 129, 131–32, 156
—Missionary impulse, 22, 71, 105, 129; domestic missions, 64, 159; foreign missions, 59–60, 64, 67–68, 73, 124; mission to enslaved people, 129, 137–41, 145, 151
—Particular, 17–20, 22–23, 31, 47, 179–80, 188–89
—Petitions, 49, 63, 77, 79, 81–83, 97–102, 118–19, 122–24, 139, 171, 195
—Primitive (Antimission, Old School), 11, 105–16, 127, 138
—Regular, 37, 43–47, 57, 182
—Segregated worship, 7, 11–12, 38, 53–55, 74, 78, 110, 116, 130, 137, 140, 146, 150–51, 159–60
—Separate, 2–3, 8–10, 37–48, 51, 57, 162, 181–82
—Sunday Schools, 71, 73, 115, 140–42
—Tension between Lowcountry and Upcountry Baptists, 1–12, 38–50, 57, 69–76, 105–16, 127, 129–37, 155–58
—White Baptist women, 6, 12, 43, 46, 60, 66, 146; deaconesses and eldresses, 39, 41–42; female domestic missionary societies, 69; female mite societies, 69, 192
—White-constructed Christian model of slavery, 1–6, 8–13, 24, 27–30, 32–35, 38, 50–51, 53–57, 77–79, 82–83, 85–91, 94–95, 97–103, 117, 120, 124, 127, 130, 138, 141, 143, 146, 150–51, 153–56, 158–60
Barbados, 13, 15, 26
Barker, Charles, 22, 31
Beaufort, SC, 66, 110–11
Bedgegood, Nicholas, 31–32, 43, 180
Bedon, Richard, 22, 31
Benedict, David, 41, 90–91, 161, 196
Bennet, Rolla, 96
Bennett, Thomas, Jr., 96–98
Bethel Baptist Association (SC), 65, 70, 79, 112, 116, 121, 148
Bethesda Orphan House, 32
Bill (enslaved person), 92
Blake, Elizabeth Axtell, 16
Blake, Joseph, 16
Blocker, Abner, 70
Boles, John B., 2

Boston First Baptist Church (MA), 15, 18, 21, 24
Boston Second Baptist Church (MA), 67
Botsford, Edmund, 21, 23, 47, 50, 53–56, 88–91, 184, 186, 188, 196
Boyce, James P., 135, 153–54, 207
Boyce, Ker, 135
Brisbane, William Henry, 204
British and Foreign Bible Society, 63
Broad River Baptist Association (SC), 70
Broadus, John A., 135, 207
Brockman, Thomas, 145
Brookes, Iveson, 72
Brown, John, 22, 30–31
Brown, Morris, 96
Brown, Nicholas, 68
Brown University. *See* Rhode Island College
Bryan, Andrew, 51–52
Bryan, Jonathan, 52

Callender, Ellis, 18
Calvinism, 8, 13, 17, 20
Campbell, William H., 155
Camp meetings, 65–66, 107
Capers, William, 64
Cates (enslaved person), 42
Chanler, Elizabeth, 33
Chanler, Isaac, 20–21, 31, 33
Chaplin, Joyce, 4
Charleston, SC, 1–2, 13–14, 16, 18, 74, 112
Charleston African American Episcopal Church, 95–96
Charleston Baptist Association, 22–23, 31, 41, 42, 45–46, 61, 63–64, 67, 70, 76, 81, 83–84, 86, 88, 98, 122–24, 139–43, 147–48, 150
Charleston Bible Society, 63, 74, 97–98
Charleston *City Gazette and Daily Advertiser*, 66
Charleston Court of Magistrates and Freeholders, 95
Charleston Orphan House, 62
Charleston Second Presbyterian Church, 95
Charleston Tract Society, 62, 74
Charlottesville First Baptist Church (VA), 135
Chiles, James, 112–13
Christian Index, 111
Church adherents. *See* Baptists in South Carolina
Church of England, 18
—disestablishment, 49
Civil War, impact of, 136, 150, 153, 156–60
Clariosophic Society, South Carolina College, 196
Clarke, Erskine, 146
Clinton, Sir Henry, 49–50
College of Charleston, 133
Colonization, 139, 196, 209
Columbian College (George Washington University), 68, 74, 133, 191, 194
Columbian Star, 98
Congaree Baptist Association (SC), 41, 45
Congregationalists, 17, 38–39, 53, 62, 67, 97
Connecticut, 31, 38, 67, 133, 186
Conventicle Act of 1664, 14
Cook, Joseph B., 64, 70, 189–90
Council of Safety. *See* American Revolution
Curtis, William, 144–45
Cutt, Robert, 15

Dago (enslaved person), 33
Dalcho, Frederick, 198, 199
Dargan, Timothy, 42
Davies, James, 109

Davies, Jonathan, 109
Davis, John, 144
Davis, Josiah, 16
Delaware, 20
Denominationalism, 2–3, 8–11, 24, 34, 59–60, 64, 66–67, 76, 103, 105, 111, 113, 129, 158
DeSaussure, William, 83, 198
DeSchamps, George S. C., 144
D'Harriette, Martha, 31
Dick (enslaved person), 147, 211
Dinah (enslaved person), 31
Disestablishment. *See* Church of England
Douglas, John, 145
Douglass, Phillip, 22
Downer, Alexander, 208
Drayton, John, 80
Drayton, William Henry, 48
Dueling, 63, 75

Edgefield, SC (Edgefield Village), 72, 75, 107–12, 131
Edgefield Baptist Association, 69–70, 108–9, 113, 121–22, 131, 140
Edgefield Domestic Missionary Society, 69
Edgefield Village Academy, 75, 108
Edisto Female Mite Society, 69
Edisto Island, 17, 50, 69
Edwards, Joshua, 22, 31
Edwards, Morgan, 20, 39–40, 42, 46
Edwards, Peter C., 133
Elliott, Stephen, 111
Elliott, William, Jr., 32–33
Elliott, William, Sr., 16, 32
England, 32, 33, 34, 37, 47, 53, 179
English Baptists. *See* Baptists in England
Enslaved men and women. *See under* African Americans
Evans, Caleb, 53
Exposition of the Views of the Baptists, Relative to the Coloured Population of the United States, in a Communication to the Governor of South Carolina, 98–102, 198–99

Fairfield, SC, 133
Federalist Party, 62–63, 80, 86, 103
Festus (enslaved person), 33
Five Mile Act, 14
Florida, 136
Ford, Lacy, 3–5, 81
Foreign slave trade, 4, 53–54, 56, 80, 84–85, 100
Fork Shoal Baptist Association (SC), 114
Fowler, James, 22, 31–32
Franklin, Benjamin, 56
Frean, Thomas, 137–38
Friday (enslaved person), 33
Frierson, John, 94
Frierson, Lydia, 94
Fripp, William, Sr., 144
Fuller, Richard, 66, 111, 125, 139, 196
Fuller, Thomas, 66
Fuller and Hodges Institutes, 131, 134
Furman, Dorothea Maria Burn (Dolly), 60–61
Furman, Elizabeth Haynsworth, 60
Furman, James Clement, 61, 108, 112, 131–33, 154–59
Furman, Josiah, 45
Furman, Rachel (daughter of Richard Furman), 60
Furman, Rachel (mother of Richard Furman), 44
Furman, Richard (son of Richard Furman), 60
Furman, Richard, 3, 5, 9–11, 19, 42–45, 47, 50, 54, 56–57, 59–70, 72–79, 81–91, 97–103, 108, 157, 162, 171, 188
Furman, Samuel, 61

Furman, Sarah (Haynsworth), 45
Furman, William, 61
Furman, Wood (father of Richard Furman), 44
Furman, Wood (son of Richard Furman), 60
Furman Academy and Theological Institution (Edgefield location), 59, 68–69, 71, 74–75, 107, 131–33
Furman Institution (Winnsboro location), 105, 131–33
Furman Theological Institution (High Hills location), 76, 105, 107–8, 110–11, 131–33
Furman University, 129, 131–36, 151, 154, 158

Gadsden, Christopher, 118
Gaffney, SC, 134
Gallay, Alan, 3–4, 170
Galphin Plantation. *See* Silver Bluff Plantation
Galusha, Elon, 124–25
Gano, John, 22, 30
General Assembly of General Baptists in England, 20
General Missionary Convention of the Baptist Denomination in the United States of America for Foreign Missions (Triennial Convention), 10, 59, 67–69, 119–20, 124–26, 139, 173
George, David, 51
George Washington University. *See* Columbian College
Georgetown, SC, 18, 19, 79–80, 88, 205
Georgetown College (KY), 68
Georgia, 9, 32, 39, 41, 42, 47, 49–52, 66–68, 72, 74, 83, 109–10, 116–17, 125–26, 135–36
Georgia Baptist Association (GA), 52
Gift, Moses, 91–92
Gillisonville, SC, 110
Glasgow (enslaved person), 44
Grahamville, SC, 110
Great Revival (early 1800s). *See* Revivals
Greenville, SC, 72–73, 75, 129–36, 151, 154–56, 206
Greenville Baptist Female College, 134, 151
Greenville Bible Society, 73
Greenville District, 57, 65, 109, 145
Greenville Female Academy, 72, 75, 134
Greenville Male Academy, 73, 75
Greenville Woman's College. *See* Greenville Baptist Female College
Greenwood, SC, 130, 132, 134
Grief (enslaved person), 138
Griffith, H. P., 109
Griffith, James, 75
Grimball, Charles, 48
Grimball, Isaac, 34
Grimball, Joshua, 34
Grimball, Paul, 34
Grosvenor, Cyrus Pitt, 204

Haiti, 95
Hamilton, Alexander, 62–63
Hamilton, James, 96–97
Hamilton Literary and Theological Institution (NY), 68, 133
Harrison, Thomas, 22, 31
Harry (enslaved person), 93–94
Harry (enslaved person), 147
Hart, Anne Marie Sealy Grimball (Nancy), 31, 48–50, 56
Hart, Oliver, 8, 13, 20–24, 31–33, 42–43, 45–50, 53–54, 56–57, 63
Hart, Sarah Brees, 21, 47–48
Hart, Silas, 48–49
Hart, William Rogers, 48
Hartwell, Jesse, 75–76, 108
Harvard University, 136

Haynsworth, Sarah, 61
Hembree, James H., 114, 138
Henry, James Edward, 145
Heyrman, Christine, 2
Higginson, Thomas Wentworth, 199
High Hills of Santee, SC, vii, 40, 43–44, 49, 61, 64, 76, 131
Hilton Head, SC, 32
Hopewell Academy (NJ), 23, 191
Hopewell Baptist Church (NJ), 19, 50, 56, 191
Huger, Alfred, 121
Huiet, John, 138

Independent Church (Charleston), 48
India, 67
International slave trade. *See* Foreign slave trade
Irons, Charles, 3–4, 170

Jack (enslaved person), 33
James, Philip, 20, 181
James Island, 21, 32–33
Jenkins, John, 34
Jersey Settlement Baptist Church (NC), 22
Jinny (enslaved person), 44
John (enslaved person), 110
John (enslaved person), 138
Johnson, Mary, 73, 192
Johnson, Nathaniel, ix, 161
Johnson, William Bullein, 66–68, 72–74, 83–84, 107–13, 121–22, 124–27, 129, 131, 134, 189
Johnson Female Seminary (later Johnson University), 131, 134, 206
Judith (enslaved person), 92
Judson, Adoniram, 67
Judson, Ann, 67
Judson, Charles H., 133
Judy (enslaved person), 33
Judy (enslaved person), 92–94
Juvenile Missionary and Educational Society, 69

Keith, Isaac, 62
Kendrick, James Ryland, 148
Kentucky, 65, 68, 136
Kingston, Jamaica, 51–52
Kittery, Maine, 13, 15–16
Kittery Baptist Church (ME), 15–16

Landrum, John G., 134
Laurens, Henry, 48
Le Jau, Francis, 26–27
"Letter to the Citizens of the Greenville District," 155
Liberia, 51
Liele, George, 51–52
Limestone Springs Female High School, 131, 134
Linia (enslaved person), 110
London Confession of Faith, 17
Lonnon (enslaved person), 33
Lord, Joseph, 17
Louisiana, 117, 135
Loveland, Anne C., 2
Lowcountry, xi, 1–14, 21, 24, 34–35, 43–46, 51, 57–58, 61–63, 83, 88, 102, 106, 112, 117, 121, 145, 151, 153, 158

McBee, Vardry, 73
McCarty, Albert, 93
McCarty, William, 88
McDonald, Mary Burn, 42
McGready, James, 65
Maine, 13, 15–16, 34, 68
Manly, Basil, Jr., 135–36, 197, 208
Manly, Basil, Sr., 21, 72–73, 75, 94, 107, 118, 121–25, 135–36, 148–49, 195–96
Manning, James, 56
Mariner's Church, 19, 31

Marshall, Abraham, 45, 47, 52
Marshall, Daniel, 37–38, 41–43, 45, 47
Marshall, Martha Stearns, 37–38, 41–42, 45
Martha (enslaved person), 147
Mary (enslaved person), 147
Maryland, 50, 79, 139
Massachusetts, 15–16, 53, 67, 68, 133, 136, 174, 204
Mathews, Donald, 2
Matthews, Edmund, 32
Maxcy, Jonathan, 189
Mercer Institute (later Mercer University), 69, 136
Methodists in South Carolina
—African American agency, 96
—Antislavery rhetoric, 79–80, 171
—Enslaved membership, 144
—Female education, 134, 207
—General Conference, 79–80
—Great Revival (early 1800s), 64–65
—Membership statistics, 25
—Mission to slaves, 117, 144–45
Mikell, John, 22, 31
Millennialism, 68, 109
Mills, Robert, 69
Mims, J. S., 133
Mission to slaves. *See under* Baptists in South Carolina; Methodists in South Carolina; *and* Presbyterians in South Carolina
Mississippi, 136, 173
Missouri, 136
Moriah Baptist Association (SC), 70
Mulkey, Jonathan, 41
Mulkey, Philip, 37, 39–43, 45, 47–48

Native Americans, 14, 22, 25–26, 38, 64, 159, 173
Negro Law of South Carolina, The, 138–39
New England, 8, 15, 16, 38–39, 68
New Hampshire, 15
New Jersey, 19, 22–23, 30, 48–50, 56, 186
New York, 22, 44, 50, 68, 121, 124, 133, 186, 193
Newman, Samuel, 45
Newton, John, 43
Newton Theological Seminary (MA), 68, 133, 136
North Carolina, 8, 22, 30, 32, 37–39, 41–43, 47, 50, 117, 133, 135–36
Notes and Questions for the Oral Instruction of Colored People, 142
Nova Scotia, 51
Nullification, Baptist divisions over, 112–13, 117, 200–201

O'Neall, John Belton, 137–39, 153–54, 209

Palmer, Benjamin Morgan, 97
Panic of 1837, 130
Parmenter, Benjamin, 22
Paternalism, definition, 3, 170. *See also* Baptists in South Carolina: White-constructed Christian model of slavery
Peart, Rev., 19
Pee Dee River, 20, 43
Pee Dee settlement, SC. *See* Welsh Neck settlement, SC
Pegg (enslaved person), 33
Peggy (enslaved person), 138
Pelot, Catherine Stoll Screven, 179
Pelot, Francis, 22, 31–33, 46, 179, 180
Pelot, Martha Sealy, 179
Pendleton, South Carolina, 73, 75
Pennsylvania, 3, 8, 13, 19–21, 24, 31–32, 34, 38, 43, 50, 53–54, 56, 67–68, 95, 186
Pennsylvania Society for Promoting the Gradual Emancipation of Slavery, 56

Perry, B. F., 137, 206
Peters, Jesse, 51–52
Philadelphia, Pennsylvania, 3, 19–21, 24, 67–68, 95
Philadelphia Baptist Association, 22–24, 46, 188
Philadelphia Confession of Faith, 182
Philadelphia First Baptist Church (PA), 54
Pinckney, Charles Cotesworth, 62–63, 83, 97
Pinckney, Thomas, 83
Pompey (enslaved person), 33
Population of South Carolina, 161–65
Presbyterians in South Carolina, 40, 145
—Great Revival (early 1800s), 64–65
—Mission to slaves, 117, 145
—Petitions to support slave literacy, 119, 209
—Response to Denmark Vesey scare, 98
—Revival of the 1830s, 110
—Women's education, 134
Primitive Baptists. *See under* Baptists in South Carolina
Princeton Theological Seminary, 135–36
Proslavery Christianity, historiography, 3–5, 171–72. *See also* Baptists in South Carolina: White-constructed Christian model of slavery
Prosser, Gabriel, 80
Pugh, Evan, 32, 42–44, 62, 180, 187
Purrysburg settlement, SC, 31, 179

Quakers, 32

Railroad expansion, 130
Ray, Thomas, 113, 138
Read, Jacob, 80
Reconstruction
—Black Baptists, 159–60
—White Baptists, 159–60
Rector, Lewis, 109
Reese, Joseph, 43–45, 47–48
Reeve, James E., 125
Revivals
—1754 (Charleston), 21
—1779 (Welsh Neck), 53
—1790 (Welsh Neck), 55
—1803–04 (Beaufort), 66
—1822 (Edgefield), 72
—Early 1770s (High Hills), 43
—Early 1800s (Great Revival), 10, 64–66
—Early 1830s, 105, 107–11
—First Great Awakening, 38–39, 170
Rewards of Grace Conferred on Christ's Faithful People, 56–57
Rhett, Robert Barnwell, 111, 202
Rhode Island, 56, 86, 90, 186
Rhode Island College (Brown University), 64, 68, 70, 135–36, 188, 205
Rice, Luther, 67, 190, 191
Richmond Female Institute (VA), 136
Richmond First Baptist Church (VA), 136
Rippon, John, 53, 55, 79, 83–84
Roberts, Isaachar J., 75
Roberts, John M., 64, 70
Roberts Academy (High Hills), 64
Rogers, William, 48, 56
Rooker, John, 64
Rose, Willie Lee, 3–5
Rush, Benjamin, 56

Saint-Domingue, 5, 80
Saluda Baptist Association (SC), 70, 73, 109, 114, 116
Saluda River, 131
Sambo and Toney: A Dialogue in Three Parts, 89
Sampson (enslaved person), 31
Sandiford, Rev., 19
Sandy Creek, NC, 8, 38–39

Sandy Creek Baptist Association (multiple southern states), 39, 41
Sandy Creek Baptist Church (NC), 8, 39, 40, 42
Savannah, Georgia, 49, 51–52, 66–67, 110, 136
Savannah First African Baptist Church (GA), 52
Savannah First Baptist Church (GA), 67
Savannah River, 41, 51, 74, 131
Savannah River Baptist Association (SC), 67, 70
Savannah Second African Baptist Church (GA), 52
Savannah Society for Foreign Missions, 67
Savannah Third African Baptist Church (GA), 52
Screven, Aaron, 18
Screven, Bridget Cutt, 13, 15, 18, 32, 174
Screven, Catherine Stoll, 179
Screven, Elisha, 18–19
Screven, Permanous, 18
Screven, Robert, 18
Screven, William, 8, 13–19, 21, 32, 174, 175
Screven, William, Jr., 22, 32, 179
Sea Islands, 141
Seabrook, Whitemarsh, 117–19
Secession of South Carolina, 153–57
—1860 presidential election, 153
—Secessionist and unionist sentiment among Baptists, 153–57
Semple, Robert, 42
Seventh-Day Baptists, 20
Sharper (enslaved person), 42
Shurden, Walter B., 2
Silver Bluff Church, vii, 51–52
Silver Bluff Plantation (Galphin Plantation), 51–52
Simkins, Eldred, Sr., 75
Simmons, Thomas, 19–20
Simons, Thomas, 75
Sirrah (enslaved person), 44
Slavery in South Carolina
—Baptist churches and (*see* Baptists in South Carolina)
—Capitalist nature of, 196
—Enslaved Africans, early colonial period, 14, 173
—Enslaved Native Americans, early colonial period, 173
—Laws pertaining to enslaved people, 26, 80–83, 96, 117–19, 138–39
Snay, Mitchell, 213
Society for the Propagation of the Gospel in Foreign Parts, 26, 187–88
Society Hill, SC, 133
Society of the Cincinnati, 62–63
Somerton, England, 14–15, 27
Somerton settlement, SC, 17, 175
South Carolina
—Baptists in (*see* Baptists in South Carolina)
—Constitution of 1776, 49
—Constitutional convention of 1790, 62
—Dissenting religions, 16, 19, 49, 174
—Lords Proprietors, 16
—Slave majority, 14, 16, 29
South Carolina College, 133, 188, 195–96
South Carolina Gazette, 33
South Moulton Baptist Church (England), 27–30
Southampton Baptist Church (PA), 20–21
Southern Baptist, 142
Southern Baptist and General Intelligencer, 205
Southern Baptist Convention, 106, 126–27, 129, 140–41, 150, 159, 190

—Committee on the Instruction of the Colored Population, 140–41
—Southern Baptist Board of Domestic Missions, 140
—Southern Baptist Board of Foreign Missions, 124–25, 127
—Southern Baptist Publication Society, 142
Southern Baptist Journal, 136
Southern Baptist Theological Seminary, 129, 135–36, 151, 154, 207
—"Report on Slavery and Racism in the History of the Southern Baptist Theological Seminary," 207
Southern Intelligencer, 98
Spartanburg, SC, 48
Springfield African Baptist Church (Augusta, GA), 52
St. Domingo, 86
St. Philip's Anglican Church, 118
Stateburg, SC, vii, 44. *See also* High Hills of Santee, SC
Staughton, William, 79, 194
Stearns, Shubal, 37–43, 45
Stephens, John, 22, 30–31
Stephens, Martha, 31
Stillman, Samuel, 21, 23, 31, 56
Stono Rebellion, 14
Summary of Church Discipline, 46
Sunday Schools, 71, 73. 115, 140–42

Temperance, 141, 209
Tennent, William, 48
Tennent, William, III, 45, 48–49
Tennessee, 41, 75
Thomas, William M., 155
Tilly, Joseph, 33
Tilly, William, 20, 33
Tilly, William, Jr., 33
Tinsley, David, 52
Titus (enslaved person), 92
Tom (enslaved person), 33
Tom (enslaved person), 92
Townsend, Hepzibah, 69, 192
Townsend, Leah, 92
Triennial Convention. *See* General Missionary Convention of the Baptist Denomination in the United States of America for Foreign Missions
Tupper, H. A., 154
Tupper, James, 141–42, 209
Turner, Nat, 107, 117

Union Theological Seminary, 133
Universal salvation, 53–54
University of Alabama, 124, 136
University of Virginia, 133, 135
Upcountry, xi, 1, 6–7, 10–11, 60, 63–74, 77–78, 103, 105–16, 119, 121, 127, 130–37, 145–46, 148, 151, 153–58

Vesey, Denmark, 95–97, 139, 199
Vesey, Sandy, 95
Virginia, 4, 8, 32, 38, 39, 47, 50, 53, 80, 107, 117, 126, 133, 135–36, 171
Virginia Baptist Missionary Society, 126

Wales, 31, 34
Warminster, Pennsylvania, 21, 50
Warne, Joseph, 75
Washington, DC, 68, 135
Washington, George, 32, 62
Waterville College (ME), 68
Waxhaw settlement, 65
Wayland, Francis, 139, 204
Welsh Neck settlement, SC, 20, 30–31
Wheeler, Daniel, 93
White, Rev., 18–19
Whitefield, George, 19, 31–32, 38, 89
Wilkinson, James G., 137

Williams, David, 46
Williams, William, 135–36, 207
Wills, Nancy, 138
Wilson, John Lyde, 98
Winchester, Elhanan, 49, 53–54
Winkler, Edwin T., 135–36, 142–43, 148
Winnsboro, SC, 131–32
Winyah Bay, 18–19
Women. *See* Baptists in South Carolina
Woodmason, Charles, 40

Yale University, 136
Yamasee War, 14
Young, Jeffrey Robert, 4